All of GOD'S WORD For All of MY NEEDS

*The Entire Bible in One Year,
Designed for Personal Spiritual Formation and
Sermon Planning*

Barry L. Callen

EMETH PRESS
www.emethpress.com

All of God's Word for All of My Needs

Copyright © 2023 by Barry L. Callen
Printed in the United States of America on acid-free paper

All rights reserved. No part of this book may be reproduced or transmitted in any form or by any means, electronic or mechanical, including photocopying, recording, or by any information storage and retrieval system, without the written permission of the publisher, except where permitted by law. For permission to reproduce any part or form of the text, contact the publisher., P. O. Box 533 Jackson, Georgia 30233, www.emethpress.com.

Library of Congress Cataloging-in-Publication Data

Names: Callen, Barry L., author.
Title: All of God's word for all of my needs : the entire Bible in one year designed for personal spiritual formation and sermon planning / Barry L. Callen.
Description: Jackson, Georgia : Emeth Press, [2023] | Summary: "This book is a guide for Bible readers taking them through the sacred text in one Christian Year. Readers are able to read in a way that brings understanding, resources for spiritual growth, and guidance for sharing the good news, whether personal evangelism or pulpit proclamation"
-- Provided by publ isher.
Identifiers: LCCN 2023033083 | ISBN 9781609471958 (paperback) | ISBN 9781609471965 (kindle edition)
Subjects: LCSH: Bible--Commentaries. | Spiritual formation. | Expository preaching. | Discipling (Christianity)
Classification: LCC BS491.3 .C35 2023 | DDC 220.7--dc23/eng/20230905
LC record available at https://lccn.loc.gov/2023033083

PURPOSE OF THE BIBLE

The purpose of biblical revelation is not primarily "informational," but "formational." Rather than giving the modern reader a detailed grasp of ancient Middle Eastern secular and religious history, Scripture seeks to prepare the believer in Jesus to grow spiritually and become equipped for mission. Following the course of one complete Christian Year, the Bible's most pivotal passages are noted, put in context, with their current spiritual growth and mission implications identified. Thanks to M. Robert Mulholland for his superb explanation of the formational purpose of the Bible (*Shaped by the Word*). See the Preface below for detail.

ACKNOWLEDGMENT

My longtime friend and Bible scholar Dr. Fred Shively consulted with me on this project. His sensitivity and suggestions proved valuable. As always, God has worked through this exceptional Christian man. Knowing him is an honor. Fred and I have instructed thousands of college students in Bible at Anderson University over recent decades. May our efforts have encouraged them to appreciate the biblical revelation and helped them find ways to incorporate its eternal wisdom into their lives. Being so incorporated means becoming shaped by the Word, being formed into the image of Jesus Christ.

DEDICATION

My sister Bonnie has faced some real obstacles in her lifetime and shown considerable discipline and courage in the difficult process. If such determined persistence would characterize the Christian reader when opening the Bible, the church soon would be much better off than it is today. I dedicate this work to Bonnie since, like her life, it is an attempt to encourage and enable more disciplined and productive reading and personal applying of the sacred pages inspired by God.

THE ALL-BIBLE READING GUIDE

                                                                             Pages

Facts of Faith	Biblical Sources	My Needs	
Beginnings—Preface...			1
1. Creation Then and Now	Genesis 1-11	Curiosity / 3	
2. God Meant It for Good	Genesis 12-50	Insight / 9	
3. God's Promise—Take It!	Joshua and Judges	Courage / 15	
4. Live "in the Spirit" or Die	Galatians	Hope / 21	
Advent—Preface..			27
5. Should I Just Give Up?	Ecclesiastes	Patience / 29	
6. Unanswered Questions	Habakkuk	Ambiguity / 35	
7. Tears Aren't Forever	Jeremiah/Lamentations	Grieving / 39	
8. On the Threshold	Numbers	Daring / 45	
9. The Bridge Between	Malachi/Zechariah	Surviving / 51	
Christmas—Preface..			55
10. Mountain Trumpets	Isaiah 40-55	Alertness / 57	
11. The Bones Will Dance!	Ezekiel	Celebration / 63	
12. The Baby in a Barn	Luke 2:1-30	Insight / 69	
13. He's God with Us!	John1/Colossians	Amazement / 75	
Lent—Preface...			79
14. Penetrating the Darkness	Job	Understanding / 81	
15. Back to the Mountain	Exodus 19-20.	Obedience / 87	
16. Act Out or Shut Up!	James, 1 John.	Living / 91	
17. Desire for Revenge?	Esther/Nahum	Forgiveness / 95	
Easter—Preface..			101
18. God of Amazing Love	Hosea/Song of Songs	Humility / 103	
19. The Messiah Killed?	All four Gospels.	Belief / 109	
20. Life Wins!	All four Gospels.	Awe / 115	
21. We're Never Left Alone	Mark 16, Luke 24.	Comfort / 121	
Pentecost—Preface..			125
22. Be Ye "Holy"—1	Leviticus	Being / 127	
23. Be Ye "Holy"—2	Deuteronomy	Doing / 133	

24. Be Ye "Holy"—3	Ezra/Nehemiah	Shining / 139
25. Be Ye "Holy"—4.	Acts 1-2 /Philippians	Learning/ 143
26. Be Ye "Holy"—5	1 & 2 Thessalonians	Submitting / 149

Ordinary Times in the Church—Preface............................ 155

A. Orientation—Getting the Story and Mission Straight

27. Songs of the Day	Psalms 1, 8, 23, 33.	Tuned / 159
28. He's Really the God-Man!	Gospel of Mark	Excited / 163
29. The Jewish Messiah	Gospel of Matthew	Taught / 169
30. The Doctor's Story	Gospel of Luke	Healed / 175
31. Echoes of Genesis	Gospel of John	Inspired / 179
32. The Gospel Takes Root	Acts 3-12	Inflamed / 183
33. Journeys with Jesus	Acts 13-28	Commissioned / 189

B. Disorientation—Trouble Inside and Outside the Church

34. Songs of the Night	Psalms13, 35, 74, 88	Encouraged / 193
35. An Earthly "King"?	1-2 Samuel, 1-2 Kings.	Humbled / 197
36. Religion of Racial Purity?	Jonah/Ruth/Joel	Cautioned / 201
37. Where's the Justice?	Amos/Micah	Determined / 207
38. Let's Get Practical	Proverbs/Philemon	Specified / 213
39. No Compromise!	Daniel	Compromised / 219
40. Christians Get "Weary"	Hebrews	Endurance / 225
41. Protecting Faith's Integrity	1, 2, and 3 John	Integrity / 231
42. Trouble in the Sanctuary!	1 Corinthians	Love / 235
43. Building Yourselves Up	Jude and 2 Peter	Strength / 239
44. Straying Churches	Revelation 1-3	Listening / 243
45. Beasts and Golden Streets	Revelation 4-22	Confidence / 247

C. Reorientation—Restored by Growth in God's Grace

46. Songs of the New Morning	Psalms 30, 40, 65, 124	Light / 253
47. Who Are God's People?	Romans	Gladness / 259
48. Proper Life in the Church	Ephesians	Unity / 265
49. Ministry of Reconciliation	2 Corinthians	Reconcile / 269
50. He's Everything to Us!	Colossians	Rejoice! / 275
51. Advice to Young Leaders	I & 2 Timothy, Titus.	Lead / 279
52. The God Who Never Dies	All of Scripture	Bow Down / 283

PREFACE

These pages guide Bible readers through the sacred text in one Christian Year. They are enabled to read in a way that brings understanding, resources for spiritual growth, and guidance for sharing the good news, whether personal evangelism or pulpit proclamation.

Christians believe that the Bible reflects reliably God's will and ways for believers. The actual reading practice of most Christians, however, falls short of this grand goal. Presented here is a fresh reading plan for addressing this hurtful failure. There's no way to be a mature Christian and remain biblically illiterate.

Being Read as We Read

Reading the Bible properly is finally *allowing it to read us!* Much too often, the Bible functions for the average Christian like a private well. We look down respectfully into its dark depths. Because of our limited sight and inherent self-centeredness, much of what we see are our own reflections. While comforting, this misses God's intention completely.

The men walking to Emmaus were struggling with the meaning of the crucifixion of Jesus. They couldn't see anything in the Scriptures that looked like this humiliated and sacrificed Jesus. Instead, they saw the smashing of their own desires and expectations. They had expected a conquering Messiah to send Romans running from Israel in fear. Someone then joined these grieving travelers and began reinterpreting the Scriptures for them. They were enabled to see the real Jesus in the divine revelation, not just their misguided hopes (Lk. 24:27).

Once Jesus had left them, they said to each other, "Were not our hearts burning within us while he was talking to us on the road, while he was opening the Scriptures to us?" (Lk. 24:32). The Bible finally had been read more properly, less selfishly, finally reading and changing them.

The Bible is really *about Jesus*. Its intention is to change us as we come to understand. We contemporary readers are so far away from the formative events and sacred writings of the Christian faith. We need a pattern of reading the Bible's many pages that provides a path to much better understanding. We need a deep immersion into God's Word that's infused with the interpretative presence of the Holy Spirit, thus reading and changing us through the reading process.[1] The need is for a process that inspires a transformative intimacy with God, thereby changing us more fully into the image of Jesus Christ.

The discipline needed is a pattern of Bible-reading *contemplation* which reminds us that personal *being* comes before "religious" *doing*. Church programming should rely on previous Scripture *"pondering."* The point isn't speed and volume of Bible reading so much as depth of hearing that leads to obeying the voice of the Spirit coming through the Word. Instructs Paul, "Finally, brothers and sisters, whatever is true, whatever is noble, whatever is right, whatever is pure, whatever is lovely, whatever is admirable—if anything is excellent or praiseworthy—*think about such things"* (Phil. 4:8). Our delight is to be "in the Law of the Lord" and on God's Law we are to "meditate day and night" (Ps. 1:1-2).

Two motives for the Bible reading are common, with one clearly best for approaching the ultimate goal intended by God. There is the surface reading motive, primarily *"informational,"* the reader looking for bits of religious quotes or concepts that support present views and fill out teaching outlines or sermon manuscripts. The second approach, quite different, is urged here. It assumes that *God is seeking to read us,* change us in the reading encounter. Rather than

---

[1] See Brian Hardin, "*Lectio Divina*: Divine Reading," in *Passages: How Reading the Bible in a Year Will Change Everything for You* (Grand Rapids, MI: Zondervan, 2011).

informational, it is *"formational"* Bible reading, being intentionally open to the God who already is wishing to be open to us.

Never should Bible readers be satisfied with a few religious "facts" and quotes. We must allow God to shape us into *new persons* who love and serve God with all we are (Matt. 22:37). Information in the biblical text is important, granted; and yet, what is of supreme importance is allowing the text to focus its attention on us and its intended role in the process—reshaping our very persons into the image of God known to us best in Jesus.

We are to go to the biblical text realizing that it intends to come to us. The nature of Scripture is "iconographic." Its text is a living reality that encounters readers and seeks to draw us into its own order of being.[1] We must read with minds fully engaged and hearts wide open to personal change as God comes and directs. We are to read *to be read*. We read *to be changed*.[2]

Admittedly, there are clear challenges to reading success. The Bible is comprised of 66 separate "books" involving 1,189 chapters as typically edited and captioned. This mass of biblical material isn't arranged chronologically or often even by themes. Some of it goes into great detail about matters that now seem completely outdated. Stories get repeated by different writers with different slants on things, even contrasting information.

If God were to write this book, surely it would be in a more consistent style, with no contrasts of viewpoint, no long sections of ancient history that readers wouldn't understand, and "some footnotes to explain the obscure bits. If God submitted the present writing for a Ph.D., it would surely fail. Fortunately, God is probably not in need of a doctorate."[3]

A book like Esther doesn't seem to belong at all—it's about ancient political intrigue with no mention of God. The last book in the big biblical collection is an "apocalyptic" presentation that reads like a Jurassic Park movie seeming to defy understanding. The story

---

[1] M. Robert Mulholland, Jr., *Shaped by the Word* (Upper Room, 2001).

[2] See Mark Maddix, "Reimaginating Christian Formation," *Wesleyan Theological Journal* (Fall 2022).

[3] Keith Ward, *Confessions of a Recovering Fundamentalist* (Cascade Books, 2019).

of the life of Jesus is told four times by different men, each with differing uses of language, reading audiences in mind, and concerns to be conveyed. The letters of Paul were composed for particular churches in given sets of circumstances, leaving the current reader to try to understand the original intent—which sometimes requires knowledge of the original circumstances.

When people step into the library which is the Bible, often they get lost among its many shelves, twisting aisles, cultural categories, literary styles, and alternate languages. Readers need skilled librarians to get around, commentaries to help interpret what is found, dictionaries to define words never heard before, and historians to explain ancient settings basic to the biblical text.

The All-Bible Reading Plan

Here is a reading plan that takes the serious Bible reader through the whole *Christian Year* (see the graphic below) and the whole Bible in the process. It highlights entire biblical books in their seasonal contexts. This way a reader is encouraged to see the big picture as biblically intended, and hopefully be inclined to personal impact and spiritual change more than private textual tinkering. This approach is less disjointed and has fewer temptations to focus on stray details or isolated verses.

Life themes faced by believers in biblical yesterdays are brought forward for the facing of today. There is constant encouragement to listen to God's Spirit who is eager to interpret and apply enduring truth in changed times and places. When finished with this year-long journey through the Bible, will every word have been read? No, but that doesn't really matter. The whole of the Bible will have been read in a more truly Bible way. Encountered will have been the big-picture texts, the central biblical truths, with everything faced that God wants known and done. Sung will have been praise to God with Jews and Christians. The psalms and hymns often appear because they address every season and circumstance of the biblical account and the spiritual journey.

One Bible scholar has organized the many psalms into three groups, *Orientation, Disorientation,* and *Reorientation*. First, one group presents things as they should be in life and faith. Then another group recognizes that things have gone seriously wrong. But even when confusion and suffering are at their most intense, there arrives the third group, the grace and guidance of God to set bleeding feet on ground higher than known before, the path of faith that leads to fresh rejoicing.[4] The composite of the groups covers comprehensively all dimensions of our spiritual journeys.

Following the Christian Year, focusing on spiritual formation, being sensitive to life themes and the range of the psalms is a plan serves well the typical Bible reader. It provides the road through the whole of Scripture as it speaks to each phase of the typical Christian's faith journey, illumined in part by the journeys of some who have gone this way long ago. Readers who employ the spiritual art of *listening* will be changed into the image of Jesus Christ. The genius of God's Word, beyond recording the critical past of Christian faith, is that it serves as a medium through which God still speaks freshly to the waiting and willing heart.

The tools of careful biblical interpretation are relied upon in presenting this reading plan, but they aren't on display. That would distract the average Bible reader. The goal is to assist with the central task of hearing the voice of God still speaking to individual hearts. Jesus joined the men on the Emmaus Road long ago, as does his Spirit on our roads today.

For each of the 52 biblical reading sessions, identified first is a "big picture" Bible verse or verses. These are worth reading multiple times, pondering prayerfully, even memorizing, encouraging God *to read you*. Second, to expand understanding, a block of surrounding verses is identified, often the biblical book in which the big-picture verses are found. Reading this larger context always deepens awareness of what God is meaning to say. The more of the context that's read and understood the greater the understanding of the big picture beginning.

A "Bit of Background" is provided for each reading, as well as "The Message in Brief," "The Present Challenge," and "Response from the Heart" that includes one growth need of every believer and a series of Bible locations where that need is addressed. All leads the

---

[4] Walter Brueggemann, *The Message of the Psalms* (Augsburg Press, 1985).

reader to a more careful listening, hearing, and understanding of the biblical revelation, and finally to a yielding to personal change. Such change is possible only because God's Spirit, who initially inspired the biblical text, now seeks to illumine it for a new reader who needs restored to the image of the Son.

On Being a Real Christian

Mere Bible reading is no guarantee of good spiritual results. It actually may be dangerous to put the Scriptures in the hands of someone whose inner self is not sufficiently awakened to experience the work of the Spirit of God. That person likely will try to use God's written revelation for selfish purposes, even if unconsciously. It's the Spirit of Jesus who leads a reader to proper understanding and use of what is read.

The tasks before us are twofold. First, life must be opened to the gracious ministry of the Spirit. Then the Bible is be read while realizing and honoring two amazing facts, namely: "The grass withers, the flower fades, but the Word of our God will stand forever" (Isa. 40:8). "Happy are those who delight in the law of the Lord and on his law meditate day and night" (Ps. 1:1-2).

The attempt in these pages resembles the earlier task of C. S. Lewis in his book *Mere Christianity*. He was chosen to introduce Christianity to the population of Great Britain during the difficult war years of the 1940s. He accepted this role not as a biblical "specialist" but as a concerned Anglican layman. Lewis wasn't setting out to tackle the correctness of debated doctrines that divided the denominations. Rather, he wanted to reveal "mere" Christianity, something that should be common to all who claim Jesus as Lord.

Christian faith at its simplest is necessarily derived from the dynamic of the biblical text properly heard and received. Martin Luther and John Calvin did not produce the Protestant Reformation. What produced that great Awakening was that Luther and Calvin had studied closely the Word of God. As they studied, with the assistance of God's Spirit, the revealed Word began to explode inside them, and they channeled that explosion into the Christian institutions and social arrangements around them.

There is enough life-changing truth and spiritual power in the Bible to produce a "reformation" in any generation willing to expose itself to the Word of God. We long for the day envisioned by Jeremiah when people will really *know God* (Jer. 31:34). The prophet uses the word "know" less like gaining knowledge *about* and more like acquiring knowledge *of* by way of personal experience *with*. The goal, well beyond information *about*, is relation *to* and communion *with*. This is why a study of the Psalms is such a good way to discover the real theology of the Old Testament. Knowing what one sings and how one prays is knowing what one really believes.[5]

Accordingly, the reading plan in these pages hopes to encourage fresh encounters with the biblical text in a relatively unstructured and non-institutionalized manner—seeking "mere" biblical truth intending to change lives. The goal is to inspire a search, not for solutions to perennial theological debates, but for openness to the God who is in search of us with good news. We are to be encountered by a gospel that offers eternal life, the very life of God, life that will alter the present and last forever! Once *informed* by such dramatic news from God, the Bible's intention is for readers to be *re-formed* into the image of Jesus Christ. May it be so!

The annual cycle of the Christian Year presents both the full range of the life of Jesus and of ours as his followers. It also serves well as a helpful guide for reading the complete text of the Bible since the Jews of generations before Jesus also experienced their times of waiting and hoping for his coming.

---

[5] A key source of what was believed is Dennis F. Kinlaw's *Lectures in Old Testament Theology* (Francis Asbury Society/Warner Press, 2010).

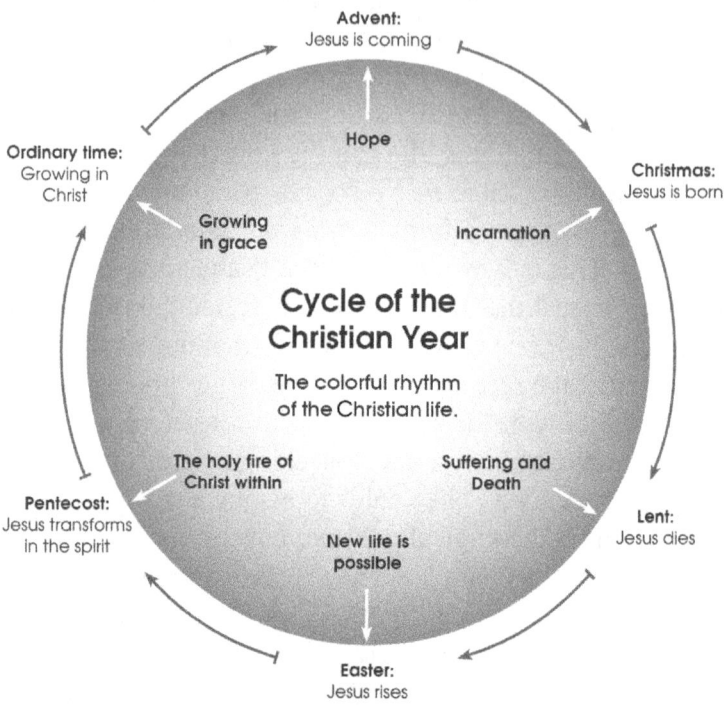

What is the Bible? It can only be stated in paradoxical terms. The Bible is God acting as the revealed and the revealer, God bearing witness to God by means of humans witnessing to their experiences of God's activities among them. It is the Word of God in the words of humans. As Jeremiah's description of his own work indicates, "the words of Jeremiah . . . to whom the Word of the Lord came" (Jer. 1:1–2).[6]

Conversation needs to continue about the nature of the Bible, its inspiration, how best to interpret it, and how Bible reading can bring guidance to many needs along our journeys of faith. Accordingly, there appears on the left-side page of the beginning of most Bible readings key thoughts that stimulate ongoing thought. Some are highlights from the Preface, some quotes from one of the more prominent books on the subject in recent decades (Pinnock/Callen, *The Scripture Principle,* 2009), and some personal spiritual growth needs and related Bible helps.

---

[6] Barry L. Callen, *Caught Between Truths* (Emeth Press, 2007).

BEGINNINGS—PREFACE

Four foundation stones of truth are essential for the house of faith to be built and stand as God intends. It's the only house that survives all the tests of life and receives all the promises of eternity. These foundation stones are identified and explored in the first four of our year's Bible readings. They are:

> • God, the original Creator, continues to create. Freedom is provided and we have abused it, but God works on.

> • God always is at work on behalf of good, even if for now it's only behind the scenes of our limited awareness.

> • God both promises and provides, but we who accept the Divine-human partnership are required to truly believe and be faithful to God's mission and expectations of us.

> • God always is the prime actor. What never must be forgotten is that our human "salvation" is less dependent on what we do *for God* and much more on what God in Jesus Christ has done for us.

So much will follow across this year of Bible reading. Throughout the reading, however, we must never forget these precious truth stones on which all else is built and depends.

The purpose of biblical revelation is not primarily "informational" but "formational." Rather than giving the modern reader a detailed grasp of ancient Middle Eastern secular and religious history, Scripture seeks to prepare the believer in Jesus to grow spiritually and become equipped for mission. Following the course of one complete Christian Year, the Bible's most pivotal passages are noted, put in context, with their current spiritual growth and mission implications identified. Thanks to M. Robert Mulholland for his superb explanation of the formational purpose of the Bible (*Shaped by the Word*). See the Preface above for detail.

Reading 1

CREATION THEN AND NOW

Who wouldn't want a new world? Can we accept by faith this basic biblical fact? The Creator of all is also a sacrificial servant, working at great cost to restore the lost and renew the creation. Amazing! Creation happened long ago and is still is going on. Can we be silent long enough to realize this, and then actively cooperate with God in the ongoing creation process? Naturally we are curious. How and when did it all happen? Can we be satisfied with what the Bible intends to tell us and not insist on claiming to find in its brief creation report what we're curious to know, even if it's not what the writer intended to convey?

1. The Big Picture Verses. Genesis 1:1-2.
The Context: Gen. 1-11, Matt. 3:1-3.

In the beginning when God created the heavens and the earth, the earth was a formless void and a wind from God swept over the face of the waters.... John the Baptist appeared in the wilderness of Judea proclaiming, "Repent, for the kingdom of heaven has come near."

2. A Bit of Background

There was creation in the distant past and then recreation in the arriving reign of God in Jesus Christ. The Bible is the drama of creation and life, with God the original creator and always the chief character. The drama begins with a prologue, Genesis 1-11, and concludes with an epilogue, the Book of Revelation. The prologue pictures everything being birthed and existing as God acted and intended, although the creation soon falls into an appalling mess. The epilogue presents the ultimate resolution of it all. What was will again be despite everything in between.

To be clear, the biblical writer's interest is not in reporting *how* things began but *by whom* and *why*. The result is a biblical report that's more penetrating poetry and superb theology than any attempt at scientific description. The Genesis focus is on *God*, not *geology*. "In the beginning *God*...." The story launches on a high point, quickly tumbles downward, and finally reaches a high point again.

Because the divine intention was corrupted by selfish humans, fresh creation would be needed. There soon would come the dramatic story of Noah and the flood (Gen. 6-9) and the doomed heights of human arrogance shown with the building of the tower of Babel (Gen. 11). Chapters 12-36 of Genesis sketch a picture of the formative ancestors of Israel, God's chosen people called to bring good news to the corrupted creation. The news? God is anxious to forgive and restore! The apex of the whole biblical account comes with John the Baptist announcing the coming of Jesus (Mk. 1:1–8). God was arriving personally to launch a restored creation, the kingdom of heaven, a new creation.

3. The Message in Brief

God brings order out of chaos at four critical points in the biblical account. It happened first at the original creation of all things, second at the Exodus of God's people from Egyptian slavery, the creation of a new people, and then when the Exile of God's people was ending and their lost freedom again was being restored. Later it would happen yet again when Jesus came signaling the arrival of the kingdom of God in the midst of human sinfulness. God's Spirit swept over the swirling waters of human beginnings and now over its lostness, bringing order out of lostness, hope and joy out of despair.

The original creation was judged "very good" (Gen. 1:31). Soon it was ruined by human disobedience. Adam and Eve tried to be "like God" by doing as they pleased in defiance of divine intentions and instructions. God responded with judgment and forgiveness, and eventually even by coming sacrificially in the person of his

Son, Jesus. In the face of human waywardness, the Creator seeks to recreate out of an abundance of overflowing love. Yes, God's creating still goes on. Love doesn't give up. Our prayer should be, in the classic words of Charles Wesley:

> Finish then Thy new creation,
> Pure and spotless let us be;
> Let us see Thy great salvation,
> Perfectly restored in Thee.

4. The Present Challenge

We scientifically-minded and self-centered people of today must be careful to read the Bible for what it is and means to be, not for what we prefer to read into it from our "modern" perspectives and "contemporary" questions. How easy reading can be like looking into a mirror—seeing only what looks exactly what we thought would be there. The Bible points to the depths of our very beings, seeing from God's perspective and exposing both our sad fallenness and great potential. We humans are hybrid beings, earthly material that nonetheless can carry the image of divinity.

William Shakespeare catches this paradox well by having Hamlet say, "What should such fellows as I do, crawling between earth and heaven?" God is the great lover who pursues the lost and seeks to repair the broken creation. The name of the prime divine workman is Jesus, God come to be with us on behalf of the salvation of ourselves and the whole creation. A big challenge of today's church is to become co-workers with the Master in reshaping the creation into more of the image of Jesus Christ. We sometimes seem inclined to do just the opposite.

One difficult but critical task is practicing "contemplation," a deliberate searching after the God who continues to search after us, promising to make all things new. This spiritual practice, rare for today's over-scheduled and sound-polluted people, has been called a "clearinghouse" of the soul, an intentional listening for the quiet voice of God amid the chaos of loud voices and rampant advertising.

A contemplative practice of some Native American Indian families has been to gather every morning and gaze eastward in silence, watching the sunrise. They are welcoming it and hoping that it will drop its fresh blessings on all people as it goes again around the globe. This simple sunrise practice is a symbol of believing that God never gives up. It's a daily recognition of the creative God working still, often in the face of our sin and refusal to listen and obey. God has said from the heavenly throne, "See, I am making all things new. I am the Alpha and the Omega, the beginning and the end" (Rev. 21:5-6).

5. Response from the Heart

My Growth Need: Curiosity not be my selfish motive.
Gen. 3:3-6; Prov. 14:12; 1 Thess. 4:11; 1 Pet. 4:15; James 1:14-15

It seems strange to say, but God is a great disappointment to most of us. God fails to answer all of our questions. God lets tyrants succeed and allows us humans to make our own choices, even ones leading to the creation's ruin. God seems a failure at protecting his own creation.

"Conservative" believers are anxious that God smite sinners, and often that seems not to happen. "Liberals" reject God because of evil being allowed to run rampant, which doesn't seem to fit the logic of who they think God should be. We all struggle with the clash between a supposedly powerful and perfect God and a stupid and badly broken creation. How I need better understanding!

Such is the way things are, in the short-term at least. God easily can be seen as a scandal, a disappointment, allowing what shouldn't be and slow to make the wrongs into previous rights. The Bible as a whole reveals a God who offers freedom, allowing the possibility of evil, failure, and sin. God, however, also is poised to triumph eventually against all contrary forces. It's natural to fear the great *Enforcer*; it's wonderful to have opportunity to be graciously related to the great *Lover*!

> God Eternal, God Almighty,
> God whose triumph is assured,

> In the course of human history,
> by your holy written Word,
> We, God's children by creation
> and redemption of the Son,
> Are upheld by faith's conviction,
> that life's battles can be won.
> "God Our Maker, God Most Holy"
> —David L. Coolidge

Personal Prayer: My amazing God, I don't understand the details of *how* all things got here in the first place, but you tell me that doesn't matter. It's enough to know that they came from your creative hand. Help me not claim to find in your Word what isn't there, mostly my own reflection. What you want me to know is that the very beginning of all things was *You* at work, creating and now re-creating in Christ despite all that's gone wrong. That includes me, of course, God. Please forgive my involvement in the gone-wrongness of your creation. May I be open to the ongoing creative work of your Spirit. Make me a willing instrument in your hands for the good of all your creation. Please channel my curiosity toward your intentions for me and not my expectations of you. Thank you for sending Jesus to bring your coming reign very near. Thank you for how your love makes all things new!

Reading the Bible properly is finally *allowing it to read us!* Much too often, the Bible functions for the average Christian like a private well. We look down respectfully into its dark depths. Because of our limited sight and inherent self-centeredness, much of what we see are our own reflections. While comforting, this misses God's intention completely.

Reading 2

GOD MEANT IT FOR GOOD

God, once having created, wasn't done. There would be recreation, and more. There would be an active caring especially for the chosen people, often done in the background where never seen even though making all the difference. Who or what is creation's ongoing director? Chance? Fate? Is evil inevitable? Is there a plan for things as they are now or is all really gone out of control? In this fallen world of today, we stressed and fearful humans should come to see as Joseph once saw. God always is at work, regardless of circumstances and appearances, and the divine intent is always for good! Many winds blow in human history. Only the wind of the Spirit will prevail, seen or unseen for now.

1. The Big Picture Verses.
Genesis 45:5, 50:20. The Context: Genesis 37-50

Do not be distressed or angry with yourselves because you sold me [Joseph] here; for God sent me before you to preserve life. Even though you intended to harm me, God intended it for good in order to preserve a numerous people, as he is doing today.

2. A Bit of Background

Genesis (Greek for "beginnings") reports the start of all things, except for God who always has been. Chapters 12-50 introduce key members of Israel's ancestors. Abraham is central (chaps. 12-25). He and his descendants are divinely chosen and called to be the special carriers of God's salvation to all people. Particular biblical space is given to the story of Joseph (chaps. 37-50). Why? To show God at work behind the scenes on behalf of his people. This is a pivotal story indeed.

Through an amazing turn of events, Joseph saves Abraham's people from near extinction. Genesis thereby takes us from the ugly story of one brother killing another (4:1-16) to the heartwarming story of an abused little brother saving his whole family. It's a foretaste of God's redemptive work in general, eventually through his sacrificial Son, Jesus.

The long Joseph story ends with one of the more tender of all biblical moments. Joseph brings close to him his guilty, frightened, and desperate brothers. He makes a dramatic announcement about loving forgiveness. It's about how God works graciously behind the scenes of this troubled world. Floods, famine, and brutal foreign occupations often have been endured by God's people. Even so, they (we) are not to despair. Somewhere there is a God-provided Joseph who brings surprising hope and healing. God intends and preserves a people, his own beloved treasure, now the church. The biblical narrative often shows God at work in spite of ourselves and in the face of circumstances that suggest that God isn't even present, let alone at work.

3. The Message in Brief

Things going wrong doesn't mean that God has ceased to work or that all hope is lost. Joseph was abused, sold into slavery, and amazingly soon was raised to great prominence in Egypt. The flow of history turned. Things worked out for good in a way not possible by mere human strategizing. Persons of faith need patience and the long view. Sometimes God works slowly and unexpectedly. Never give up hope. Suffering could be the path to resurrection. God always is somewhere behind the scenes, lovingly even if invisibly at work.

Is our human history finally *HIS-STORY,* God at work guiding the complex events that form the flow of time? If so, then surely we have an obligation to pay attention, look beneath the surface of things, reconsider the road now traveled, "look back for the distinctive marks of God etched along our paths."[1] God's footprints aren't always noticed at first. Keep looking. They are there!

Chance? Fate? Is evil inevitable? Is there a plan for our lives or is all really haphazard, accidental, truly out of control? Here's the answer. God is active, even if behind the scenes, and has clear intentions for our well-being. There is our freedom of action, given by God, and now considerable evil because of our selfish choices. Does that mean that what we have wrongly set in motion will be the inevitable future despite God's intent otherwise? Not necessarily, because God still is at work, graciously active for good in the midst of all the evil. Although often out of sight, God's ongoing grace and forgiveness intend to have a large role in what yet will be.

4. The Present Challenge

The three faith traditions emerging from Abraham, Judaism, Christianity, and Islam, continue to struggle over who is the intended recipient of the legacy of God's promises found in Genesis, especially the part about the "promised land." Abraham ventured into the unknown by faith in God's promise. His legacy is yet to be fulfilled. Jews and Moslems at times fire rockets at each other in the name of God! In modern Israel, dramatic mosques are being built alongside classic Christian sites, partly to compete for public attention. In the twentieth-century, "Christian" Germany was responsible for the murder of a shocking number of Jews.

Things haven't gone well for today's church in the Western world. "Christian" societies have secularized significantly. Beautiful cathedrals sit almost empty, except for tourists admiring the stunning architecture. Should a faith community seek to control society, forcing its standards on unbelievers? Can faith communities avoid being "infected" by surrounding non-faith cultures? Where is God in the midst of all this change, much of it seemingly opposed to God's will?

Our fragile human bodies weaken and die despite modern medicine. No matter! God still lives and is at work, seen or unseen, and

---

[1] Barry L. Callen, *A Pilgrim's Progress* (Anderson University Press and Emeth Press, 2019).

death does not possess the last word. In the meantime, believers are to focus on *faithfulness* and not *success*. Arranging the apparently impossible is God's ordinary business. "We cannot *attain* the presence of God because we are already totally in the presence of God. What's absent is *awareness*. We have to learn to see what is there."[2] What's there is God at work for our good. Praise God!

5. Response from the Heart

My Growth Need: Insight into behind-the-scenes history.
Ps. 119:105; Jer. 29:11; Jn. 7:17; Col. 1:9-10; 1 Tim. 2:3-4

"Light, space, zest--that's God! So, with him on my side I am fearless, afraid of no one and nothing…. Stay with God! Take heart. Don't quit. I'll say it again: Stay with God" (Ps. 27:1, 13-14, *The Message*).

Now to him who is able to keep you from falling and to make you stand without blemish in the presence of his glory with rejoicing, to the only God our Savior, through Jesus Christ our Lord, be glory, majesty, power, and authority, before all time and now and forever. Amen. (Jude 24-25, NRSV)

> Immortal, invisible, God only wise,
> In light inaccessible, hid from my eyes,
> Most blessed, most glorious, the Ancient of Days,
> Almighty, victorious, Thy great name we praise.
> "Immortal, Invisible, God Only Wise"
>
> —Walter Chalmers Smith

Personal Prayer: My precious God, I admit that it's easier to be one of the brothers selfishly pushing around the kid in the house than being Joseph, the abused kid. By your grace, functioning somewhere behind the scenes of my life, I truly believe that you are more powerful than all other forces. You persist in loving, forgiving, and restoring. While I believe this wonderful thing, I admit that too often I have trouble actually being aware of it in action. I'm beginning to

---

[2] Richard Rohr, *What the Mystics Know* (A Crossroad Book, 2015).

see that the kid brother in the Joseph story is a picture of your Son, Jesus. He's the One in whose image your Spirit wishes to reshape my life. Help me yield willingly to this wonderful process. May it be creation day for me again, with your Spirit sweeping over my troubled waters with fresh order and peace! Give me eyes to see it happening, even right now, even if only behind the scenes.

The Bible is really *about Jesus*. Its intention is to change us as we come to understand. We contemporary readers are so far away from the formative events and sacred writings of the Christian faith. We need a pattern of reading the Bible's many pages that provides a path to much better understanding. We need a deep immersion into God's Word that's infused with the interpretative presence of the Holy Spirit, thus reading and changing us through the reading process. The need is for a process that inspires a transformative intimacy with God, thereby changing us more fully into the image of Jesus Christ.

Reading 3

IT'S GOD'S PROMISE—TAKE IT!

We each report the past as we are able to recall it, given our limited perspectives and points of view. Often we miss the whole of the truth since our memories tend to serve personal preferences and agendas. Here's one critical thing that must be remembered by us all. God has chosen us and invites us into partnership with the ongoing divine work. We are invited to cooperate in a "covenant" relationship that is aimed at the world's re-creation. Let's celebrate the promise of being in community with and on mission for God. Two related questions must be answered. Exactly what have we been promised by God and exactly how are we to go about claiming it? Promises are of little value if not embraced and activated. Sitting on a gold mine is hardly the same thing as having extracted and marketed the precious ore.

1. The Big Picture Verses. Joshua 1:9, Judges 2:22. The Context: Books of Joshua and Judges.

Be strong and courageous; do not be frightened or dismayed, for the Lord your God is with you wherever you go. Challenges come in order to test whether or not God's people will take care to walk in the way of the Lord.

2. A Bit of Background

The books of Joshua and Judges go together. They recount essentially the same story, although from somewhat differing angles. For the full picture, both books are necessary. It's the dramatic and complex story of God's people leaving the wilderness and entering and claiming God's promise of their own land, Canaan.

Following the first five Old Testament books, the "Torah," these two books begin the section of the "Prophets." We must be clear about one thing. The prophets of the Bible were not focused on predicting the future so much as recalling and interpreting the past properly in the light of God's intentions and the people's faithfulness—or lack of it.

The "facts" of history come to life only when surrounded by reflection and interpretation of their real meaning. They are specific events and broad stages in God's overall plan of saving and employing his people for the good of all humanity. The chosen people are called to receive the goodness of God and carry forward the divine plan of the restoration of all things. They are promised all that's necessary to accomplish this task. However, promises are of little meaning if not received in joy and used well for their intended purpose.

In Joshua, God's people enter and soon dominate the promised land and its former people. In Judges, this "conquest" is seen as taking longer because it's filled with problems "in order to test Israel, whether or not they would take care to walk in the way of the Lord" (Jud. 2:22). Sometimes the people failed the test and God had to raise up "judges," temporary heroic leaders sent to deliver them from the faithless chaos of their own making.

3. The Message in Brief

God promises his people a home and rest from their hard and long wilderness journey. They will be divinely assisted in securing their new home, although it may be a difficult process and they must remain faithful to their covenant with God. Temptations and opponents are numerous, as is the adequacy of the saving grace of God. How easy—and dangerous—it is to yield to the surrounding non-faith culture, wanting to be accepted, safe, and a part of what seems to work locally, like "fertility gods" in the eyes of inexperienced farmers like the arriving Jews.

Common wisdom often is assumed to go something like this. "When in Rome, do as the Romans do." However, God says that the covenant people always are to be faithful to the divine will and ways or severe consequences will follow. The final "conquest" of the promised land foreshadows the eventual arrival of the Christ in an age to come (Josh. 21:44; Heb. 4:8-9). The key to survival and success is not depending on military might in doing God's work. Central must be faithfulness to life in God's Spirit, and thus doing God's will in God's way. Divine life is offered to God's people. To refuse it is to lose everything.

4. The Present Challenge

What geographic "land" has God promised his people, if any? The church of Jesus exists in many countries and cultures, each potentially enriching and threatening to the life and mission of the church. Success is possible with God's help, as is failure if faithfulness to God's expectations is sacrificed to local distractions and temptations. Unfortunately, the church in the past sometimes has identified sections of "sacred territory" as necessarily promised to God's people and has launched brutal crusades to capture it from occupying infidels. Many have died, supposedly on behalf of God, in capturing some little piece of land in God's name.

What of the modern nation of Israel and its belief that a particular strip of land on the eastern Mediterranean belongs to them by divine right? Jesus, a loyal Jew, seems to have redefined the "kingdom of God" in other than geographic terms (Jn. 18:36). Is the church to be judged successful when it controls particular territory or dominates a given culture? In Christian faith, what constitutes "success"? The faithful certainly have received much and at times have occupied what it has assumed was divinely promised. Exactly what has been promised?

Might God sometimes want to give and we don't want to receive, being too comfortable where we are? Do we gladly receive divine gifts, but on our own terms and used for our own ends? There is the story (not in the New Testament) of a man with a chronic illness who met Jesus. Jesus offered healing and the man protested. "Why not receive my healing gift?" asked Jesus. "Because I'm on disability!" In what ways are God's people settled into chronic church illnesses and somehow receiving enough twisted satisfactions that they aren't prepared to go on to available higher ground?

5. Response from the Heart

My Growth Need: Courage to cling to God's promises.
Deut. 31:6; Josh. 1:6; Ps. 23:4; Jn. 14:17; 1 Cor. 16:13; Eph. 6:10

In our attempt to understand true strength, there are contrasting definitions. The Hebrew name *Yeshua* is rendered in the Old Testament as Joshua, the successor to Moses, and in the New Testament as Jesus our Lord. Joshua looked to God to give military insight for conquering land whereas Jesus exhibited the inner power of the Spirit to enable spiritual victory. The Quaker hymnist Jenny Evelyn Hussey composed the poem "The War Dog," the story of a soldier's dog during the Civil War.

> Sally was a lady;
> She was a soldier too.
> She marched beside the colors,
> Of our red, white, and blue.
> It was in the days of our Civil War
> That she lived her life so true.

Sally was so faithful to her soldier friend that, when he was felled in the battle at Gettysburg, she stayed until he was buried. She later became the mascot of the Pennsylvania 11th regiment, so well known that in 1863 President Lincoln saluted her as the regiment passed by. A bronze statue of Sally memorializes her today at the Gettysburg battlefield. Both the dog and the poem's author are examples of faithful service. Even so, is war the best way to be faithful to God?

> Not to the strong is the battle;
> Not to the swift is the race,
> But to the true and the faithful
> Victory is promised through grace.
> —Fanny Crosby

Personal Prayer. It's easy, Lord, to fall into the trap of thinking that we need military might to accomplish your holy work. I repent of such thoughts and commit my mind to realize more fully that you dwell within us and, in your own time and way, will meet any challenge that we face. Arm me with your Spirit! What I so need is the courage to cling to your promises instead of reverting to the ways of the world. My promising and conquering God, help me see what "land" you actually have promised and then help me be faithful in occupying it as you truly intend.

The discipline needed is a pattern of Bible-reading *contemplation* which reminds us that personal *being* comes before "religious" *doing*. Church programming should rely on previous Scripture *"pondering."* The point isn't speed and volume of Bible reading so much as depth of hearing that leads to obeying the voice of the Spirit coming through the Word. Instructs Paul, "Finally, brothers and sisters, whatever is true, whatever is noble, whatever is right, whatever is pure, whatever is lovely, whatever is admirable—if anything is excellent or praiseworthy—*think about such things"* (Phil. 4:8). Our delight is to be "in the Law of the Lord" and on God's Law we are to "meditate day and night" (Ps. 1:1-2).

Reading 4

LIVE "IN THE SPIRIT" OR DIE

True Christianity begins and proceeds faithfully only when believers gladly receive and live in God's saving and restoring grace. Once received, there comes the great privilege of new life "in the Spirit" of Jesus. It is essential, requiring a death to self-centeredness that willingly yields to "eternal" life, God-like life, re-created life on mission for the creating and re-creating God. Such new life dares to look ahead hopefully despite circumstances. It looks through the eyes of the Spirit and functions by the divine gifting of the Spirit. The person with the perspective of Christ's Spirit seeks what pleases the Spirit of the Lord, yearns to know where Christ's Spirit is at work, and seeks to be part of what Christ is doing now in the world.[1] Anyone with another (alien) spirit is hardly one of Christ's living children.

1. The Big Picture Verses. Galatians 2:19-20.
The Context: The Book of Galatians.

I have been crucified with Christ and it is no longer I who live, but it is Christ who lives in me. And the life I now live in the flesh I live by faith in the Son of God who loved me and gave himself for me.

---

[1] For a book-length exploration of being alive in God's Spirit in today's secular setting, see Barry L. Callen, *The Living Dead*.

2. A Bit of Background

The letter of Paul to the Galatians is among the earliest writings of the young Christian community. It brings into view the central theological issues faced by the earliest church, including how Christian people are to understand themselves. Paul insists that the church must be an "inclusive" community, a loving fellowship made possible by the gracious love of God. His letter has been likened to a sword flashing in the hands of a great spiritual warrior. Some old barriers among humans had to go.

Paul and the good news he taught were under attack. If the attack had succeeded, Christianity likely would have been nothing more than another Jewish sect. He insists that his message came from God and is truly good news for all people, not just Jews. Opposition to Paul's ministry naturally arose from ultra-loyal Jews defending the view that God already had decided on the chosen people, and most people of the world were unacceptable outsiders to God's sacred community. Surely God wouldn't accept belief in Jesus Christ unless first a person agreed to become an obedient Jew.

To be a true Christian "apostle" originally was thought to require having been with Jesus personally and witnessed his resurrection appearances. Paul met neither of these qualifications. However, he insisted that he was a true apostle because Jesus had chosen to meet him personally on the road to Damascus. He hadn't gained favor from God by being Jewish and obeying the Law but by having faith in Jesus the Christ.

After all, Abraham had gained God's favor by faith before there ever was the Law of the Jews. Salvation isn't dependent on what we do *for God* but on what God in Jesus has done *for us*. This is a basic assumption of Christian faith and Paul was defending it against all comers. Salvation and membership in the true church is dependent on new life in the Spirit of Christ, not on any ethnic identity or heritage.

3. The Message in Brief

As with the creation itself, our human salvation begins with God and not ourselves.

Our sinful fallenness has disabled us, rendered us unable to perceive properly our spiritual condition and reach out humbly in faith. God moves first, reversing this inability and opening the door to possible salvation for all persons. The Law of the Jews was valuable indeed, but only to point the right way and convince us of our insufficiency of following it as God intends. The Law forced us to admit that the only thing that can save is the unmerited grace of the sovereign God.

To really come alive spiritually requires being resurrected into life *in the Spirit of Jesus.* It requires receiving God's enabling grace that highlights the saving work of Jesus. We cannot save ourselves, including by our best efforts. But there is good news! We *all* can be saved by the grace of God.

Salvation in Jesus Christ is available to all people who will reach out to their Creator and Savior in repentance and faith. Once having reached out, we are enabled to become alive "in the Spirit," crucified to our selfish selves, resurrected with Jesus to our true selves, "sanctified," set apart to and for God. Christian life means accepting the rule of love and not merely the detailed obligations of law. True Christian life is grateful response to God's love, bringing freedom in Christ, although certainly never an uncontrolled yielding to moral license. The new life is superintended by the Spirit, kept in line with the standards and mission of Jesus.

4. The Present Challenge

A struggle with Jewish law is hardly a common threat to Christians today. Still, the core issue remains. God alone is the Creator and the re-Creator, with the new creation based on divine love, grace, and forgiveness, life *in the Spirit* and nothing else. Earning restoration into God's favor is beyond the capacity of fallen humans, although we persist in efforts to "please God" as though that gives us acceptability.

Religious institutionalism is always a threat to true salvation. It's a human replacement for the pure grace of the saving God. We humans try working our way to heaven, earning our salvation, honoring the standards that supposedly please God, and keeping the privileges for ourselves and our kind. God already has opened the door to all people, most being unlike us in many ways. We tend to resist, preferring to choose our spiritual brothers and sisters according to our selfish human standards. Such is so unlike Jesus. It's Christianity gone wrong. Paul fought this tendency in Galatia and so should we wherever we live. Salvation is by God's grace alone and available to all.

Augustus Toplady's great hymn "Rock of Ages" expresses well the burden of Paul's message to the Galatians:

> Nothing in my hand I bring,
> Simply to Thy cross I cling;
> Naked, come to Thee for dress;
> Helpless, look to Thee for grace;
> Foul, I to the fountain fly;
> Wash me, Savior, or I die.

5. Response from the Heart

My Growth Need: Hope that life finally wins.
Isa. 40:31; Rom. 15:13; Eph. 1:18; Col. 1:27; 1 Thess. 1:3; Heb. 10:23; 1 Pet. 1:3

Jenny Evelyn Hussey was born into a New Hampshire Quaker family. She was an invalid with rheumatism, and yet cared for her sister who had the same disease. Out of her suffering she expressed her faith by composing numerous hymns, the best known being:

> King of my life, I crown Thee now,
> Thine shall the glory be.
> Lest I forget Thy thorn-crowned brow,
> Lead me to Calvary.
> Lest I forget Gethsemane,
> Lest I forget Thine agony,
> Lest I forget Thy love for me,
> Lead me to Calvary.

The beauty of these words invite deep reflection. Inspired by Luke 9:23 (the call to take up our crosses daily), Hussey wrote: "May I be willing, Lord, to bear daily my cross for Thee, even the cup of grief to share; Thou hast done all for me." Even though Quakers did not baptize, she requested baptism before she died, saying, "I want people to know that I love Jesus." Her life was filled with the life of the Spirit of Jesus. Whatever the death brought on by sin, hope persists that life can win!

> Did we in our own strength confide,
> Our striving would be losing.
> Were not the right man on our side
> The man of God's own choosing.
> —Martin Luther

Personal Prayer. God, sometimes I feel stuck, mired in a difficult situation, unable to decide or move forward. Help me trust you and hope in the outcome you desire for me. Give me strength and courage to overcome. May your voice become clearer, and your Spirit energize me from within. I'm grateful for the gift of life which I know comes from you. Lord, I long to be free from all prejudice, anxiety, and the self-preoccupation that clings to me. I long to love my neighbor as I love myself, to do unto others as I would have them do to me. May I live on behalf of others and dare to hope that my feeble efforts will make a difference for your kingdom. May I be truly alive in your Spirit.

ADVENT SEASON—PREFACE

"Advent is the Christian season of the hopefully soon-coming of God. As we seek to wait patiently for this divine coming into our troubled human circumstances, there are five difficult spiritual experiences that must be faced. They are encountered by all believers and featured prominently in Readings 5-9.

> Should we just give up?
> We are so tired of unanswered questions!
> Can we really believe that tears aren't forever?
> We are on the threshold, at least that's what we hope!
> Despite the dangerous distance, there is a bridge between!

As we keep waiting for what we're confident is God's soon coming, there is a good biblical place to linger. It's in the "Wisdom Literature" of the Old Testament, Job, Proverbs, Ecclesiastes, and various of the psalms. The Bible is a living, real-life, multi-dimensional document. We sometimes find in it cross-currents that seem to move against each other. Those are our mixed emotions. We must read carefully and think deeply in order to find the larger biblical wisdom, the comprehensive view that reconciles what sometimes appear to be diverse moving parts.

Life in this world has become tangled and we search for the "hidden order" that we hope is somewhere beneath the chaotic surface of everyday life experiences. There's an emphasis in Ecclesiastes on life "under the sun," looking at life from below, in the midst of its immediate anomalies and relativities, sometimes without even taking God into account. Then there comes a balancing, the dominant biblical emphasis on rising above to the sun, managing to grasp the fuller truth.

There is a tendency in parts of the Bible to seek for truths that emerge from the actual life we know, as opposed to what we hope is coming from divine revelation not yet fully received. We humans must look real life square in the face and find answers that are adequate for the harshness of our experienced reality. Advent is the "in the meantime" season, a time of patience and persistence, of waiting and hoping, of still seeing more from under the sun than yet from above.

Reading 5

SHOULD WE JUST GIVE UP?

The old saying isn't working for many people. "Ready, set, go!" Given how real life often is, we're not ready, can't quite manage to get set, and seem to be going nowhere fast! Is life just so much "vanity," ultimately an unfair and unsatisfying waste of time? Apparently, but not really. Sometimes, but surely not always. Are we to give up in frustration or keep looking up, knowing by faith that the fuller truth is almost here. Make the best of the moment. Solutions will be arriving shortly. Look up!

1. The Big Picture Verse.

Ecclesiastes 12:13. The Context: The Book of Ecclesiastes.

Here's the end of the matter after all has been heard. Fear God and keep his commandments, for that is the whole duty of everyone. For God will bring every deed into judgment, including every secret thing, whether good or evil.

2. A Bit of Background

The *Kuyasa Kids* is an African children's choir sponsored by Horizon International. It's toured the United States for many years, encouraging new child sponsorships of AIDS orphans. They feature the energetic singing and dancing of young Africans who have lost much and yet now have gained health, education, and hope in Jesus Christ. Their theme song is *Never Give Up!*

Yes, never, although in the adult worlds experienced by many in biblical and present times, circumstances push toward giving up.

Hopelessness comes easily and can be deadly. The writer of Ecclesiastes, *Qohelet*, is a "gatherer," a teacher who accumulates bits of wisdom and collects students for life instruction. He shares reflections of an aged and sometimes crabby Hebrew "lecturer," supposedly King Solomon.

This book of "wisdom" likely was composed when the Greeks were ruling Israel in brutal ways disastrous for the Jewish community's active faith in God. Cruelty and injustice were everywhere, with no hope seen. An old man looks back over his life and reports that bad luck finally overtakes even the swiftest and strongest. Life's lessons and pleasures have their advantages, but they also have their limitations that finally fail to last or satisfy. Sometimes things just make no sense, are going nowhere, and people are on the edge of giving up. What's the alternative? Is there one?

Ecclesiastes is sometimes confusing and depressing. Explained at one point is how our human bodies eventually fall apart (12:1-7). The frequently used phrase is "under the sun," considering only the present and visible aspects of life. This religious exclusion may be key to understanding why this writing belongs in the Bible. Including God in the picture (*beyond the sun*) may be the only place where hope comes when all underneath the sun, on their own, seems senseless, useless, and hopeless. With a God exclusion in place, all that's left is chasing the wind, "pointless" (1:2), a word used thirty times in this biblical book.

There is a redeeming epilogue to this strange biblical book (12:13-14). Introduce God to the picture of life's perplexing and painful experiences and suddenly all can make some sense. Reverence God, be faithful to the One behind all things, and some day questions will be answered and justice will be done. In the meantime, under the sun, do the best you can and be satisfied as much as possible.

3. The Message in Brief

Life as we experience it tends to encourage disillusionment. Things seem to be merely puffs of wind, meaningless. Generations come and go and the wrong people often come out on top. There's little apparent connection between what we do and what we get. A closer relation between them is judged in Deuteronomy 7:12-14 and Proverbs 2:21-22, where it's said that a high price is paid for wickedness. Whatever the case, death is certain for all, righteous or wicked.

A living dog is said to be better than a dead lion (Ecc. 9:4). That's hopeful, at least a little. We are advised to practice moderation in all things and get what joy we can out of daily events. We should reverence God, keep his commandments, and believe that, when it's all over, life won't have been totally in vain after all. Things can be seen from under and maybe also from above the sun.

Mixed messages? Maybe, but that's how real life in this world usually is experienced. A full biblical view sometimes requires a balancing of different emphases found in different places. Ecclesiastes stresses the painful point that immediate observation sees no apparent relation between what we do in life and how we prosper or even survive. So much in life seems like the vanity of chasing the wind.

Biblical indications of hope do appear in Ecclesiastes (3:17; 8:12; 12:14). Oddly, a reading of this book is traditionally associated with the Jewish celebration of *Sukkoth*, the Festival of Booths. People are encouraged to enjoy the festival and all of life as best they can (2:24-26; 3:1-13, 22, etc.). With God in view, the fullness of joy can come. Having a reason for faith in tomorrow can make endurance possible today.

4. The Present Challenge

Views of life in this present world are dominated by widespread despair. Many say, "Live now and for here because there may be no other time or place." On all hands are bombs and missiles of massive destructive potential and a human-worsened climate change bringing pain and poverty worldwide. People are critical of their inept governments and seeking pleasure and safety wherever they can, including fleeing across national borders. Despite all the technological advances, death still is certain for all, regardless of titles or wealth or place of residence.

Our big telescopes now can see well beyond the sun. Have we yet seen God and gained substantial reason for hope? Are we looking in the right place, in the right way? The Christian church is to be a beacon of light in this sea of our darkness of unknowing. It's to be proclaiming and modeling Jesus Christ as the only way out of empty and useless living (1 Pet. 1:18-19). Is the church widely viewed as such or mostly ignored as irrelevant to the big issues of the real world we can see and in which so many suffer?

Human life on its own is not self-explanatory or ultimately satisfying. Without the light of special revelation, God's Word from beyond the sun, life easily becomes an endless round of nonsense on its way to nowhere. The Bible offers key glimpses of truth from *beyond the sun*, glimpses desperately needed. Love, seen in the life and through the lens of Jesus, is the best means we humans have for rightly understanding God and approaching life.

Divine love is the intended way humans are to relate to each other. We are to dance with loving joy as reflections of the image of God implanted in us at creation. This joy and love are to be refreshed in us by the sacrificial work of Jesus and extended through us to others by the ministry of the Spirit of Jesus.

5. Response from the Heart

My Growth Need: Patience while waiting for meaning.
2 Chron. 1:9-12; Ecc. 7:8; Rom. 12:12; 1 Cor. 13:4; Phil. 4:6; Rev. 21:4

The film *The Thin Red Line* intersperses haunting voice-overs with awful World War II battle scenes from the fight to control the South Pacific island of Guadalcanal. The voice is of a young soldier pondering the "thin red line" of war that separates life and death. His questions are haunting. "This great evil. Where's it come from? Who's doing this? Who's killing us? Does our dying benefit the Earth? Does it help the grass to grow or the sun to shine? Is this darkness in you [God] too? Have you passed through the night?"

> While life's dark maze I tread,
> And griefs around me spread,
> Be Thou my guide;
> Bid darkness turn to day,
> Wipe sorrow's tears away,

Nor let me ever stray, from Thee aside.
"My Faith Looks Up to Thee,"
—Ray Palmer

Personal Prayer: Looking at things "under the sun" fills me with nothing but confusion and doubt, my God. I realize that what I can see is so shortsighted and won't last. Help me learn how to gaze in faith "beyond the sun." Are you there, loving Jesus, somewhere I can't see? Speak to me, You who are the only One behind and before and eventually beyond all time. The dark maze of life is all around me and my tears aren't going to be wiped away unless you appear and do it for me. Come, Lord Jesus! Make me into a beam of light and not just more of the spreading darkness.

Never should Bible readers be satisfied with a few religious "facts" and quotes. We must allow God to shape us into *new persons* who love and serve God with all we are (Matt. 22:37). Information in the biblical text is important, granted, and yet what is of supreme importance is allowing the text to focus its attention on us and its intended role in the process—reshaping our very persons into the image of God known to us best in Jesus. We are to go to the biblical text realizing that it intends to come to us. The nature of Scripture is "iconographic." Its text is a living reality that encounters readers and seeks to draw us into its own order of being. We must read with minds fully engaged and hearts wide open to personal change as God comes and directs. We are to read *to be read*. We read *to be changed*.

Reading 6

TIRED OF ALL THOSE UNANSWERED QUESTIONS?

Have you seen the sign "Jesus Is the Answer"? I've heard this response to it. "What's the Question?" For people in real trouble, they certainly know their questions. What they don't know are the answers that can make a difference. One biblical prophet struggles to respond to the big life questions that seemed to him resistant to all available answers. He was tired of waiting and insisting that God finally respond. I want a God who answers now! Does God sometimes answer and we are not really listening, or might the answer be something we just don't want to hear?

1. The Big Picture Verse.

Habakkuk 1:2. The Context: The Book of Habakkuk.

O Lord, how long shall I cry for help, and you will not listen? Or cry to you "Violence!" and you will not save? The righteous must live by their faith, not their sight.

2. A Bit of Background

The little book of Habakkuk likely arose during the Babylonian captivity of God's people, a difficult time indeed. All "why" and "how long" questions seemed urgent but unanswered. Would answers ever come? The recent past was awful and the future seemed likely to be no better. Had the Babylonian gods put the God of the

Jewish tradition to sleep or rendered him helpless, deaf to the cries of his people?

The answers are conflicting. Yes, Maybe, No! See the struggle of Job found in Reading 14. We humans have to learn to live with some questions that are bigger than the answers we get while in this life. The awkward circumstance of God's seeming silence demands patience of the faithful, which for many struggling believers is in short supply. The questions nag and disturb.

How can "bad" people prevail and the good suffer at their hands, with a powerful and good God seeming to do nothing about it? How could an evil empire like Babylon be used as an instrument of God, the godless being the sword of God judging his own wayward people?

We need this kind of wisdom: I trusted God's mercy and believed profoundly in grace. I learned not to carry the crushing burden of believing that I had to nail every question to the ground. Mature believers in the biblical God learn to live with doubts and unanswered questions. At least for now, it's part of the human condition. "Now I know only in part; then I will know fully, even as I have been fully known" (1 Cor. 13:12). Faith fills the gap created by our continuing and sometimes painful ignorance. We may be closer to God and the truth when asking hard questions than when parading arrogant and inadequate answers. There likely is more genuine faith in honest doubt than in some blind believing of a conventional creed.

3. The Message in Brief

Our prayers in times of distress sometimes meet with frustration. The prophet Habakkuk knew such pain and yet also received key answers from God (1:5–11, 2:2 ff). He realized that, whatever the circumstance, the Lord is from everlasting (1:12). God still is in his holy temple (2:20) and "enables me to go on to the heights" (3:19) regardless of limited understanding. The righteous must live by faith (2:4). With faith, we believers can go on despite unanswered questions and unresolved problems.

Knowing that God *is* assures us that one day answers *will come*. Meanwhile, faith can bring endurance and even joy. "Though the fig tree does not bud and there are no grapes on the vine . . . and the fields produce no food, yet I will rejoice in the Lord, I will be joyful in God my Savior" (3:17-18). We who believe can be confident that God ultimately will triumph over all evil. Hope need not be destroyed by difficult present circumstances.

John Wesley's sermon "Walking by Sight and Walking by Faith" makes the essential point. We believers must judge things good or evil not by reference to the presently visible but by the things invisible and eternal. Mature faith will adjust to lingering paradox and unrelenting mystery. We are to relax and leave room for the freedom of God to act when and how it seems best. Divine thoughts and strategies are not always ours to know.

4. The Present Challenge

Habakkuk 3:2 is an ancient prayer worthy of repeating today. The prophet stands in awe of God's past deeds and asks, "Renew them in our day, in our time make them known." Patience may be required and the answers that do come may be somewhat different than the past deeds of God that we know. Even so, there is hope that soon "I will rejoice in the Lord" because "the Sovereign Lord is my strength" (3:18-19). Answers always will be consistent with the loving nature of God who is from everlasting to everlasting.

It's time to go when God calls, regardless of the swirl of confusing events, unresolved issues, and unanswered questions all around us. These hymn lines are Christian marching orders:

> Jesus calls o'er the tumult
> of our life's wild, restless sea;
> Day by day I hear him saying,
> "Christian, come and follow me."
> In our joys and in our sorrows,
> Days of toil and hours of ease;
> Still he calls in cares and pleasures,
> "Christian, love me more than these."
> "Jesus Calls Us O'er the Tumult"
> —Cecil Frances Alexander

5. Response from the Heart

My Growth Need: Ambiguity--learning to live with it.
2 Sam. 12:13-14; Lk. 9:44-45; 1 Cor. 14:8; Gal. 1:6-7

> Lord, speak to me, that I may speak
> in living echoes of Thy tone;
> As Thou hast sought, so let me seek
> the erring children lost and lone.
> "Lord, Speak to Me"
> —Frances R. Havergal

Often what we need aren't answers so much as an unmovable rock on which to stand while questions remain unanswered.

> We have an anchor that keeps the soul,
> Steadfast and sure while the billows roll,
> Fastened to the rock which cannot move,
> Grounded firm and deep in the Saviour's love."
> "Will Your Anchor Hold in the Storms of Life?"
> —Priscilla J. Owens

Personal Prayer: Lord, how can I talk on your behalf until you've first talked to me? I need to know your answers before I can share them with the hurting and lost questioners of this world. Please do for me at least what the prophet requested. Help me recall and stand in awe of your work in the past, and then revive it in my present so I can rejoice and make it known to others (3:2). Keep me humble and make my faith strong enough to go on believing even when I find it necessary to keep asking and still not knowing some things. My precious Lord, protect me from disillusionment. Help me take the struggle of unanswered prayer and turn it into an opportunity to grow in intimacy with you.

Reading 7

TEARS AREN'T FOREVER

God may be known best at the point of pain. Tears often are the telescope by which persons see beyond the moment, even as far as heaven. To see God best, we are invited by the Bible to look at the cross on which Jesus once hung for our redemption. It's natural to shed shocked tears on seeing that execution hill. However, great wisdom can come in the midst of such tears. Suffering can lead to our healing. Tears need not be forever, and they can be telescopes of great insight. The death of Jesus turned out to be the potential of life for all the creation. Few saw that coming! Do you see it?

1. The Big Picture Verses.
Jeremiah 31:31-33. The Context: The Books of Jeremiah and Lamentations.

The days are surely coming, says the Lord, when I will make a new covenant with the house of Israel and Judah. It will not be like the covenant I made with their ancestors that they broke. I will put my law within them and write it on their hearts, and I will be their God and they shall be my people.

2. A Bit of Background

Jeremiah sometimes is called the "weeping" prophet. It might be more accurate to call him the prophet of the weeping God. A large portion of his prophetic book deals with the themes of trauma, God's judgment, and hope despite all. The tearful reputation of Jeremiah led to the assumption that he also authored the book of Lamentations. It narrates vividly the desolation of the downfall of Jerusalem, the holy city, which fell to Babylon in 587 B.C. This prophet says at one point that he ate God's words and was disappointed: "You have become for me as unreliable as a spring gone dry!" (15:18). Advanced pain can bring awful despair. It also can finally perceive the larger truth. For children of God, tears aren't forever.

The big story told by Jeremiah shows Judah and Jerusalem dragged into the tragedies of defeat, destruction, and exile, and finally God bringing them out on the other side. Judgment and promise interplay in eyes often filled with tears. Jeremiah witnessed and railed against the awful reign of Manasseh, and even the partial reforms of Josiah, while the evil empire of Assyria was on its last legs and Babylon was rising and threatening God's people. This weeping prophet once appeared in public with a yoke on his neck, dramatizing God's impending judgment. Jeremiah was charged with blasphemy and barely escaped with his life (chap. 26). How vigorously people sometimes deny their own wrongs.

People resist bad news. Judgment did come and Jeremiah was able to see and report this national disaster as the mysterious work of God's judging and redeeming providence. There was purpose and intended wisdom in all the tears. If only the people would acknowledge their fault and regain their faith and practice faithfulness. There's always hope for the future (3:20–36).

What might come after the shaking of all these human foundations? According to Jeremiah, Messiah will come, the One who will present a new covenant and save the people by his own voluntary suffering. Through his pain will come our new possibilities. In that divine suffering of the Son on a cross, the true light of understanding will shine directly on the loving reality of the Father. Can we see this big picture through our tears? God is loving grace, the divine One who voluntarily suffers on our behalf. Amazing!

3. The Message in Brief

A grand promise shines through all the pain and turmoil, especially as reported in Jeremiah 31. There is hope beyond all the judgment and suffering. There will be a "new covenant" (New Testament), which later appears in Luke 22:20. The big truth, the reality through and beyond the tears, is that love is the fundamental character of God. God is "intimately connected with the world, caring for it, committed to its good, and sometimes also grieving because of our waywardness. God is necessarily sensitive to this world and vulnerable to its developments. God suffers in our suffering and rejoices in our joys."[1]

This fundamental truth about God's character and working is revealed in the Christian "Negro spirituals."[2] They are "songs from the night," "outcries of longing for needed change." They have a persistent perspective regarding God. It's a profound conviction that "no problems or masters have the last word where faith reigns." This is "the music of searchers who had found something eternal and Someone immortal." Tears aren't forever!

Israel and now the church of Jesus have experienced great pain, and through it they have evolved a distinctive understanding. It's about the God who identifies with and even shares our pain. God is neither immune to the evil and suffering of our world nor trapped in any co-dependence with them. The God who is utterly free and sovereign also is responsive and vulnerable, suffering from our sin and paying the necessary price for our redemption. In the reality of who God is lies our hope that stretches beyond all tears and deserved judgment.

4. The Present Challenge

Tears of repentance can send one's sight to the very heart of a forgiving God. On the other hand, tears often are signs of being broken, reaching out and seeing nothing hopeful at all. Too many of us Christians today have become so absorbed in the surrounding secular context that we are functioning as aggressive capitalists in our spiritual lives. We strategize, count, plan, produce, consume, invest, and think of time as money. If, however, we are to survive as God intends, we must focus, listen, and learn to live *by grace*, quietly practicing the presence of God. Many of us devote years to education and hardly minutes to serious spiritual formation.

---

[1] Delwin Brown, *What Does a Progressive Christian Believe?*
[2] James Earl Massey, *Sundays in the Tuskegee Chapel.*

An insightful autobiography includes this delicate wisdom from early years spent in Missouri:

The River Meramec is a winsome old stream—one of nature's most enchanting gifts to mid-America. On long and lazy summer days, the Meramec is the picture of peace and quiet and rest. I love to linger on her bank and hear the music of her waters. They seem to be singing about the meaning of things. Men have come to her banks, and gone from her banks, but she just keeps rolling quietly along. And in her music there seems to be reason as well as rhythm.[3]

With today's personal schedules jammed full, will we find time to "linger," hear the quiet "music," and catch glimpses of the "reason" and "rhythm" in the ultimate meaning of things?

Tragedy may be right before us, while triumph lies just beyond. How far are we seeing through our tears? As C. S. Lewis once observed, "At present we are on the outside of the world, the wrong side of the door. But all the leaves of the New Testament are rustling with the rumor that it will not always be so. Someday, God willing, we shall get in."[4]

5. Response from the Heart

My Growth Need: Grieving and knowing ongoing grace.
Ps. 34:18; Matt. 11:28-30; Heb. 8:6-13; Jn. 16:22; Rom. 8:18; Rev. 21:4

Tears and temptations won't last forever for faithful disciples of Jesus. In fact, they can be of spiritual benefit while they last. Grief can spur growth, increase insight, and make us more like our Master who also struggled. Jesus faced his very private temptations alone in the desert. How then do we even know about them? He must have thought it important to share his struggles with his disciples. The point was to help them (us) deal with hours of temptation, turning trouble into triumph by the grace of God.

Perhaps the greatest lessons in life are those learned in difficult and painful times. Pain and tears come to us all, but God has given

---

[3] The autobiography of John A. Morrison, *As the River Flows*.
[4] C. S. Lewis, *The Weight of Glory and Other Addresses*.

gracious promises and is faithful to them. Jeremiah calls it a covenant that will be written in the heart. Faithfulness to that covenant keeps hope alive.

Poet Robert Frost pictures a covenant between neighbors as they rebuild the stone wall separating their properties. Frost is dissatisfied. Why do they even need a wall? His apple trees will never eat his neighbor's pinecones. The neighbor insists, "Good fences make good neighbors." The poem invites a deeper understanding of covenant.

> Something there is that doesn't love a wall....
> Before I built a wall I'd ask to know
> What I was walling in or walling out,
> and to whom I was like to give offense.

Personal Prayer. Lord, help me be aware of the promise of your covenant within. I accept your promise, O God, and am gladly open to your healing presence. Do your work in me. Help me hold still and not get in the road. Tear down any walls between us that I've built and bring to reality in my life what you are pleased to do. As Jeremiah finally helped your people of old see hope through their tears, help me, precious Jesus, see through my tears to your intended future.

When people step into the library which is the Bible, often they get lost among its many shelves, twisting aisles, cultural categories, literary styles, and alternate languages. Readers need skilled librarians to get around, commentaries to help interpret what is found, dictionaries to define words never heard before, and historians to explain ancient settings basic to the biblical text.

Reading 8

ON THE THRESHOLD

Instead of standing on the promises of God, are we believers in Jesus spending too much time just sitting on the church premises complaining, idealizing yesterday, and fearing tomorrow? If so, promised lands can evaporate before our eyes. God says that we are standing on the threshold of a marvelous divine gift. Are we ready to go and claim it? Can we trust that God is adequate for all our needs as we dare to venture out on the divine mission? We are nearly there. No stopping now!

1. The Big Picture Verses.
Numbers 14:18; Hebrews 3:7-8. The Context: The Books of Numbers and Hebrews.

The Lord is slow to anger and abounding in steadfast love. If you hear the voice of the Holy Spirit, do not harden your hearts as in the days of testing in the wilderness.

2. A Bit of Background

Found in Numbers are narratives of the long journey of the ancient Jews to Canaan, from Egyptian slavery and the receiving of the Law of God at Mt. Sinai (Num. 1:1-10:10) to being on the plains of Moab, the very threshold of the promised land (22:1-36:13). A census of the people was taken twice somewhere along the way (chaps. 1 and 26), thus the book's name, "Numbers." The Hebrew designation is "In the Wilderness." The journey of the freed people stretched into decades, with numerous obstacles encountered, complaining and dissension erupting, and stories dramatically told—a golden calf, spies sent ahead, Balaam's talking donkey, and Moses and Aaron bringing forth water by striking a rock. What a trip!

By the end of this long process, with the initial generation of Egyptian slaves now dead in the wilderness, the Jews had become a strong fighting force ready to invade and claim what had been promised by God. The old had grown weary but the new were ready to march. The sacred Ark of the Covenant, carrying the agreement made with God at Mt. Sinai, was the symbol of God's presence. It always was taken with them to guide and protect (10:1-36). Moses would die, while the people, after all their disobedience and desert experiences, finally would move into the land of God's promise, now guided by others.

Much later there would come an unlikely scene, an almost absurd glimpse at a possible new future. Two women were on another threshold of entering in. They were marginalized, pregnant women, one young, poor, and unwed, the other beyond the age of conceiving. They met in the hill country of tiny Judea, celebrating and consoling each other. What could their surprising pregnancies really mean? This strange picture was of an upside-down world intending shortly to be set right-side up in a most unlikely way. In this case, receiving the promise meant nothing less than arrival of the long-expected Messiah. The time of God was arriving. No stopping now!

3. The Message in Brief

The blessed people, freed from Egypt and now formally in covenant with God after Mount Sinai, should be expected to be grateful, faithful, and hopeful. The story of the spies scouting out the land ahead, however, reports quite the opposite. Although the promised land indeed was "flowing with milk and honey" (13:27), and God's people were capable of occupying the land, there would be great challenges. Fear and doubt prevailed. Many are condemned to die in the wilderness because of unfaithfulness, although their children would make it to the promised land—God both judges and graciously provides. Moses was the great leader of the Jews, although he would die before the promise was realized. Sometimes faith leaders see the vision and pay the price of blazing the trail, having to leave to others the days of victory.

Even a brief glance at Christian church history makes clear that the followers of Jesus often have been unworthy of receiving from the gracious hand of God. We have wandered in circles, questioned divine promises, and defied the wisdom of church prophets. The presence of God with us has never faltered, even though our vision and faith often have. Fortunately, God's grace is a demonstration of divine generosity and forgiveness, never a reward for moral perfection.

There was in the ancient desert where the Jews wandered, and there always is where we stumble along, the overshadowing cloud, symbolic of God's unchanging presence with his people (Num. 9:15-23; 10:11-12, 33-36; 11:25). Our spiritual lives are an accompanied pilgrimage, not a meaningless maze. There is a land promised, a destination assured, and constant progress forward as our faithfulness allows.

4. The Present Challenge

The church of Jesus always must confront the reality of its huge task and many opponents, realizing its own weakness and dealing with times of discouragement. As did Moses for the people in the wilderness, it must recall the message that "God is merciful and gracious, slow to anger and abounding in steadfast love and faithfulness" (Ex. 34:6, Num. 14:18). We must not refuse to go forward for fear of the unknown (Num. 13-14). The God who promises also provides. Staying on the threshold means that the people wind up nowhere, still outside. The promise must be claimed.

We Christians, like the Jews of old wandering in the desert wilderness, will be denied entrance into our promised land if we cling to the security of the present or long for the idealized security of the past. Warns the writer to the Hebrews, "Today, if you hear the voice of the Holy Spirit, do not harden your hearts as in the rebellion, as on the day of testing in the wilderness" (Heb. 3:7-8). Fear hardens while faith follows on. Times change, as do spiritual leaders and mission strategies. Even so, God is constant, available, adequate, and eternal.

> Standing on the promises of Christ, the Lord,
> Bound to him eternally by love's strong chord,
> Overcoming daily by the Spirit's sword,
> Standing on the promises of God.
> > "Standing on the Promises of God"
> > —R. Kelso Carter

5. Response from the Heart

My Growth Need: Daring to step forward when God calls.
Isa. 54:2; Matt. 17:20; Phil. 3:14, 4:13; Eph. 3:20-21; Heb. 10:35-36

The Hebrew people on their way to the land of Canaan could well have been singing, "I am bound for the promised land. Oh who will come and go with me? I am bound for the promised land." They had come to the brink of entering the land for which they longed. From the time they had left Egypt, God had demonstrated his faithfulness to the people. Now they had reached a crucial point in their journey. Could they still trust God? Here's the risk of inaction at the most critical moment:

> Once to every man and nation
> comes the moment to decide,
> In the strife of truth with falsehood,
> for the good or evil side.
> Some great cause, some great decision,
> Offering each the bloom or blight,
> And the choice goes by forever,
> Twixt that darkness and that light.
> > —James Russell Lowell

The moment to decide requires a steady mind, a clear memory, and a soft heart. God was with us then; God is with is with us now, and God comes to us with great compassion, always working for our good.

O Jesus, I have promised to serve Thee to the end;
Be Thou forever near me, my Master and my Friend.
I shall not fear the battle, If Thou art by my side,
Nor wander from the pathway, if Thou wilt be my Guide.
—John E. Bode

Personal Prayer. My Father in heaven and on my pathway, I realize that my response to your call requires courage, faith, hope, and community support. Will I honor my commitment? "Faithful" is such a beautiful word, Lord. You always have been faithful to me. Am I prepared to be faithful to you? Am I willing to stand with you, no matter the circumstances, claim your promises no matter the challenge? These questions haunt me. Please give me inner spiritual stamina to bear whatever it takes to be faithful to you. After all, you are the future and I am your humble servant. Move me from threshold to fulfillment!

The attempt in these pages resembles the earlier task of C. S. Lewis in his book *Mere Christianity*. He was chosen to introduce Christianity to the population of Great Britain during the difficult war years of the 1940s. He accepted this role not as a biblical "specialist" but as a concerned Anglican layman. Lewis wasn't setting out to tackle the correctness of debated doctrines that divided the denominations. Rather, he wanted to reveal "mere" Christianity, something that should be common to all who claim Jesus as Lord. Christian faith at its simplest is necessarily derived from the dynamic of the biblical text properly heard and received.

Reading 9

THE BRIDGE BETWEEN

The spiritual life is endangered by deep crevices that block the way. We selfish humans build too many walls and not nearly enough bridges that open the way forward. Bridges of forgiveness and love can cross the deepest of ravines, connect kindred souls, build communities, and launch new worlds. The coming of Jesus would reconnect God and his people with a redeeming new covenant. Now is the time to prepare the way and cross God's bridge into new lives and futures!

1. The Big Picture Verses.
Malachi 3:1, Mark 1:3. The Context:
Books of Malachi and Mark.

Says the God Almighty, "Suddenly the Lord you are seeking will come to his temple; the messenger of the covenant, whom you desire, will come." The voice of one crying in the wilderness says, "Prepare the way of the Lord!"

2. A Bit of Background

The prophet Malachi takes us back to Jerusalem sometime after the Jewish exiles had returned from Babylon. Sadly, their high hopes for a bright new future after the exile hadn't worked out very well. Nehemiah and Ezra had drawn restrictive lines around the returned people, supposedly protecting them from the contamination of "outsiders."

By contrast, the stories of Ruth and Jonah had leaned in a more open and "progressive" direction, seeing the offered grace of God as for all people, Jew or not. Over time, however, a narrow and defensive nationalism took root in Israel. The people had begun generations of frustrated waiting for their Savior Messiah to finally arrive. The gap between what was and what should be was great. Would it ever be bridged? Bridge builders were in short supply.

Despite failed experiments and new threats, the heart of the Jewish heritage managed to keep beating, leading finally to the time of Jesus. He would be the needed grand link between the people and their God. He would bring a fresh awakening with a call for the needed heart-cleansing. Meanwhile, the prophet Malachi functioned as a bridge between the times, a bridge between the Old and New Testaments, a memory of the faltering old and an anticipation of the liberating new surely to come soon. Yes, says Malachi, the Lord we are awaiting *will come!* Its first announcement would be by John the Baptist, a voice "crying in the wilderness."

3. The Message in Brief

We must have eyes of faith to see the purposes of God working out in ways beyond typical human perception. Otherwise, skepticism and religious apathy take hold, moral standards drop, and even the leaders of the faith community lose their sense of true identity and vocation under God. The prophet Malachi saw the despair and compromise, and also the wonderful work of God just on the horizon.

What we so desire is on the way! Even so, do we see it coming or are we blinded, dulled, and even deadened as we keep waiting? Zechariah, the prophet just before Malachi at the end of the Old Testament, shares in chapter 2 a vision critical for New Testament believers. A man is seen with a measuring line trying to map out the plan for building the new Jerusalem.

Zechariah's vision is based on the assumption that the past must be honored but not allowed to dictate details of the future. Instead of being another city with high defensive walls, the new Jerusalem was to be more of a network of united, interdependent villages, diverse in their unity and defended less by walls of stone and more by the presence and power of a surrounding "ring of fire," God's indwelling Spirit.

There was to be a new day functioning in a new way, grounded in the unchanging divine Word and constant presence of God. More important than the details of the reconstructed dwellings where God's people would live should be the people's focus on the divine One who is prepared to live in and serve through the Jews for the sake of a lost world. Bridging ahead, that One would be named Jesus.

4. The Present Challenge

The big story in the world news as I wrote this page was about a huge explosion on the bridge connecting Russia and occupied Crimea. It's twelve miles long and vital for transporting military equipment and troops from Russia to support its ongoing invasion of Ukraine. Now it's suddenly a damaged symbol of Russia's dramatic attempt to bridge the big gap between itself and the key portion of Ukraine it had annexed.

A challenge we all face is bridging the gap between where we are now and the goal we hope to reach under God. Malachi saw the gap and the poor attempts to bridge it. He scolds the priests of his time for being bored with their holy office and content with many things far beneath divine standards. He even dares to say that the worship of the Gentiles was more acceptable to God than that of the Jews (1:6–2:9). What bridge there was had been damaged severely. How different is today? What should be characterizing ministers and ministries? How should they be filling the gap between what we have and what we really need?

Insists the prophet of old, there is to be a reverence that stands in awe of God's very name. There must be true instruction, turning away from sin and walking in the ways of peace (2:3-6). Elijah would be sent ahead to prepare the way. A day was coming when John the Baptist would appear in the wilderness with a sharp tongue and fresh hope for the arrival of the Lord (Mark 1:4-8). He would be proclaiming an exciting truth. God's kingdom is coming near! The troubling gap between us sinning humans and the holy God is about to be filled! Are we listening? Is that word still true? Can we believe it and begin to act accordingly?

5. Response from the Heart

My Growth Need: Surviving the shadows of the waiting.
Ps. 63:1-8, 51:11-15; Isa. 55:1-5; Rom. 12:2; Eph. 6:10-18; Rev. 12:9.

> Renew Thy church, her ministries restore,
> both to serve and adore.
> Make her again as salt throughout the land,
> and as light from a stand.
> Mid somber shadows of the night,
> where greed and hatred spread their blight,
> O send us forth with power endued;
> Help us Lord, be renewed!
> "Renew Thy Church, Her Ministries Restore"
> —Kenneth Lorne Cober

Personal Prayer: I know the frustration of endless waiting, and I see the compromises some church leaders are making. I so want to be part of a healing force in today's wasteland, someone who can see the soon-coming of the Lord and can transfer that hope into action! Renew Thy people, dear Father, as we travel through the long night of today's "somber shadows." Shine your light over the horizon so that we can see that your new day indeed is on the way. Help me to be part of that light and not just more of the frustrated darkness. If I am a wall blocking your future, make me a bridge!

CHRISTMAS SEASON--PREFACE

Advent was the season of waiting and Christmas now is the celebration season. The anticipated arrival of God with us is actually here! The Old Testament is the story of God with Israel so that together they could face this world's evil and convey good news. However, failure came. Even so, God worked on, determined to restore even if it cost a great Self-giving, the coming of Son Jesus to live and die on behalf of a new creation. In this regard, the Bible reveals four critical truths . . .

> God continues to reach in love, wanting to save this fallen world;
> Salvation will not be accomplished from heaven alone, but with willing human involvement;
> There is no salvation inherent in us humans, so not one of us was found able to accomplish the intentions of God;
> There was need for an "incarnation," a God/man, God willing personally to become one of us on behalf of us!

Thus, God acted and the baby Jesus was born. The very idea of an "incarnation," God arriving "in flesh," is so dramatic and unprecedented that it was and still is difficult to believe. Most people didn't accept the idea when Jesus first came. God choosing to arrive as a helpless baby in a stinking barn? Really? The God of all power voluntarily suffering by our sinful hands? Could such a God actually be?

It's time for Christmas, the actual birth of Christ among us. Readings 10-13 address these demanding questions as they report this dramatic event.

> Can you hear the trumpets sounding on the mountain?
> Look out on the desert--the bones are dancing!

What should we make of this baby in the barn?
The baby is none other than God with us!

Reading 10

TRUMPETS ON THE MOUNTAIN

God a "Suffering Servant"? We humans prefer a "god" who is all-powerful, meets all our present needs, and conquers all our threatening enemies as we anxiously request. Could a suffering servant also be all powerful? The Son's name is Jesus. If he really is God with us, then what must be the heart of the Father? It must be Self-giving love! God's very being must be loving grace.[1] Listen for the trumpets—they are blasting out notes of great joy for all people. God is love. God has come for us. God will suffer as necessary on our behalf. It's Christmas!

1. The Big Picture Verses.
Isaiah 40:1-3, 53:5. The Context: Isaiah 40-55.

Comfort, O comfort my people, says your God. A voice cries out: "In the wilderness prepare the way of the Lord." Surely he has borne our infirmities and carried our diseases.

2. A Bit of Background

Judah had ceased to exist, Jerusalem was in ruins, and the Babylonians were holding God's people captive, although they were about to be replaced by a new power, Persia. The Jewish exiles were despondent, some thinking God had abandoned them forever. Many

---
[1] See Barry L. Callen, *God As Loving Grace*.

still wept when remembering Zion, their beloved Jerusalem (Ps. 137). Are world events just the playthings of the rich and powerful?

Suddenly the prophet Isaiah pictures a miraculous highway opening up across the massive, trackless desert separating the captives from their homeland. God was about to lead his people home as a loving shepherd leads his needy sheep (40:3–11). They could hear the heavenly trumpets sounding. Good news! What do you hear?

Isaiah has been called the "Shakespeare of the Old Testament" and the "Fifth Gospel of Christianity." This is a biblical book well known and loved by Jesus. It covers three large sections of Israel's history, thus the speculation of three Isaiah writers. This prophet(s) initially was seized in the Temple by a dramatic experience of the holy God (chap. 6). Overwhelmed, he confessed his unworthiness, was renewed, and committed his life to represent the divine holiness he now knew. His trembling lips had been touched by God's cleansing power and he had become a willing messenger of the Word of God.

Isaiah stood in the center of public affairs as an advisor to kings and statesmen. He denounced injustice in his time (5:1–12) and called for repentance and a true serving of God (1:11-18). He sounded a warning as Assyria was a coming instrument of God judging his people, even while assuring the people that God would be faithful and restore (10:20-22). With God, there is both justified judgment and a lasting love always willing to forgive. Isaiah's chapter 53, a centerpiece of the entire Old Testament, announces that God is pure love and willing to suffer on our behalf. It's an amazing trumpet sound of hope, a foretaste of the horizon over which Jesus soon would rise.

3. The Message in Brief

About 7,000 people were at the Ringling Brothers and Barnum & Bailey circus on July 6, 1944, in Hartford, Connecticut. Suddenly, nearly 200 were dead, many of them children. A fire had broken out and the giant canvas tent roof was quickly engulfed in flames and collapsed on the crowd below. It was the day "the clowns cried," including a picture of clown Emmett Kelly carrying water in a futile attempt to stop the blaze. Tents in this world do burn and collapse.

What about trumpets on the mountain announcing unbelievably good news? Many had died before they finally sounded. The silence had seemed deadly.

God brings order out of chaos at four critical points in the biblical account. It happens first at the original creation of all things, next at the exodus of God's people from Egyptian slavery, and then again when the exile of the people was ending and their lost freedom being restored. Great news of the coming freedom was trumpeted from the mountain. Then surprising news was tacked on. God one day would come to earth as a "Suffering Servant" (chaps. 42-53)—a dramatic and not necessarily welcome portrait of God at work for us at great cost.

This would be the fourth bringing of order out of chaos. It would happen when Jesus was born as that Servant, signaling the early arrival of the active reign of God in the midst of the watery waste of human sinfulness. God's Spirit again would sweep over the swirling waters of human lostness with waves of redeeming love. Trumpets would sound on the mountain, signaling the saving presence of the holy God (Lk. 24:13-34, Acts 8:26-39).

Paul makes the central point. There would sound a cry of coming justice on the wayward, and also this welcome word. While judgment may fall on some, "whoever trusts in God *will not be put to shame*" (Rom. 9:27-33). Even in the worst of circumstances, there is hope! Can you hear the trumpets blowing such good news? They are for you. Jesus is arriving!

4. The Present Challenge

How does the God of amazing love prefer to work in this world? By bringing harsh judgment when deserved? Yes, eventually, even if reluctantly. By showering forgiveness when's the guilty repent? Yes, happily and joyfully. By arriving as a mighty army to smash all enemies? Rarely, and certainly not initially. The Almighty is gentle, has a loving heart, and prefers persuasion to displays of raw power. The Creator might well come to this world as a helpless baby in the stench of a Bethlehem barn. In fact, God would do just that. It's Christmas!

Now comes our turn. God's church must learn to be obedient children of such a "suffering servant." We who claim the name of Jesus as our Lord "must let the same mind be in us as was in Christ Jesus, who emptied himself, taking the form of a slave, and became obedient even to the point of death" (Phil. 2:5-8). Living in that humble way would be unusual good news in our self-seeking and power-hungry world. We are to let our lights shine, our self-less trumpets blow. The widow, orphan, prisoner, and homeless must know that help is on the way. The God of love, who once came in Jesus, is arriving again in the lowly persons of his servant people.

5. Response from the Heart

My Growth Need: Alertness when God is speaking.
Isa. 53:7-12; Matt. 27:45-50; Lk. 21:34-36; Acts 20:29-31; Eph. 6:18

The healing process is real. I have experienced healing personally. God enters our experiences, our suffering, and suffers with us. God enters our hearts and understands all that we go through. What God enters God can change.

> I was sinking deep in sin, Far from the peaceful shore,
> Very deeply stained within, Sinking to rise no more;
> But the Master of the sea heard my despairing cry,
> From the waters lifted me, now safe am I.
> "Love Lifted Me"
> —James Rowe

I also know that God calls those who have been healed. We are to join God in the healing of others, leading the blind through darkness to the light. As healing takes place, we sing to the Lord a new song. It's all because of God's love. Bring out the trumpets; we have an exciting song to share!

Personal Prayer. Lord, I am filled with gratitude for the promise and the healing. I want to be a part of Your great ministry of healing brought to others. Take whatever gifts I have and transform them into instruments of care so that others can be made whole. When you came in Jesus, it was Christmas. Somehow allow Christmas to come in me. Give me the mind of Christ so that I can be part of the ministry of Christ. This is for me to be and do, and yet it's too much for me to manage. Help me, Lord!

Martin Luther and John Calvin did not produce the Protestant Reformation. What produced that great Awakening was that Luther and Calvin had studied closely the Word of God. As they studied, with the assistance of God's Spirit, the revealed Word began to explode inside them, and they channeled that explosion into the Christian institutions and social arrangements around them. There is enough life-changing truth and spiritual power in the Bible to produce a "reformation" in any generation willing to expose itself to the Word of God. We long for the day envisioned by Jeremiah when people will really *know God* (Jer. 31:34). The prophet uses the word "know" less like gaining knowledge *about* and more like acquiring knowledge of by way of personal experience *with*.

Reading 11

THE BONES WILL DANCE!

The ancient scene was of the lost and hopeless. It was gruesome and depressing. God's faithful people had failed in their high calling. Their bones lay bleached on the desert floor. It was mass death rarely rivaled in scale. Then a voice from above spoke new life and called for the skeletons to rejoin their parts, become enfleshed again, and start dancing on the hot sand. Impossible, undeserved, unbelievable? Of course, although apparently not for a forgiving and renewing God!

1. The Big Picture Verses.
Ezekiel 37:11-14. The Context: Book of Ezekiel.

They say, "Our bones are dried up and our hope is lost." God says, "I am going to open your graves and bring you up, O my people. I will put my spirit within you and you shall live!"

2. A Bit of Background

The first group of exiles deported to Babylon in 598 B.C. included the prophet Ezekiel. He soon would begin to encourage belief that there was hope for the future, replacing the considerable despair that naturally had evolved over time. Another prophet, Isaiah, helped them realize that their God was clearly superior to the gods of Babylon despite their suffering circumstance. What a scene the prophet pictures, the annual celebration day of the Babylonians when their helpless gods were on parade and fell off their carts, with God commenting: "I have made and will bear; I will carry and will save" (46:4). The pretending gods would have to be dug out of the gutters and stood back up on their carts.

Jewish nationalism was revived. Sabbath practice grew as a faith distinctive, circumcision became a patriotic ritual, and synagogues developed in the absence of the Temple. As opposed to earlier generations wanting to be "like the nations" by having their own king, the Jews now were anxious to be distinctive from the nations in order to survive as a particularly called people. Could their poor bones ever dance again back home in Jerusalem or were they doomed to exist as lifeless captives in a foreign land?

The Book of Ezekiel contains oracles against foreign nations (chaps. 25–32) and glimpses of the coming new Jerusalem (chaps. 33–48). Certain of his prophetic utterances were "ecstatic" in nature, with some verging on being sheer nightmares. Classic among these are the "wheel within a wheel" (chap. 10) and the "valley of dry bones" that suddenly stand up and begin to dance. The wheels are cherubim appointed as guardians of the holiness of God (1:4; 10:5-20). They were able to move in any direction that the wheels moved, with this mobility likely symbolic of God's constant presence and full awareness of the plight of his people.

Ezekiel provides a truly dramatic scene, one of mass death about to turn into dancing new life. It's the vision of the valley of dry bones (37:1-14) that comes after God had directed Ezekiel to prophesy of the coming rebirth of Israel (chap. 36). God was having his servant announce that Israel soon would be restored to her own land in blessing.

3. The Message in Brief

God's people are to be faithful to their mission of being a light of hope to all nations. Ezekiel teaches that the God of Israel is no tribal deity but Lord of all people, including being sovereign over life and death, despair and hope. The mighty king of Babylon, seemingly invincible, finally would be obligated to whatever the God of Israel decrees (21:19-23; 30:25). When all is said and done, God alone stands and reigns, while the pretenders of this world sway awkwardly on their fragile carts and finally crash helplessly to the ground.

Later, Jesus would instruct his disciples to speak boldly to all people. He would assure them of the gifting necessary to accomplish this great mission. "You can make it. Help is on the way. What looks like cosmic chaos is actually the arena in which my Father is delivering your redemption. He is sovereign even in the worst of times and places. Go, therefore, with courage and good news."

The arrival of God's kingdom was near at hand. The faithful were to believe this and move forward gratefully and boldly. Delay was unacceptable. Failure must not be a concern. The time was *now*, right in the jumble of life as it is. Be alert and expectant, Jesus would say. When the future of God starts happening, hold your heads high and stand firm. You are mine, says the Lord. When I come, join me! (Luke 21:25-36).

4. The Present Challenge

Great wisdom comes to today's church from another vision of Ezekiel. It's about how to lay the foundations of a new Jerusalem after the Exile is finally over. The church can find its own intended future when it focuses on being protected by the divine Presence, suffused by the divine Spirit, and worshiping the Name of our God. Today's church needs a radical God-centeredness. The God presented in Ezekiel is utterly transcendent, perfectly holy, and truly merciful. In spite of the people's faithlessness, God was not abandoning them but preparing to sprinkle them clean and give them new hearts (11:19-20; 36:25-26).

Rather than be defensive and build protective walls, the church is to be Spirit-filled and Spirit-propelled. We live in an age of God-minimization. Read the classic little book *Your God Is Too Small* by J. B. Phillips. Vincent Miceli agrees, critiquing modern tendencies to "do theology" through introspection, relying on non-transcendent categories. Earth-bound theologians have a preoccupation with the human, constantly reducing God to ourselves, making theology a mere extension of anthropology.[1]

---

[1] Vincent Miceli, *The God's of Atheism* (1971). See also Barry L. Callen, *Discerning the Divine: God Through Christian Eyes* (Westminster/John Knox, 2004).

The global church today must hear this urgent message: *Our God reigns!* He rules over all in power and might, and one day judgment will fall upon those who cling to the things of this world. Meanwhile, God invites into his storehouse of goodness any who will bow the knee in reverence and obedience (37:23). To those who do, their sun-bleached bones will be given fresh life and infused with the very breath of God (37:1-14).

Let the celebration begin. Since no time is ideal, the best available time is *now*. Someone claimed hearing a minute say to an hour, "without me you are nothing." "Salvation" for Christians is not merely the notion of deliverance from hell and going to heaven, but a present deliverance from sin, a restoration of the soul to its original purity, and the renewal of our souls in righteousness and true holiness, in justice, mercy, and truth. It's time to dance with new life—*now*.

5. Response from the Heart

My Growth Need: Celebration in the face of a miracle.
Ps. 150; Jn. 3:16; Jn. 11:25-26; Jn. 16:21; 1 Cor. 15:54-55.

When the prophet Ezekiel writes of the glory of the Lord, he is referring to the presence of God. (chap. 43) How could the prophet write of such wonderful presence when the temple had been destroyed? The clear reference is to God *with the people,* temple or no temple. God will bring new life to the people, reconstitute the body of the people, and give them a new song that's fulfilled hope. God will breathe new life into the bones scattered on the floor of the valley. God opens graves and renews life.

The words "breath" and "spirit" are the same (*nephesh*). It's the breath of God within the spirit of the people that gives them life and hope. God has created a sanctuary among us. In it we are to worship, "lost in wonder, love and praise." Ezekiel is a great prophet of new life, a gift from God. We can begin the dancing, celebrating the gift, being people where God is pleased to dwell.

> Lord, prepare me to be a sanctuary,
> pure and holy, tried and true.

> With thanksgiving I'll be
> a living sanctuary for you.
> —Randy Lynn Scruggs and John W. Thompson

Personal Prayer. Lord, help me be open to your presence within. Breathe your spirit through my bones. Help me to celebrate you and dance with joy. I join my brothers and sisters in the Lord, anxious to experience your constant presence, your enabling love, and your overwhelming joy. While we are ever aware of our past unfaithfulness, we know by faith that you, our gracious God, loves and comes. It's Christmas. May its joy spill over to many others.

> Joy to the World; the Lord has come;
> let earth receive her King.
> —George Frederic Handel

The reading plan presented in these pages hopes to encourage fresh encounters with the biblical text in a relatively unstructured and non-institutionalized manner—seeking "mere" biblical truth that intends to change lives. The goal is to inspire a search, not for solutions to perennial theological debates, but for openness to the God who is in search of us with good news. We are to be encountered by a gospel that offers eternal life, the very life of God, life that will alter the present and last forever. Once *informed* by such dramatic news from God, the Bible's intention is for readers to be *re-formed* into the image of Jesus Christ. May it be so!

Reading 12

THE BABY IN A BARN

Joseph and Mary were doing what they had to do, go to Bethlehem to register for the census as required by law. It was a difficult journey, partly because Mary was close to giving birth and on arrival there was no place for them to stay other than with the animals. Regardless, it was a journey of destiny for all humanity. As they arrived in Bethlehem, God was newly coming to all humanity! It's the greatest and most unlikely story ever, God being born in a barn!

1. The Big Picture Verse.
Luke 2:7. The Context: The Gospel of Luke.

Mary gave birth to her firstborn son and wrapped him in bands of cloth and laid him in a manger because there was no place in the guest houses.

2. A Bit of Background

The powers in control of Palestine at the time of the birth of Jesus cared only that their control not be threatened. Nor was the main leadership of the Jewish community prepared to welcome gladly this baby Jesus as their Messiah. Why did they miss and turn away from him? Because he didn't appear and then function as they expected and desired. They misunderstood the grand prophecy of Isaiah 53. While it suggests that the Messiah would act in self-denial, humiliation, and personal loss on behalf of others, most Jews expected and certainly wanted one who would deliver them from the oppressive power of Rome. Wasn't Rome the most serious problem of the Jews? They judged "yes" and baby Jesus would judge "no."

The facts are straightforward enough. A long time ago Jesus was born in one little town and grew up in another. They both were mere dots on the map of a marginal Roman province called Palestine. Jesus started out following his earthly father's manual trade. Soon gripped by some powerful convictions, however, he moved from settled obscurity to roving notoriety. His popularity with the area masses skyrocketed, and then it all went sour. He ended up hanging on a Roman cross in apparent disgrace, executed on false, politically inflammatory charges. So how does this seeming tragedy of one man's failed life relate to the eternal being and activities of God?

The very appearance of Jesus among us was dramatic indeed. Mary was the mother, but it's reported by Matthew and Luke that neither Joseph nor any other human male was the biological father. The biblical narrative reports simply that the conception of Jesus occurred because of the Spirit's overshadowing. This virginal conception means that the male, traditionally considered the specific agent of human action and history, in this case must retire into the background as the powerless figure of Joseph. The point of the biblical story is that, from the very beginning of the earthly existence of Jesus, the Holy Spirit was the direct agent in the dawning of a new age. It's God who takes the initiative for our salvation. God has come to us in Jesus by the sole initiative of God.

3. The Message in Brief

This man Jesus appeared on the human scene in a very humble way, a baby born in a barn. Even so, no more extensive claim could be made concerning him than the one recorded in the Gospel of John. This humble baby Jesus is said to be in some profound sense the very Word of God who always has been (Jn. 1:1, 14). The central teaching of the Christian faith is none other than that recognizing the true identity of Jesus is finally coming to know God. Put more properly, discovering the identity of Jesus is actually being found by God.

God arriving as a baby, a helpless beginning in a poverty setting for the Sovereign of the universe? Yes, precisely. Paul explains that

Jesus "though he existed in the form of God, did not regard equality with God as something to be grasped, but emptied himself, taking the form of a slave, assuming human likeness" (Phil. 6:6-7). Jesus, on our behalf, would know all of our pains and suffer intensely unto death on our behalf. That's who God is. That's what God came to do. That's the meaning of Christmas.

A key function of the material world is to mediate the presence of God. That presence, however, often is hard for us humans to see. The highpoint of Christian faith, therefore, is God's actual and very visible "enfleshment" in Jesus. The Messiah, arriving as a baby born in extreme poverty, was a dramatic act of the Self-revealing God. In Jesus, God was making visible and understandable in our terms the largest of all truths—who God is and what God is prepared to do on our behalf. These truths, with their excitement and joy, may be expressed best in the wonderful words of Charles Wesley:

> Veiled in flesh the Godhead see,
> Hail the incarnate Deity;
> Pleased with us in flesh to dwell,
> Jesus, our Emmanuel.
> Hark, the Herald Angels sing,
> Glory to the newborn King!

4. The Present Challenge

Many Christians look the wrong way and try to make divine what is only a medium of the message. For instance, they insist on an "inerrant" Bible, one without error, doctrinally precise, above reproach of any kind, almost a literary deity. In fact, that isn't the nature or purpose of the biblical text we have, although as ancient literature its human frailties are strikingly minimal, understandable, and really of no significant consequence. Observes Eugene Peterson, beloved author of *The Message* paraphrase of the Bible, "If God had wanted to communicate with us 'inerrantly,' he would have used the language of mathematics, which is the only truly precise language we have. But, of course, you can't say 'I love you' in algebra." What God could do is say it *in person*, especially in the person of a lovely baby boy.

The Christmas message is redeeming love, the carrier of the message is the Lord of creation himself, and the way we tend to hear the message of Jesus is through the book, the biblical record of the coming of Jesus. We must learn to trust the book, even while allowing it to be what it is, a medium of the message and not the message itself.

5. Response from the Heart

My Growth Need: Insight into who Jesus really is.
Jn. 1:1, 1:14; 10:30; 1 Cor. 8:6; Col. 2:2-3; Heb. 5:5-6.

> What child is this who, laid to rest,
> On Mary's lap is sleeping?
> Who angels greet with anthems sweet,
> While shepherds watch are keeping?
>
> This, this is Christ the King,
> Whom shepherds guard and angels sing:
> Haste, haste to bring him laud,
> The babe, the son of Mary.
> "What Child Is This?"
> —William C. Dix

The shepherds joyfully made their way into the village to find the family and worship the baby. The worship of God who now was with us in flesh is the miracle of the Christmas story. May it be so for you, not just at Christmas, but as each new day dawns.

> O come to my heart, Lord Jesus.
> There is room in my heart for Thee.
> —E. S. Elliot

Personal Prayer: Oh Lord, help me walk in the footsteps of the shepherds who heard the announcement of the angels and responded joyfully. They left their work to find a miracle, and in a surprising way they found this miracle in a humble place with a lovely couple and a little baby. May this miracle overwhelm and renew me now, and may Jesus come to dwell not just in a humble birthing place but within my very heart. May I not fear the worldly powers that oppose his coming or the religious establishment that expects someone else and rejects their own Messiah.

Reading 13

HE'S GOD WITH US!

It's so dramatic a claim that it's nearly unbelievable. Still, the church of Jesus Christ always must believe that the vulnerable little infant of long-ago Bethlehem is indeed the very One who presides over the affairs of the universe and one day will implement judgment and justice for all the creation. Baby Jesus was none other than God with us. He was both present at the time of creation (Jn. 1) and is set to preside at creation's ending (Rev. 1:4–8). Either this is sheer nonsense or the greatest of imaginable truths.

1. The Big Picture Verses.
John 1:14; Colossians 1:15, 19-20. The Context:
John 1 and Colossians.

The Word became flesh and lived among us, and we have seen his glory, full of grace and truth.... Jesus is the image of the invisible God. For in him all the fullness of God was pleased to dwell, and through him God was pleased to reconcile to himself all things.

2. A Bit of Background

Many early Christians tried to adjust their faith in Jesus to fit whatever was acceptable in their time and place. One adjustment tried in Colossae was to give the faith more presumed intellectual depth, trying to make it more attractive to religious highbrows. These supposedly more sophisticated thinkers were speculating on the existence of a range of mysterious forces that supposedly control life and deserve to be reverenced, even worshiped alongside Christ.

On hearing of this dangerous heresy, Paul reacted vigorously. His letter to the Colossians offers a breathtaking analysis of the significance of Jesus Christ and what it means to be a faithful Christian. In looking for depth without straying into pools of intellectual heresy, there are no better places to land than the letter to the Colossians and the opening verses of the Gospel of John.

In this Gospel is found the most familiar verse in the New Testament, John 3:16. It echoes Paul's strong emphasis. The amazing news is that "God so loved the world that he gave his only Son that everyone who believes in him may not perish but have eternal life." None is comparable to Jesus Christ, the singular divine Son, the baby in the Bethlehem barn, the presence in flesh of the Divine who will shape the eternities yet to come.

3. The Message in Brief

Jesus Christ is God present and in action on our behalf. He is the creative purpose that (Who) shaped the universe, the very meaning of its existence. He is totally supreme over all orders of being and is the unifying principle that underlies and holds together all things. We believers will be able to resist the allurements of futile speculations and false mysteries only by being fully grounded and rooted in the historical reality who is Jesus Christ, the man in who God was with us.

Here's the most important of all questions: "Was Jesus the son of Mary who became the Son of God, or the eternal Son of God who became the son of Mary?" If you choose the first, you have no good news because there is nothing saving in us humans. Salvation is in God alone. "So if Jesus emerged *out of us*, he can do nothing more for us than we can do for ourselves. But if he came *to us* out of the loving nature of the eternal Deity, then he can do for us what only God can do."[1]

Once we know that Jesus really is the One "coming down from the Father above," we can grasp by faith that the Prince of Peace will sweep over and transform our spirits forever.

---

[1] Edwin Lewis, as quoted by Dennis Kinlaw, *Lectures in Old Testament Theology*, 54.

> Peace, peace, wonderful peace,
> coming down from the Father above!
> Sweep over my spirit forever, I pray,
> in fathomless billows of love!
> "Wonderful Peace"
> —Warren Cornell

There can be a new birth, a new identity, an inheritance received that is beyond imagination. Peter writes "to God's elect, strangers in the world who have been chosen and given a new birth and an inheritance that can never perish" (1 Pet. 1:1–4). How can this be? Only because the presence with us in Jesus is actually God.

4. The Present Challenge

It seems that we humans are destined to shape our thinking to whatever is prominent at the time. The church exists in the world and is hardly immune from its most popular assumptions, however wrong they may be. Attractive or not, human ways of thinking and acting are typically faulty and keep changing. The only satisfactory stance is a constant focus on Jesus Christ and devotion to who he is and the life he defines and makes possible.

Mountain views are the very best. Moses ascended Mt. Sinai and encountered God. Disciples went up the Mt. of Transfiguration with Jesus and suddenly realized who he really was. In his last sermon before being assassinated, Martin Luther King, Jr., spoke of the threats of violence he had received. Even so, he affirmed that God "allowed me to go up to the mountain top. And I've looked over, and I've seen the promised land. My eyes have seen the glory of the coming of the Lord!"

Today's culture is loaded with "data," tiny bits of electronic information. They are held by the billions in databases and stored in "the cloud." What used to be found only in libraries is now packed away in little smartphones in our pockets and purses. Access is immediate. Here's the problem. While now knowing so much, it's not clear that we are that much wiser. If our hearts remain twisted, we tend to use for ourselves and against others whatever we supposedly know. By contrast, knowing Jesus Christ doesn't yield answers to all our questions, at least not yet. What it does do is put our understanding in proper perspective. And that's more than enough!

5. Response from the Heart

My Growth Need: Amazement at revealed truth.
Matt. 7:28-29; Mk. 6:2; Jn. 1:18; Jn. 5:20; 2 Tim. 3:16

Perhaps the greatest miracle of Christmas is what we call the "incarnation." God so loved human beings that the ultimate gift was given, God present as a human being, *"God with Us. Emmanuel!"* We can say, as did the disciples of the New Testament, "I have seen him, I knew him, I heard him, I responded to him, I followed him."

The miracle is that in the face of Jesus we can see God. No one has ever seen the very heart of God fully, except in the face of Jesus. Jesus enabled blind eyes to be opened. He provided a new experience for Christians, enabled by the Spirit within. It's the removal of our desire for revenge, bringing new relationships between ourselves and all others. Forgiveness brings a newness of life. Have you been forgiven? Have you found ultimate wisdom? His name is Jesus.

Personal Prayer: I'm slow to understand, I realize, especially when the issue is as big as the source, meaning, and destiny of the whole universe. I'm only a limited human, Lord, and you know my great limitations so well. I don't want to know everything, only one thing. I want to know *who Jesus really is*. If he really is what the New Testament claims, that's more than enough for me!

> Open our eyes, Lord, we want to see Jesus,
> Reach out and touch him and say that we love him.
> Open our ears, Lord, and help us to listen.
> Open our eyes, Lord, we want to see Jesus
>
> —Robert Cull

LENT: PREFACE

Lent is a the period in the Christian Year of preparation for facing the coming suffering and death of Jesus, and for beginning our own sacrificial service for him in the world. Moses had remained on Mount Sinai for forty days waiting for the word of the Lord. For forty days Jesus had been in the wilderness sorting out the motives and means of his coming mission. Forty days of self-denial before Easter is therefore an appropriate annual discipline for Christian believers. It's a time of cleansing, strengthening, clarifying, and refreshing the soul—and especially bracing for whatever is to come—and it's both awful and wonderful!

Readings 14-17 illumine four dimensions of this difficult season and its especially challenging tasks of self-discipline and sometimes painful preparation.

>
> Penetrating the darkness
> Going back to the mountain
> Acting out or shutting up
> Dealing with the desire for revenge

Reading 14

PENETRATING THE DARKNESS

Let's be done with simplistic answers to profound questions. They tend to bring more confusion than wisdom, extra pain instead of relief. Job is one of the great wisdom books of the Bible. He represents all of us as we face the harshness of existence in this world of injustice and pain. His well-meaning "friends" wore him out with their trite and inadequate answers to life's big questions about the sources of our suffering. We must pick our consultants with care and realize that full understanding of the most difficult mysteries of life lie only in the mind of God.

1. The Big Picture Verses.
Job 42:3, 28:28. The Context: The Book of Job.

Admitted the finally humbled Job: "I have heard what I did not understand, things too wonderful for me." Reverencing the Lord, that is wisdom, and to depart from evil, that is understanding.

2. A Bit of Background

The dominant viewpoint at the time of the writing of Job was that misfortune is the result of a person's sins, committed knowingly or not. Prosperity, on the other hand, is the reward of a well-lived life of virtue. This simplistic solution to understanding life's paradoxical realities, including the problem of evil, is one that the book of Job finally rejects. Penetrating the darkness of this mystery must be done some way other than listening to simple answers common on the streets. Supposed "common" sense often is as wrong as it is everywhere.

Presented through three cycles of speeches, the "friends" of Job try to convince him that the tragedies suddenly burdening his life somehow were his own fault. Job knows better and keeps insisting on his innocence. Surprisingly, no final answer to the problem of unjust suffering is given in this book, although the proper path to the answer is identified. It comes in a magnificent poem on wisdom (chap. 28). Job is overwhelmed by the majesty, power, and creativity of God. This causes him to confess his sin of presumption in daring to argue with God (40:3-5) about things he really didn't understand.

The Book of Job can be a difficult book to understand, partly because Job asks the obvious question and never receives a direct answer from God. He didn't understand why he suffered so much. He, and we, may not understand what's happening or why, but we are being called to learn at least this. We are not to ask "why" but rather "what." "What are you trying to teach me, Lord, about the struggles of this life?" The lesson appears to be this. God knows what He's doing, so we must trust when there are no answers yet available. God's work and its final outcome are sure and just and will be *wrapped in love.*

3. The Message in Brief

The providence of God should not be doubted even when not understood (42:1–6). God is love and always is working for good (Rom. 8:28). We mere humans must discipline ourselves to increase our awareness of God's gracious presence in life's circumstances, even when God's will and ways of working remain in the darkness of our limited awareness. Demanding to know answers tends to frustrate more than resolve our concerns. A much better approach is Job's dramatic statement of humble praise: "Naked I came from my mother's womb and naked shall I return there; the Lord gave and the Lord has taken away; blessed be the name of the Lord!" (1:21).

When we frail humans suffer, insist on answers to our "why" questions and don't get them, the best response is to echo Job's words to God: "I know that you can do all things and that no purpose of yours can be thwarted" (42:1-2). With such words of assurance comes this by faith: "God sets on high those who are lowly, and those who mourn are lifted to safety, for I know that my Redeemer lives, and at last he will stand upon the earth, and then I shall see God" (5:11, 19:25-26).

Is that comfort enough in the face of ongoing evil in the present? It must be because that's all we have for now. Added to this, of course, is the cross of Jesus, God's dramatic and wholly unjust suffering on our behalf. On that ugly hill of execution is the greatest darkness—which turns out to be the brightest light. The One who knows all willingly submitted to suffering, standing by our sides, and finally raising the Son and all who belong to him to resurrected victory. Praise the Lord!

4. The Present Challenge

We must guard against assuming that the conventional thinking of our time is necessarily the proper approach to understanding God's nature and ways of working in a world full of evil. Spiritual advisors can be well-meaning and quite wrong, and there always are many of them. After reviewing the numerous creeds and traditions of the churches and absorbing their assurances, people of faith still must proceed humbly in the face of life's mysteries. One day God will turn mourning into dancing, tragedy into joy, and wrongs into proper paths of right.

Night is a disturbing book that tells the story of Eliezer Wiesel, a studious Orthodox Jewish teenager living in Hungary in the early 1940s. He was sent by the Nazis to the Auschwitz concentration camp and struggled there to maintain his faith as he witnessed other prisoners lose their lives from inhumane treatment that God presumably could have but clearly did not stop. Had even God died in this awful place? How, in such terrible circumstances, can believers say with Job, "Though he slay me, I will hope in him" (13:15)? Wiesel's faith faltered.

In our "advanced" time with the Lord not returning yet and horrific genocides still happening around the globe, can we still believe in the all-powerful God of all goodness? Where is God when terrible evil isn't being stopped? Various answers are floated, some by popular preachers, but none seem adequate. Can we learn from Job to be humble, realizing that we are not equipped to think God's high thoughts after him? Can we find some comfort in going on without all the answers? Does Christian maturity include not needing to know what can't yet be known?

5. Response from the Heart

My Growth Need: Understanding the reason for suffering.
Gen. 3:14-19; Isa. 53:3; Rom. 5:3-5; Phil. 1:29; 1 Pet. 3:14; James 1:2-4

Many people ask why there's so much suffering in the world. The book of Job never answers this question. Rather, it asks, "How can I best respond properly to the inevitability of suffering?" It seems that suffering is a consequence of being human. People cry out to God, "Why me?" The question should be, "Why not me? I'm human too."

> And in despair I bowed my head.
> "There is no peace on earth," I said,
> "For hate is strong and mocks the song
> Of peace on earth, good will to men."
>
> Then pealed the bells more loud and deep:
> God is not dead, nor doth He sleep,
> The wrong shall fail, the right prevail,
> With peace on earth, good will to men.
> —Henry W. Longfellow

> There is a place of quiet rest, near to the heart of God;
> A place where sin cannot molest, near to the heart of God.
> Oh Jesus, blessed Redeemer, Sent from the heart of God,
> Hold us who wait before Thee, near to the heart of God."
> "Near to the Heart of God"
> —Cleveland McAfee

Personal Prayer. O Lord, I know you are with me, and I am to trust that you are at work in my life even when I cannot see or feel you. But sometimes that's hard! Continue to teach me to know that your love never ends. Whether life is good or filled with suffering, Lord, help me not be judgmental when those around me are suffering and crying out, or prospering when they are very undeserving. Help me be patient with injustice, knowing that one day, somehow, you will judge justly and make all things right. Keep me appreciative of the cross of Jesus. You've endured suffering, dear Savior, and you did it for me. Knowing the why of your cross helps me go on when much in my life remains so unknown and seemingly unfair.

We must avoid the disobedience of religious liberalism with regard to the givenness of the biblical text and the inflexible legalism of some conservatives who overreact to the liberal's misuse of Christian freedom. There is a playing field on which the process of biblical interpretation is to be to be played. As we get into the specific cases of our study of the Bible, there is no way to predict what joyful discoveries, as well as painful struggles, we will experience. This is the way of our whole life with God. *It is a journey with the Spirit.*

Clark H. Pinnock and Barry L. Callen,
***The Scripture Principle*, 257-58.**

Reading 15

GO BACK TO THE MOUNTAIN

How we humans hate being enslaved, and yet how readily we find ways to enslave others and become victims of our own addictions. Can it be true that the greatest possible freedom is a particular form of slavery? God's creation is intended to operate according to the laws built into its very nature. The biblical call is back to the holy mountain where the Law was given to Moses. It had been violated and things now had to change. God is the Liberator. Being alive in God is to be holy, truly happy, and really free.

1. The Big Picture Verses.
Exodus 20:2-3; Deuteronomy 5:24. The Context: Exodus 19-20, Deuteronomy 5:6-24.

I am the Lord, your God, who brought you out of the land of Egypt, out of the house of slavery; you shall have no other gods before me. This can be the day that God will speak again, and persons still may live.

2. A Bit of Background

An event central to the entire Bible is the "Exodus," God freeing his people from Egyptian slavery. Fifty days from this miraculous "escape" brought them to the base of Mount Sinai. There Moses, their leader, climbed the mountain, interacted with God on their (our) behalf, and received the *Law* of God. It's highlighted by the

"Ten Commandments." God had saved the people to be his own, and now the Commandments are given to make clear how these people are to behave as God's own in the world. These Commands are the terms of the "covenant," the agreement between God and the people, sent out on behalf of others.

Unfortunately, a "going back" has been a frequent need of God's people. It's seen many times in the Bible and church history. There have been compromises and apostacies, revivals, reformations, and "great awakenings." We stray and must return to sure foundations. What we learn from the past is that, much too often, we don't learn from the past and have to endure the sad process of relapsing and then repenting, falling back and needing to be jerked forward anew.

Psalm 19 describes the law as "reviving the soul." Typical today is the assumption that law is restricting, hardly reviving. Nonetheless, human beings find themselves caught in various forms of self-chosen servitude. Freedom is never absolute. The big question is what or whom one serves.

3. The Message in Brief

God has acted on our behalf, *therefore*.... That's the sequence. We are shown mercy before being asked to show it to others. God acts first when we cannot, and only then asks us to act with divine enabling. Being set free should lead to the grateful discipline of obedience. Obedience to what? To the commands God has given that show what life should look like when divinely directed, when we are freed from our selfish selves and on mission for God. We must be God's people by living in God's way in response to God's prior action and ongoing direction.

The Commandments were given to our ancestors long ago. Time has hardly eroded their value or our responsibility. "Not with our ancestors (only) did the Lord make this covenant, but *with us* who are here alive today" (Deut. 5:3). God is unchanged. Neither is there be change in how we are to live in obedience to God's will.

Taking God's name "in vain" always has meant much more than avoiding vulgar language. It's also making God's name little more than a religious slogan, baptizing whatever fits our human agendas. Keeping a "Sabbath day" is more than giving all Saturdays to God's service alone (or Sundays in Christian tradition). It's to break the hold of abusive production schedules by declaring periodic freedom from an overwhelming consumption culture, allowing needed rest for our bodies and souls, enabling opportunity to focus on God.

4. The Present Challenge

People intending to be true followers of Jesus are not merely to be "saved" by God's grace. After experiencing forgiveness of sin, we then are to live as God's redeemed people, behaving in God-like and God-directed ways. Jesus fulfilled the Jewish Law by his life and death, and on occasion corrected false understandings, sometimes separating the Law's mechanics from its intended spirit. We deceive ourselves by thinking we are in charge of our own destiny. Jesus is the "way, truth, and life."

To be avoided are the modern "gods" of racial purity, wealth, personal ambition, and nationalism. Another meaning of not taking God's name "in vain" is refusing to take seriously the claim of God in all our social, economic, and political affairs. There are to be "no other gods" that dictate our lives. God has called into being a covenant community, the church, formed around the knowing and doing of the divine will. As opposed to conventional human communities, the church is to avoid all exploitation of its own members or of the neighbors and environment around it.

5. Response from the Heart

My Growth Need: Obedience to God's commands.
Ex. 19:5; Deut. 11:1; Jn. 14:15-17; Jn. 15:9; Heb. 13:17

The central message of the Exodus story is that the liberation was *God's* doing. God rescued the people and led them out of Egypt, performing great miracles in the process. Once in the wilderness, God provided food and safety. However, the people were not always faithful in return. It's such a human tendency to forget and go our own way. How could the Jews forget such great miracles as these? As with children who want to express their own independence, we talk back to God and get lost in the wilderness of our own making.

The need certainly is not to return to Egyptian slavery but to the mountain where God initially spoke and gave the keynotes of the liberating way of life. God had redeemed the people and rescued their spirits from self-serving. Would they remain free? Are you free? We need constant reminders to renew our commitments to love God and each other, and to walk God's way.

> Consecrate me now to Thy service, Lord,
> By the power of grace divine;
> Let my soul look up with a steadfast hope,
> And my will be lost in Thine.
> "I Am Thine O Lord"
> —Fanny J. Crosby

Personal Prayer. O Lord, help me to remember how you acted on my behalf so many times in the past. May I not forget the lessons that came and that still can bring hope and help today. I need You, Lord. I realize that I cannot live in the Spirit without You and without these reminders. Teach me through the Spirit to honor You for bringing hope and help in my times of need, and for just being who you are, the ultimate, pure love, giver of the laws of life at its best. Help me to relish and not strain against the very idea of "law." Yours, I know, is the source of life itself.

Reading 16

ACT OUT OR SHUT UP!

There is no apology for the harsh language. The Bible is bluntly clear. Act like a child of the loving God or surely you still are a child of the devil! The stakes are high and the choice clear. Act in love or except that your Christian testimony will be viewed by God as a sham. Of course, salvation is by faith alone, but saving faith is never alone. It's always anxious to act in accord with the wonderful new reality of being in Christ, and thus necessarily active with Christ on a mission of love. Don't speak as though you are God's representative unless you are acting like you really are.

1. The Big Picture Verses.
James 1:22, 1 John 5:2. The Context: The Books of James and 1 John.

Be doers of the word and not merely hearers who deceive themselves. By this we know that we love the children of God, when we love God and obey his commandments. The authenticity is in the action.

2. A Bit of Background

The "Wisdom" literature of the Old Testament encourages the people of God to think and act like God's people. James and John echo this in the New Testament. Martin Luther, the great Protestant reformer, referred to the book of James as "an epistle of straw." Since his reforming emphasis was on salvation by faith *alone*, the focus of James on practical "works" seemed to Luther questionable at best. He lamented the absence of a strong theological presence like appears in the "purest gospel," the book of Romans. Still, Paul wrote more than Romans and often stressed vigorously the needed practical applications of true Christian faith. Theology not lived out is shallow theory at best.

Lying behind First John and several other New Testament books is a dangerous line of religious belief that threatened to swamp the early Christian church. This "Gnostic" stance stressed a special religious knowledge which supposedly was all one needed to gain—personal conduct was relatively unimportant. Religion is a thing of the spirit, some taught, and not a thing of the material world, with spirit good and material evil.

The real humanity of Jesus was denied by these new teachers. John wrote to Christians to protest such dangerous thinking seeping into and spoiling the faith in Jesus. Our Lord indeed did come in the flesh (4:2). He is not some grand mystery that only philosophic specialists can comprehend. Jesus was real and action-oriented. He is none other than God acting in love toward us so that we can act in love toward others. If we wish to be attuned to God, we must not be preoccupied with probing the secrets of the mysterious, but actually doing God's loving will as Jesus did and his Spirit still calls us to do.

3. The Message in Brief

Here is the great Christian paradox that must not be diluted or destroyed. Salvation is indeed by faith alone, although real faith is *never alone*. Truly "saved" people are eager to act in accord with their new life in Jesus. According to Jesus, entering the kingdom of heaven requires *doing* the will of the Father (Matt. 7:21). Faith without supporting deeds is an empty shell (James 2:1–26).

We cannot claim to love God and act like pagans (1 Jn. 1:7--2:16). Living a Christ-like life is the only sure proof that we have been made new persons through the Spirit of Jesus. Caring for each other brings us into God's very presence. When there, we learn that God's very being is love. If there is no love in our hearts and none seen in loving actions toward our neighbors, any claim to be loving God is a living lie (1 Jn. 4:17-21).

4. The Present Challenge

Christian "holiness" must be more than abstract intellectual theory. Here are some very practical life issues that James insists we must face with integrity--how we treat the less fortunate, how we speak to others, our use of money, and our reactions to misfortune. Non-believers will know we are Christian only by our wise and loving *actions*. Accurate theology is important, although of little evangelistic value apart from loving relationships and actions. It's as simple as that. Act in love or shut up about assured dogmas. People will judge you more by the work of your hands than the words of your mouth.

The Message paraphrase of 1 John 3:18 summarizes things well. "Let's not just talk about love; let's *practice* real love. This is the only way we'll know we're living truly in God's reality." Put another way, we'll only really *know* as we actually *do*. To really know a loving God, we must start loving like God. It's as simple and yet as blunt and demanding as this. "Put up or shut up!"

The greatest credibility gap within our society is the one that exists between what we say and what we do. If we speak one way and act otherwise, we negate any potential impact for good. The central message in the Hebrew Scriptures is that we are to love God with all our heart, soul, mind and strength, and love our neighbor as ourselves. The Scriptures do not concentrate on intentions but on the way we live, the ways we respond, and the good we do.

> To serve the present age,
> my calling to fulfill;
> O may it all my powers engage
> to *do* my Master's will.
> —Charles Wesley

5. Response from the Heart

MY GROWTH NEED: Living and affirming the faith.
Phil. 1:27; Hebrews 11:2-10, 15:22; Jam. 2:21-26;

Rev. 14:12-13

If you promise to pray for others, you must follow through. Henri Nouwen said, "Prayer without action grows into powerless pietism, and action without prayer degenerates into questionable manipulation. Our actions, like our prayers, must be a manifestation of God's compassionate presence in the midst of the world." The story of the "Good Samaritan" is central to the teachings of Jesus. When need appears, the Christian must go into selfless action.

> Lord, whose love through humble service
> bore the weight of human need,
> Who, upon the cross, forsaken,
> offered mercies, perfect deed;
> We, your servants, bring the worship,
> not her voice alone, but heart,
> consecrating to your purpose,
> every gift that you impart.
>
> "Lord, Whose Love through Humble Service"
> —Albert F. Bayly

Personal Prayer. O Lord, I react against blunt statements that demand something of me. Still, I do want to witness for you, not only by talking about faith but through loving deeds inspired by faith. Help me to receive this message from James and John and do something about it. If I don't act out in love, I should shut up about how wonderful God's love is. Give me wisdom and strength to be true to my promises to pray and find compassionate ways to live out my prayers in actions. "Breathe on me, breath of God, fill me with life anew, that I may love what Thou dost love, and *do* what Thou wouldst do."[1]

---

[1] Words by Edwin Hatch.

Reading 17

WHO DOESN'T WANT REVENGE?

Is a Christian faith community obligated to full obedience to the political state wherein it resides? Yes and No. Should Christians take direction from Paul or John on this difficult citizenship question (Rom. 13 or Rev. 13)? Yes, both. It's a difficult paradox indeed. The politics of this world can be a respected instrument of public order, although too often it can and does devolve into a tool of the worst kind of human tyranny. Nahum saw the worst of the possibilities and shared the harshest of judgments. Some things do belong to Caesar and others clearly don't. Regardless, if revenge for previous injustice ever is acceptable, it should be left to God.

1. The Big Picture Verses.
Nahum 1:7; Romans 12:17-18.
The Context: The Book of Nahum.

The Lord is good, a stronghold in a day of trouble; he protects those who take refuge in him, even in a rushing flood. Repay no one evil for evil. If possible, so far as it depends on you, live peaceably with all.

2. A Bit of Background

The Assyrian Empire was especially ruthless, terrorizing so many over several generations. God is pictured by Nahum as calling an end to this horror. The prophet graphically describes an avenging God. Nineveh is stormed and sacked (2:1-13). It's not unlike the eventual fate of the Beast reported in John's Revelation. The world then and now tends to breathe a sigh of relief when seeing the ugly giant fall. Even so, some account must be made of the sharp contrast between this view of God and the one shown to us by Jesus. Is God the great avenger, the prince of peace, or somehow both?

The early Christian church was a marginal social group in the surrounding Roman Empire, totally outside the circles of power. The later church in the West, however, became virtually one with the reigning "worldly" powers, often with results quite negative for the church's integrity. Cooperation of Germany's main church bodies, at least by silence in the face of the Nazi regime, is one embarrassing example of how unholy church-state alliances can come to be.

A man who had seen the unholy German church accommodation firsthand tried to warn young Eugene Peterson. His boyhood pastor had been a fervent Nazi. All the German churches Peterson knew had "played cozy" with the Third Reich. That kind of compromised church would ruin young Peterson. It tends to reduce pastors to functionaries in a bureaucracy where labels take the place of faces and rules trump relationships and total devotion to the gospel of Christ.[1]

Paul calls believers in Rabbi Jesus to be responsible citizens of their nations—they should add to peace and order, fulfill obligations and respect government leaders (Rom. 13). However, the New Testament also recognizes that sometimes political powers emerge like a beast that is determined to devour the church (Rev. 13). Ultimate loyalty, then, must be to God, whatever the cost. This is a painful paradox, sometimes spawning persecution or worse.

The ancient Jews increasingly blended the faith community and the ruling state. David is pictured as the rightful ruling power of his time, king and chief representative of God. The psalmist sings of Jerusalem, the Jew's national capital and religious center, symbol of God's ruling righteousness in this world. But being "like the nations" often is also to be quite unlike God. God is to be the refuge in times of trouble, but the people often are anxious to fortify them-

---

[1] See Eugene Peterson's biography, *A Burning in My Bones*, by Winn Collier.

selves with the big guns of others in hope of survival. That soon brings disaster, the fury of the avenging God according to Nahum.

3. The Message in Brief

A wind of fury can blow like the tornado of an angry God, crushing Nineveh (1:1-6). Even so, the tender heart of the same God can smile on those who wait for him.

The more a believer truly prays, the more she or he realizes that God really is, that actions will have consequences, and that all persons are equally loved by their Creator. That brings a "political" dimension to prayer, one that easily comes into conflict with the world's ruling powers. "Repay no one evil for evil. If possible, so far as it depends on you, live peaceably with all" (Rom. 12:17–21).

The powers that be in this world want--sometimes demand--full allegiance of its citizens, but Christian allegiance ultimately lies in another direction. It must be offered to the Divine who transcends all human nations and political structures with their sometimes brutal ways. Christians are to be obedient, respectful, cooperative citizens where they live, yes, but only as much as possible. The big question becomes, "What belongs to Caesar and what only to God?" (Matt. 22:21). What must be learned is the "political" meaning of Jesus when he taught: "Blessed are the poor in spirit for theirs is the kingdom of heaven" (Matt 5:3).

4. The Present Challenge

One small piece of classic poetry states both the problem and eventual solution:

> Truth forever on the scaffold,
> Wrong forever on the throne…
> Yet that scaffold sways the future,
> and behind the dim unknown,
> Standeth God within the shadows,
> keeping watch upon his own.
> —James Russell Lowell

Nahum, some six centuries before Christ's coming, watched the ebb and flow of evil empires. He concluded that there is a moral law woven into history which works inexorably to a certain climax. It's a reflection of the justice of God who, although sometimes seeming to tarry, inevitably will move to the proper and overwhelming end. Rudyard Kipling warns in his *Recessional*:

> Lo! All our own pomp of yesterday
> Is one with Nineveh and Tyre.
> Judge of the nations, spare us yet,
> Lest we forget, lest we forget!

5. Response from the Heart

My Growth Need: Forgiveness in the face of evil.
Deut. 32:35; Prov. 10:12; Mk. 11:25; 1 Thess. 5:15; 1 Pet. 3:9; 2 Cor. 13:11

My life is filled with choices between good and evil, sometimes between good and better, and sometimes between bad and worse. How can I know God's will? What will be the result of my decision, short-term or long-term? Will what I decide bring hurt or help? What are the implications of maturing into the image of Christ?

The meaning of the name Nahum is "comfort." Nehemiah means "My comfort is Yahweh." For whom do we request comfort? Where do we turn for refuge when our own circumstances sour? Do we allow the desire for revenge to creep into our consciousness? Nahum's vision, typical of the prophets, predates the downfall of Nineveh, the city that becomes predominant in the story of Jonah. Do we, God's faithful, yield to the desire for revenge against the evil or persist in praying for repentance and redemption of even the worst of sinners?

Personal Prayer. Lord, speak to my heart when it aches for revenge. Redeem and purify it for your sake. Teach me the reality of forgiveness. The headlines are full of news about evil national leaders and hateful policies and programs. Should I respond vigorously and to try right things? What would Jesus do? Cleanse my heart, Lord, so I can represent you properly. Teach me the boundaries of the world's political jurisdiction. Help me determine to be a citizen of the kingdom of God before all else, doing what social good I can and accepting the consequences of backing away when necessary.

The work of biblical interpreters involves taking a text that was intelligible in one ancient culture and situating it in another. We start with the original communication and determine what was being said; then we attempt to encode that message in the modern hearer's frame of reference. Because translation always will be culture specific, we must be open to unfamiliar ways of doing the translation in contexts other than our own.

>Clark H. Pinnock and Barry L. Callen,
>*The Scripture Principle*, 256.

EASTER SEASON--PREFACE

Love always will rise from the dead because good is more powerful than evil and faithful love is the very heart of God. The mystery of the death and resurrection of Jesus Christ tells us that "this finally is a benevolent universe. God is on our side, we belong here, and there is no basis for existential fear. Something much better already is in the works. The beginning anew is always happening! Power cannot see that. Love can see nothing else."[1]

Jesus had warned his disciples that evil was gathering and his violent death was inevitable. They didn't understand and couldn't allow themselves to accept such a terrible thing. Kill our Messiah? Unthinkable! What they couldn't see was the big picture. God was at work and some awful things apparently were necessary. The bottom line would be that no human power or action could prevail in the long run. Even the darkest of Fridays would have to yield to the bright sunshine of a divine Sunday. Despite anything, resurrection was already in the wind!

The church year begins with Advent. We wait and hope and believe, and sometimes we struggle with our belief when days are yet dark. Finally, the child is born, clear evidence that God indeed is with us and at work. And yet, we still have to watch and wait. How will things play out? How do we deal with our own sin that keeps obstructing the way of God among us? That's the season of Lent.

Now it happens. Jesus is dead! Is this the end of what we were so sure was the final answer to the human dilemma of all the evils of sin, sickness, and death? They killed our Rabbi Jesus! Then comes the news, so dramatic that all else now hinges on whether it's true.

---

[1] Richard Rohr, *What the Mystics Know*, 132.

God had acted again, choosing the dead no longer to be dead, but alive forevermore, alive *for you and me!* It's all highlighted in Readings 18-21.

Reading 18

GOD OF AMAZING GRACE

John Wesley made clear that "orthodoxy" is only one part of religion. We are not to get hung up on mastering the fine details of belief, thinking that getting all our theology exactly right is the prime goal of authentic faith. Beliefs are important, yes, but they must not be mistaken for the substance of the faith, which is *holy love reigning in the heart*. Can it be? We know that love indeed is reigning because *Christ is risen!*

1. The Big Picture Verses.
Song of Songs 2:1, 8; Hosea 6:1, 3. The Context:
The Books of Hosea and the Song of Songs.

I am a rose of Sharon, a lily of the valleys. The voice of my beloved, look, he comes! Come let us return to the Lord. His appearing is as sure as the dawn; he will come to us like the spring rains that water the earth.

2. A Bit of Background

The Song of Songs is a very different biblical book. Certainly not a manifesto for "free love," it's an exploration of the possible beauty of erotic love when between lovers passionately committed to each other. Such whole-life passion mirrors the ideal "covenant" relationship between God and human beings who have been created in love and for love. Given Solomon's checkered personal history on the sexual front (a royal harem), and this book not declaring its authorship, it's probably best not to feature Solomon's name in the title.

Hesed is one of the great Hebrew words found in the Bible. It means "undying love," what God is constantly and what his people often fail to be. Alongside God's great love is the more romantic kind that's affirmed here as proper for humans under proper circumstances. It's part of the goodness of the good creation that the divine *hesed* has provided.

Love poetry belongs in the Bible even though it surprises and even shocks some readers. A young couple sing of their love and how they overcome obstacles to being together passionately. Some interpreters have preferred to understand the book allegorically. For Jews, the woman embodies Israel being loved by God. For Christians, often it's the love relationship between the church and Jesus. This is true, but not all the truth.

God is a passionate lover and has fallen in love with Israel, whom he wishes to be his own. God is looking for children for the Father and a Bride for his Son. A self-giving love is the basis for all desired relationships. In the time of the great Hebrew prophets, the divine--human courtship had broken down and the prophet Hosea probed deeply the meaning of the love of God in the face of human disloyalty to the sacred relationship.

While Amos thundered coming judgment, Hosea announced that judgment isn't the final word of God. The ultimate truth about God is an infinite love sometimes played out in the oddest of love stories. The prophet is directed by God to marry an unfaithful prostitute. Hosea does and longs for the day when Israel will come to her senses and return to the purity of her covenant with our ever-loving God.

3. The Message in Brief

The Song of Songs sometimes is read by Jews at the Passover celebration, thought of as the beginning of God's courtship with Israel. In a male-dominated world at the time of its writing, the Song shows a remarkable equality and mutuality of the lovers. In fact, the woman speaks most and has the first and last words (1:2, 8:14). Erotic sexuality, when between a couple deeply in love and fully life committed, is far from pornography. It's part of God's good creation. The divine seal is set on physical human affection when it dignifies rather than spoils the intent of the creation, when it's intense and faithful as is God's love for his people (Eph. 5:22–33).

Implied is the fundamental fact that love is built into the very fabric of the creation. "Evil," "live" spelled backwards, is very real now. One day, however, God will straighten out all things. Life and love will win! No more clearly would this be seen than on the day when Jesus, God-with-us, would be brutally killed and then his tomb becomes empty. Defiance of God's will is doomed from the beginning, whatever its apparent little victories in the meantime. Regardless of the darkness, Easter daylight is on the way! God's love cannot be kept down and finally defeated.

4. The Present Challenge

Far too many Christian believers are "religious" in a traditional, "orthodox," institutional sense, but not as they need be. Adequacy of faith comes only when one actually *falls in love with God*. Of course, not in the sentimental or erotic sense but in what happens when humble sinners begin to become "saints." How? By rejoicing in the fact that God loved them when they were unlovable, trusted them when they could not trust themselves, and forgave them when no one else would or could. Christian congregations, when filled with people truly in love with God, will become powerful change agents in any love-starved community.

Our time is mired in many debates about matters of sexuality, gender identity, and the meaning of marriage. Christians need to be more than merely voices denouncing practices they understand to be wrong. Here's the positive thrust so needed today. If God created us humans so that we could be sons and daughters, children of the Father, and if we were created so that everyone ultimately could be part of the Bride of the Son, the church, then human sexuality can be viewed as a positive force in the arena of faith.

No wonder the Song of Songs is in the middle of the Old Testament. We need wholesome presentations of family metaphors and paradigms of marriage and selfless yearnings for oneness with each other and God. When we talk about human love, we should be speaking profoundly about how it's at its best when corresponding to the love that defines the Creator of our universe—who is love in redemptive action. Evil is headed for death; love is on the rise!

5. Response from the Heart

MY GROWTH NEED: Humility that experiences God's love.
Zeph. 3:14-17; Deut.7:9; Jn. 14:21; Eph. 5:25-27; 1 Jn. 3:1

Love is giving, and the giver is primarily concerned about the other's well-being. Love is expressed and enjoyed whether reciprocated or not.

> I love you Lord and I lift my voice to worship you;
> Oh, my soul, rejoice.
> Take joy, my King, in what You hear.
> There's a sweet, sweet sound in my ear.
> —Laurie Klein

> There is a name I love to hear; I love to sing its worth.
> It sounds like music in my ear, the sweetest name on earth.
> It tells of one who's loving heart can feel my deepest woe;
> who in each sorrow bears a part that none can bear below.
> —Frederick Whitfield

The story of Hosea and Gomer is an enactment of God's love for the people of the Northern Kingdom of Israel. Even though those people had been unfaithful to God, God's love for them never wavered. Hosea, representing God, loved Gomer and redeemed her, giving her new life. There is no end to the power of true love. How can you and I do any less than respond with our own love toward God?

Personal Prayer: O Lord, I am overwhelmed by the beauty and power displayed by You. You love me even when I'm completely unworthy and don't know how to love back. You love me when I cannot fully understand, but still I know you do. I love you, Lord, and I'm so grateful that you love me. Make me a love agent in my world, always confident that, no matter what, love finally wins. Resurrection is rooted in the very fabric of creation. Ad yet, I know people all around me who see only the grave ahead. May I somehow show them that the stone has been rolled away!

The Bible is to be regarded as a creaturely text that is at the same time God's written Word. We consult this Word believing that it reveals the mind of God. It communicates authoritatively to us on those subjects about which Scripture teaches, whether doctrinal, ethical, or spiritual, and we believers willingly subject ourselves to this rule of faith. The Bible is the informative Word of God to the church.

    Clark H. Pinnock and Barry L. Callen,
      The Scripture Principle, 92.

Reading 19

THE MESSIAH KILLED?

All four of the New Testament Gospels tell this brutal story, a shocking injustice that tended to shatter the faith of the first disciples of Jesus. Yes, he tried to warn them, but they couldn't believe it. How could the real Messiah let this awful thing happen? Must we now wait for another, the real one who will save us instead of being hurt by us? Is death really the end? Is there hope beyond the grave? Jesus said he'd be back. Did he really mean it? How could that be possible? What happens now that our supposed Savior is dead?

1. The Big Picture Verses.
Luke 23:33-34. The Context: Matthew 27, Mark 15, Luke 23, John 19.

When they arrived at the place called "The Skull," they crucified him. Jesus said, "Father, forgive them for they don't know what they are doing."

2. A Bit of Background

Jesus had spent his ministry trying to help his disciples understand the arrival of the kingdom (the reign) of God. Finally, they had begun to understand. But now their Master, the supposed beginning and even center of this dramatic new reality, was being brutally hung on a Roman cross! Was that the end of all hope, an ultimate mocking of the teachings of Jesus, the time to scatter and deny that they had ever known him?

When it was all over, there would be a day when Jesus would appear alive in the midst of the bewildered and fearful disciples, devastated because of the unbelievable crucifixion of their Master. He would complete the task of helping them become a true and united community of faith on mission. He would bring them the gifts of peace, well-being, and joy. Then they would find the way to come together and go to the ends of the earth "in the Spirit" of the *living* Christ.

This new-life, God-infused community of the Spirit would be in stark contrast to the competition, conflict, and brutality so characteristic of the numerous tribalisms of this world. The church is to be a realization of the arriving reign of God on a grand redemptive mission. That realization was still in the unimaginable future. For now, it was looking more like all was over. The world had won!

3. The Message in Brief

It's frequently hard to see life's larger picture. Where's God when things are going very wrong? The psalmist gives us permission to be angry at the things that anger God (Ps. 4:4). God will put in our hearts a peace and joy adequate to sustain when we can't understand and it's not clear that God has even heard our prayers. As an old hymn puts it, "trust and obey for there's no other way." Often we can't make sense of the ways of God, causing our prayer to be, "I believe, help my unbelief!" (Mk. 9:24).

God is real and yet still uncomfortably mysterious and seemingly unpredictable. The joy that's possible isn't a shallow "happiness" when all tensions have been resolved. Rather, it's a settled sense of eternal safety despite the ongoing depth of life's hard experiences. While besieged by evil, we also can be embraced by love. Jesus returned to his disciples from death to embrace them with an eternal love that was very much alive.

What's the hardest experience to imagine? How about standing before a cross on which humans are appearing to conquer God! How about finally believing in the Nazarene who said he was God with us for our salvation, and now having to watch arrogant humans mock and murder him! Faith requires listening to the man on that cross, praying that the evil ones be forgiven for they don't understand what they are doing—and the disciples didn't yet understand what they were seeing.

The God of infinite love was *voluntarily* Self-giving for our salvation. Jesus hadn't been forcibly, helplessly nailed to that tree. *He chose to be there for us!* The crucifixion event obviously was tragic when seen only from the human perspective. Seen through the Spirit's eyes, however, it was God willingly suffering on our behalf, and thus it was something amazing indeed. The old, ugly cross was actually wondrously beautiful indeed!

4. The Present Challenge

We are children of God with limited knowledge. What we eventually will be hasn't yet been revealed. We do know at least two very important things as faithful followers of Jesus. A day will come when, despite death, we again will see Jesus face-to-face, and by his transforming grace we will be like him (1 Jn. 3:1-7). Meanwhile, to ensure that day, we must dedicate ourselves to maturing into the image of Christ. The world badly misunderstood who Jesus really was and as his representatives we also risk being misunderstood.

Our choice, therefore, is simple. Honor the world's values and mirror its spiritual blindness or enter the danger zone by determining to mature into something the world doesn't see, understand, or easily tolerate. This world is a place of desired and exercised power. We tend to think of God as the One with all power who always will control and conquer. Then we recall Jesus on the cross and know that his church is to be a place of love and sacrifice, not a proud and conquering community feared by the world. Love has its own way of conquering, although there's a price to be paid on the way.

Sacrifice was a key element of ancient Jewish worship, but God never wanted sacrifice if it meant our trying to placate him with our efforts. God wanted the hearts of the worshippers, not their selfish gifts. When people kept their hearts to themselves and went through what they assumed were God-pleasing routines they called worship, God found it disgusting. When Jesus died, it was not to placate his Father. It was his Father giving himself to us in love, still seeking our hearts. It was a loving process of reconciliation which we are invited to receive gratefully and then extend to others through our own loving and self-giving. Is that what we see the church now being and doing? Nothing else is acceptable.

5. Response from the Heart

MY GROWTH NEED: Belief even when surprised.
Matt. 17:20; 2 Cor. 5:7; Heb. 11:6; Jam. 1:6; Heb. 3:19; 1 Jn. 4:1

A recent visitor to the crematorium ovens of Auschwitz came away with this. "The God I see after Auschwitz is not the comforting, rescuing God I wish for in my weakness. Instead, when my heart is broken open by suffering, I need a more complex God: simultaneously truthful, powerful, vulnerable, suffering, and commanding, a God whom I can love and trust completely, but who also makes me quake. An uncomforting God does not provide easy, consoling answers to our pleading question. Why? A truly vulnerable God suffers with those who suffer and risks everything for the ultimate victory of justice, wholeness, and peace. A discomforting God demands our participation in the establishment of divine justice in the world."[1]

In a famous sermon, Peter Marshall, then Chaplain of the United States Senate, asked, "Were You There When They Crucified My Lord?" He describes those who were there and suggests what they might have been thinking as they watched Jesus suffer and die. At the end, he repeats the question. So I now ask, Was I there? Were you? Are we able to realize the meaning of the death of Jesus? Some celebrated his death, others wept bitterly. Some didn't know what it was about and just went on their way. The truest test of an event is to be able to see it "in the Spirit." The Spirit hovered nearby, feeling the great pain and prepared to blaze a divine light into the darkness of our ignorance and grief.

Personal Prayer: Oh God, it's dark, but I know that you hold my hand and intend to instruct and comfort me. Thank you for being lovingly by my shaking side. I'll hold tightly to your strong hand. And thank you for your love. I feel it and am enabled by it. It's my only hope, my promised future. Yes, I was there at the cross—we all

---

[1] Elaine Emeth, "Lessons from the Holocaust," *Sojourners* magazine.

were. No, I didn't understand, nor did anyone else. Death is frightening, seemingly so final. Is resurrection only a dream or an actual coming reality? With you close by, I know that my Savior lives!

The term biblical "inspiration" occurs only once in the Bible (2 Tim. 3:16), and then without a definition. It's probably best to think of inspiration as divine activity accompanying the production of the Scriptures. We are not privileged to know how in hidden and mysterious ways the Spirit worked alongside human agents in the creative literary work. Inspiration seems to have been a quiet and long-term affair as faith traditions were shaped into texts and brought to final form. We may speak of the social character of inspiration, the work and gifts of many people doing their part, under the care of the Spirit, to achieve the desired result. God was at work in the community of faith to produce a normative text to serve as the community's constitution.

Clark H. Pinnock and Barry L. Callen,
The Scripture Principle, 93-94.

Reading 20

LIFE WINS!

Celebrate God's love and faithfulness. They form a goodness that has no limits. They can turn broken stones into cornerstones, loss into new gifts, despair into hope, graves into celebrations of life. God the Creator never tires of re-creating. Every day is the Lord's Day, God's acting day, a day of new life and the dawning of hope that can stretch even beyond the binding limits of our fallen world. Death rips at our very souls. No matter. There is One who extends beyond death. Eventually, life wins!

1. The Big Picture Verses.
Mark 16:6, Luke 24:5. The Context: Matthew 28, Mark 16, Luke 24, and John 20.

Don't be alarmed! You are looking for Jesus of Nazareth, who was crucified. Why do you look for the living among the dead? He has been raised!

2. A Bit of Background

We all know that death is real, all too real and inescapable. Today, however, comes dramatic good news. Even death can be overcome, no, *has been overcome!* The unexpected and unprecedented emergence of Jesus from his tomb is the event on which all else now hinges. Because he lives, we too can live, his teachings can be believed, and his promised return can be trusted. In his living, *death has died.* In the Resurrected Son the Father promises to make all things new. The new life is "eternal" life, meaning more than life everlasting beyond death. It's the *God-like* quality of life that's like the Eternal One, and it's to exist before our deaths as well as ever after.

Now that's good news! What can be later is to begin right now. Jesus lives! So can we, and so will we by faith in him, beginning on this blessed Easter day. Paul says it in several places. Our former selves already have been crucified (Rom. 6:6). In other words, if we will die before we die, then we will know how to live resurrected lives in the present. There no longer will be fear of death because we, along with Jesus, will already have been there and back. By God's grace, we will have taken our place in the "force field" of resurrection where we are working out our salvation as God works in us (Phil. 2:11-12). The breathing into Adam long ago is now the breathing of Jesus into us as we share in the life-giving breath of his Spirit (Gen. 2:7, Jn. 20:22).

Mary Magdalene came looking not for Jesus but for his remains. Soon he turned that into her joyfully announcing that she had seen her Lord himself and he was very much alive. Her beginning logic had been the usual. If his remains are gone, someone must have taken them, and they must be gotten back so that proper grieving can proceed. However, Jesus assures her that the usual human logic fails in this case. *I'm alive!* It's a new day, a new world, a new future, a new reality. We shocked humans are to forget about the missing corpse and focus on the living Lord.

Everything now hinges on our managing to do this amazing forgetting and focusing. We are to be God's Easter people now destined to live no longer in the world of the merely what has been. The possible was limited by the known rules of science and logic, generally dependable but inadequate when it comes to the God for whom all things are possible. The resurrection of Jesus would initiate a new day, a new way, a new set of values and possibilities for human life now and hereafter.

3. The Message in Brief

All women and men who wish to belong to Jesus must see the much larger picture, adjust everything by is new light, and dare to start living accordingly. Mary Magdalene learned quickly that she was not involved in a typical religious discussion. Her relationship to Jesus was deeply personal. The best and only way to really understand the new Easter truth is to relate personally to the Risen Lord. After all, he is truth and life itself. He invites us to come, touch, awaken, and believe that he's real and here and ours forever. He's in a realm beyond death and invites us to join him.

Christians today are a diverse crowd in skin color, geographic location, culture, and even religious practice. Paul is bold to insist that at least on one point the church's diversity must end (1 Cor. 15:1-11). Confusion about resurrection, that of Jesus yesterday and the potential of ours tomorrow, must not be a subject that divides believers. Belief in the resurrection of Jesus is foundational to all else.

To deny the witness that Jesus was raised from the dead is to undercut the credibility of all the teachings and the entire mission of Messiah Jesus. To deny the resurrection is to question the power and intent of God to one day complete the grand plan of making all things new. Easter is chapter one in the larger story of the release of all creation from the grip of sin and death. All parties originally involved had strong motivation to recover the "remains" of Jesus. Now, after multiple centuries, nothing has been found. What remains is the new people of God who have been raised to new life and have stayed to serve after Jesus has returned to the Father.

4. The Present Challenge

Being confronted by news of the resurrection of Jesus and believing its dramatic implications is always a big challenge for us humans stuck in a web of apparent impossibilities. The twenty-first century is proving to be one of exciting thrusts forward and yet, unfortunately, developments happening under a dark cloud of widespread violence and despair. The resurrection of Jesus is a large neon sign that keeps flashing, inviting us to see history moving forward toward God's grand conclusion. The risen Christ is the brilliant light set as the Omega point of time and history. It keeps reminding us that love, not death, is the eternal reality.

We moderns are privileged to realize the truth found in the classic words of Martin Luther. We are being invited to open ourselves to a new life that is without limits.

> It was a Strange and Dreadful Strife,
> When Life and Death Contended;
> The Victory Remained with Life,
> The Reign of Death was Ended.
> Stripped of Power, No More It Reigns,
> An Empty Form Alone Remains,
> Death's Sting Is Lost Forever! Alleluia!

5. Response from the Heart

My Growth Need: Awe in the face of wonder.
Lk. 24:6-7; Jn. 11:25-26; Acts 4:33; Rom. 1:4, 6:19-21; 1 Pet. 1:3.

The most important word of the good news in Christ is the word LIFE. Jesus is alive, and his disciples discovered that, because he came to them and was alive, they too could be given new life. This message has come down through the centuries and brought life out of death many times over. The Spirit of God in Jesus is alive today. You ask me how I know he lives. I know because he lives within my heart! Is he alive in you?

Jesus has defeated sin and death. The Apostle Paul closed his famous eighth chapter of Romans with this: "Who shall separate us from the love of God in Christ? I am convinced that neither death, nor life, nor angels, nor demons, neither the present, nor the future, nor any powers, neither height nor depth, nor anything else in all creation will be able to separate us from the love of God that is in Christ Jesus our lord." We know that Christ is raised and dies no more. Death's fearful hold is broken and our despair has turned to blazing joy. Hallelujah!

> With a mighty hand and outstretched arm,
> His love endures forever;
> For the life *that's been reborn*,
> His love endures forever.
> —Chris Tomlin

Personal Prayer. Oh Lord, the ringing testimony of believers throughout the ages and around the world has been "Hallelujah! Christ is risen!" The echoing reply is, "Christ is risen indeed!" I gladly join this mighty chorus of thanksgiving and praise. This witness and the faith it represents enables us believers everywhere to live in you, our Christ, by the power of your Spirit. Let that life pulsate throughout my very being. Let it be seen by others, who then will long for it themselves. Thank you Lord. It's Easter. Life wins!

The Bible makes a strong claim to be true in a particular way. We have no basis for being dogmatic when we encounter perplexing features in the text. We cannot say that this is an apparent error that sooner or later will be solved by our scholarly efforts; nor can we confidently say that this is a flaw for which there can never be a solution. We have to take the evidence as it comes, not rush to judgment, and rest in the marvelous gospel of Christ that shines clearly through the divinely revealed biblical text.

>Clark H. Pinnock and Barry L. Callen, *The Scripture Principle*, 161-62.

Reading 21

WE'RE NEVER LEFT ALONE

We disciples of Jesus can't accomplish God's work alone, but we're never alone even though Jesus now has returned to heaven. The crucified One is the resurrected, departed, and yet ever-present One. Today is the time of the Spirit. To be truly Christian is to be a member of the community of the Spirit, the church, that is living out before the world its witness to the Risen Lord. This witness is possible only as it's enabled by the gifts of the Spirit being employed faithfully in the mission of the Spirit. Jesus promised that his Spirit would be with us to the very end of time. We never need be left alone!

1. The Big Picture Verses.
Luke 24:50-51, Matthew 28:20. The Context: Luke 24 and Matthew 28.

Jesus led them as far as Bethany, where he lifted his hands and blessed them. As he blessed them, he was taken up to heaven. We must remember that Jesus said to them and now to us, "I am with you always, to the end of the age."

2. A Bit of Background

The early Christian movement was an outbreak of the Holy Spirit. This outbreak was experienced by many non-believers as a dangerous wildfire, and thus became a risk to the messengers of love. The disciples of Jesus were being called by their faith to put themselves out there, clearly in the way of possible danger. Why? It's out there that the many opportunities lie for needed witness and service. It's out there that love calls and sin lingers. Jesus regularly opened himself to misunderstanding and even dangerous opposition because that's where the need was, risk notwithstanding.

It was made obvious soon after the resurrection of Jesus. Following Jesus would hardly be an exercise in soft sentimentality, feeling good while helping others feel good about themselves. Caring for lost sheep and wayward societies would be costly. Jesus made two things clear. Really loving, being faithful to the loving Father, can be both a glorious and a dangerous business. Those who first heard often reacted with division and even violence. Regardless, there was made clear that the Master of time and eternity, the survivor of the cross and victor of the tomb, would be a constant presence and strength and hope for the faithful. We are in this together, always accompanied by the Spirit.

3. The Message in Brief

The divine mission at first was through the physical presence and sacrificial work of Jesus. Then, after his ascension, that work was transferred to those of us who are his faithful disciples, his Spirit-filled disciples. The Spirit comes and is anxious to birth in us the will and means to continue fulfilling the mission of Jesus until he comes again. Jesus may be gone in a physical sense, but is never absent from his disciples, never!

The Spirit comes to continue teaching us on behalf of Jesus, guiding our minds and hearts to understand properly the biblical revelation and engage effectively in the Christian mission. The Son of God has ascended, returning to the universal presence of God who is active in the whole world on behalf of the whole of lost humanity. The Easter reality now is a life-generating mission, every day and everywhere!

4. The Present Challenge

The ascension of Jesus following his resurrection is less about his going *from* this world and more about our going *into* it well prepared because of his continuing presence. What we were promised at his departure was his ongoing presence and continuing power in the midst of the church's urgent mission. Jesus leaves, and remains, and we begin, but not alone. God sent his Son, Jesus; now Jesus has left us his Spirit who gifts and comforts and sends us.

We who believe have become the body of Jesus, his hands and feet traveling this world, fulfilling our responsibility for doing the ongoing work of God. We can't do it alone, of course, and there's no need to even try. We aren't alone! Jesus directed that we wait on his Spirit to come and indwell our very beings, setting us spiritually on fire and accompanying and enabling us as we go in his name.

5. Response from the Heart

My Growth Need: Comfort provided by the Spirit.
Jos. 1:5; Ps. 91:1-2; Jn. 14:16-17; Acts 9:31; Rom. 8:26; 2 Cor. 3:17

Jesus promised his disciples, "I will never leave you." That promise is true now and will be at the moments of our death. Not only is the Spirit of Jesus with us, but the Spirit lives within and seeks to shine outward on others through us. The Comforter is with us, especially when we are faithful in comforting others.

> I stand amazed in the presence of Jesus the Nazarene,
> And wonder how he could love me, a sinner condemned, unclean.
> How marvelous, how wonderful, and my song shall ever be,
> How marvelous, How wonderful is my Savior's love for me.
> —Chris Tomlin

In 2019 we lost a dear friend, Phyllis Kinley, career Christian missionary to Japan. She was a wise and spiritually sensitive woman who left behind this bit of verse. She knew that, despite death, she never would be left alone or ever really be dead.

> As I grow older and wiser,
> sometimes in the night,
> I find myself longing for other shores
> where the sun shines on an Eternal Sea,
> on the other side of the soul,
> where another self will be born,
> and time will begin again.

Personal Prayer. I praise you, Lord, for your love and mercy. Thank you for your constant presence with me and all my sisters and brothers in Christ who know and love you. We are surrounded by your wonderful and sustaining love, filled and gifted by your comforting Spirit. Fill the eyes of our souls with that vision of rebirth when "time will begin again," and allow your loving Spirit to conceive that rebirth in us *this very moment*. May we be resurrection disciples, agents of the Spirit, comforted and sent on your life-giving mission.

PENTECOST--PREFACE

Large sections of the Old and New Testaments express concern that believers learn about and appropriate the will and character of God, "the Holy One." Holiness is being and living on God's terms, sharing in God's likeness as made visible and possible for us in Jesus Christ. Paul says his goal was "that we may present everyone mature in Christ" (Col. 1:28). Peter's word is similar: "God has given us his precious and very great promises so that through them we may become participants in the divine nature" (2 Pet. 1:4).

God has ordained that those who surrender to His love come to share in His likeness. Becoming a Christian involves both a change in one's experience and a resulting alteration in one's very being. This is the grand goal of the gospel of Christ. We are privileged to look to Jesus since he is "the reflection of God's glory and the exact imprint of God's very being" (Heb. 1:3). Jesus himself made the claim that "whoever sees me sees him who sent me" (Jn. 12:45). Further, Jesus has given us "power to become children of God" (Jn. 1:12).

Pentecost is the Christian season highlighting distinctive spiritual possibilities. Prominent among them are said by Jesus to be "the promise of the Father," a potential "baptism with the Holy Spirit" (Acts 1: 4-5). The Christian life is not to be only a moment of sins being forgiven. It's to move on to a state where sin no longer dominates the values and motives of life. Believers can walk in newness of life by being "conformed to the image of God Son" (Rom. 8: 29, 6:12-14). John 3:34 describes this endowment with the Spirit as "without measure." With these great truths and Spirit possibilities in mind, following are five Bible readings of the Pentecost season that explore the dimensions of this promise of the Father.

These five readings, while diverse, focus at one central point. Since God is holy love, "holiness" is being expected of believers and enabled by this divine love, implanted in us by the Spirit of Jesus. As redeemed children of the Great Lover, God, we who call ourselves Jesus people are supposed to become great lovers, reflections of our Father in heaven. Our congregations are called to be Schools of Love, places that model love in action and prepare people to be messengers of divine love. Holiness is divine love gratefully received and generously shared for the benefit of others.

To understand the intended Christian life requires understanding the Hebrew word "ruach." The English equivalent, "spirit," is misunderstood when thought of as something immaterial, disembodied, beyond normal earthly life. Rather, it's to be recognized as the breath of God that actively infuses love and life into the full reality of our earthly existences. To be a child of God is choosing to hoist one's personal sails into the rushing wind of God. Paul's instruction to "pray without ceasing" (1 Thess. 5: 17) is the call to open all of one's life to the power and direction of God's moving Spirit. See Readings 22-26 for details of this essential opening.

Reading 22

YOU SHALL BE HOLY--#1

Leviticus is a biblical book few readers ever manage to get through to the end. After all, it narrates in seemingly endless detail religious rituals connected to the Temple in Jerusalem that was destroyed in 70 A.D. It dwells on a sacrificial system of worship that is very foreign to contemporary Christians. Christian holiness lived out in contemporary life surely wouldn't look anything like what's being described. What meaning could all this possibly have in the twenty-first century? Just this. It's at least the ancient base for what turns out to be one of the biggest themes in the whole Bible, holiness. The mechanics of what God expects may not now involve sacrificing animals or living in Jerusalem. Still, there are basic meanings found here that eventually would inform the holiness that Jesus still has in mind for us who believe.

1. The Big Picture Verse.
Leviticus 19:2. The Context: Book of Leviticus.

You shall be holy, for I the Lord your God am holy.

2. A Bit of Background

Here we find the religious outlook and worship practices of the little Jewish community in Jerusalem in generations long before the coming of Jesus. Israel had lost its kingdom, known the pains of exile, and now had returned to a fragment of its former territory. The overpowering concern was to repair and rebuild the shattered structure of its national life and worship culture.

Israel's prophets had thundered that the past disasters were judgments of God on a failure to fulfill its side of the covenant of Sinai. Now it was determined that such failure must not happen again. The Lord had said, "You shall be for me a priestly kingdom and holy nation" (Ex. 19:6). Leviticus, then, is essentially a manual for the sacrificial system designed to teach how to follow the paths of righteousness in formal worship, and exactly how to make sacrifices of atonement to cover the sins of the people. The word "holy" occurs in this book more than any other in the Bible.

This community of God's people was trying vigorously to maintain its distinctiveness in light of the critical memory that had brought it into being originally. "You shall not cheat in measuring length, weight, or quantity: I am the Lord your God who brought you out of the land of Egypt. You shall keep all my statutes and all my ordinances and observe them: I am the Lord" (19:36).

The Jews were to remember who they were and act accordingly under the eye of their loving and saving Sovereign. This suggests why this book of Leviticus comes so early in the Old Testament collection, in fact right after Exodus. God's people, once freed from Egyptian slavery and Babylonian exile, are expected to reflect in all their ways the very nature of the Holy One, their God. "You shall be holy, for I the Lord your God am holy" (19:2).

Admittedly, the cultural particulars of worship obedience may change over time, but not the basic holiness demand. Christian life over the generations has witnessed numerous denominations dividing over the detail of religious practice, the whats, whens, and wheres of being holy. Baptism by how much water and performed by whom? Spiritual gifts of which kind received by whom? Unfortunately, purity *codes* have abounded more than has purity *of life*.

Paul captured the core truth, apart from the confusing cultural particulars. What really matters is not whether one is circumcised or not, but that one becomes a genuinely *new creation* (Gal. 6:16). Beyond rules of holy behavior, it's our actual identity that needs radically changed. After real "conversion," a true life turning around, one then is to be enabled to look with eyes other than their own and love with an intensity that comes only as a gift from the loving Father.

3. The Message in Brief

The New Testament book of Hebrews rightly reports, "It is not possible that the blood of bulls and goats should take away sins" (10:4). Still, we must recognize the earnest desire of those before Christ to treat sin seriously, to understand all aspects of their lives as "religious," and to find some way to restore the relationship with God which had been constantly broken in pride and folly. The Jews were in search of a workable "mediation" between a holy God and an unholy people, one which eventually would turn out to be the man Jesus who "gave himself up for us, a fragrant offering and sacrifice to God" (Eph. 5:2). It would take the church of Jesus time and struggle to sort out the details of the old categories and prejudices, like the "clean and unclean" groups of animals and people and practices (Acts 10:1-16). Holiness is a process as well as the goal.

This holiness quest requires a fundamental life change and therefore can be most difficult. There are two forms of religion. One assumes that God will love me *if I change*. The other assumes that God already loves me *so that I can change*. The first, most common, is a wrong and dangerous idea. Real Christian faith is less any correct religious *ideas* and more a life-changing *encounter* with Jesus who is the truth. Religious ideas, right or wrong, can *inform* us; encountering Jesus person-to-person alone can *re-form* us into his gracious image by the power of his Spirit. The Old Testament religious "system" sought to accomplish the right thing but lacked the power to complete the task.

4. The Present Challenge

Granted, by modern standards some of the worship practices detailed in Leviticus are repulsive and even grotesque at times. Even so, this must not blind us to the zeal with which the priestly mentors of Israel sought to bring the whole of their society under the sovereign will of God. Today's church still struggles with old worship categories and prejudices of people and methods. What about the leadership of women in church life? Remove the organs and choirs in favor of drums and dance? Do we please God best by staging a high mass or sitting in simple silence? No animals are seen at the altars of today's churches. Is that where we should be instead?

Cultural commitments intrude on religious zeal and go in various directions. Jesus said he had come not to destroy the Law but to restore a proper perspective on its intentions, especially its spirit as opposed to its rigid legalisms. It takes the work of the Spirit of God in us to avoid our justifying personal preferences and calling the result God's real intention.

The second half of Leviticus, called the "Holiness Code" (chaps. 17-26), details a range of deviant sexual practices prohibited and still widely practiced. Which ones are truly deviant? Sorting this out is still high on the agenda of the church. Are we turning to idols and making cast images of ourselves (19:4)? Which of our festivals are "holy"? What about God's warning that if we defile the land he will "vomit us out" (18-28). A holy God birthed a holy creation and expects holy people to care for it lovingly. We still seem a long way from that expectation.

5. Response from the Heart

My Growth Need: Being a reflection of God's nature.
Lev. 20:7; Mt. 5:48; 2 Thess. 2:13; 2 Tim. 1:9; 1 Pet. 1:15-16.

> Holy Holy Holy! Lord God Almighty!
> Early in the morning our song shall rise to Thee.
> Holy Holy Holy! merciful and mighty!
> God in three persons, Blessed Trinity.
> —Reginald Heber

Holiness, the prime characteristic of the God our songs celebrate, is shrouded in mystery. God is beyond full comprehension. Making relatively clear the nature of God was an important purpose in the ancient law (*Torah*) of the Jews. It sought to spell out in detail a list of forbidden and expected behaviors. A holy witness was to be the result. We must become a visible expression of God's loving nature reaching toward a lost world.

From pride and pretense set us free
to walk in truth's integrity.
O grant us grace to reach, to give,
to touch the dream by which we live.
—Kenneth E. Morse

Personal Prayer: O God of mystery and might, great Mover of the stars in flight, alert my heart to apprehend the silent witnesses you send. What I receive may I also live, your gifts to me may I freely give. Help me shine on your behalf, brightening this dark world. Move me from believing with my mind only to becoming an actual new being with my whole person. Dear Lord, please keep me from cultural prejudices that lead me to judge others who worship in ways slightly differing from my standards. Don't allow me to ignore parts of your biblical revelation because I judge them totally outdated.

The "Scriptural Principle" is the assertion that the Bible is the primary and fully trustworthy canon of Christian revelation, the reliable medium for encountering and understanding the God who seeks to transform all persons who read the sacred text into the image of Jesus Christ. In this regard, we mean by the Scripture Principle the belief that Scripture never leads one astray in regard to what it intentionally teaches.

    Clark H. Pinnock and Barry L. Callen,
      The Scripture Principle, 11

Reading 23

YOU SHALL BE HOLY--#2

The questions are easier to state than the answers are to live out. Since being "holy" means that I'm to become like God in some important ways, then we must know exactly what is God like. Precisely what does God expect sincere believers to say and do in their everyday lives? Surely we are to follow faithfully the divine "Law," but which set of regulations really makes up God's Law today? Aren't there a variety of laws even within the Bible itself, let alone in the churches across the centuries since? Precisely how shall I go about being holy?

1. The Big Picture Verses.
Deuteronomy 6:4; Micah 6:8. The Context: Books of Deuteronomy and Micah.

Hear, O Israel: the Lord is our God, the Lord alone. You shall love the Lord your God with all your heart and with all your soul and with all your might. What does the Lord require but to do justice and to love kindness and to walk humbly with your God?

2. A Bit of Background

The word "Deuteronomy" means "second law." It concludes the group of books called the *Torah* (the first five books of the Old Testament), each tending to repeating and occasionally supplement and even alter what's been said before. King Josiah carried out a series of needed reforms guided by this second law, which recently had been rediscovered or freshly written. It includes the great *Shema*

(6:4–10), calling the people to hear God's voice and obey his commands as their very way of life.

Coming after the Book of Numbers and before Joshua, we can picture Israel camped in the plains of Moab, poised to enter the promised land across the Jordan River. Before the people plunge forward, however, the death of Moses is reported after he has delivered a series of valedictory addresses to the people. The great leader of the desert journeys urges that once in Canaan the people will be strictly obedient to the Law of God. Unfortunately, often they would not be. The prophet Micah later would come from a village in the foothills of Judah in the promised land. He saw the Jerusalem of his time as a sick parody of what it should have been. His faith reached out to the possibility of a real renewal, with God actually reigning over Israel's life (2:1-3:12). A cleansed remnant there will be, gladly offering the service due to her Lord (4:1-5:15).

This service is given definition by the prophet Micah, one excellent statement of the practical meaning of Christian "holiness." It comes in the form of a question. "What does the Lord require of you but to do justice and to love kindness and to walk humbly with your God?" (6:8). How can that actually be? Paul makes the answer clear when later writing to the Roman church. True life in Christ involves a divine implanting, a "sharing in the divine nature," an indwelling of the Holy Spirit (Rom. 8:16–17) who will enable humility, kindness, and justice.

Richard Rohr rather sarcastically suggests the possible reason we have to keep coming back to church each Sunday. It's because "last Sunday's message did not work at any deep level."[1] I sometimes have wondered why it was typical for holiness congregations of Christians a generation or two back to routinely schedule two "revivals" each year, fall and spring. Was it that the people were known to keep dying spiritually every few months? Holiness isn't easy, automatic, or a one-time-only event.

---

[1] Richard Rohr, *Immortal Diamond*, 121.

3. The Message in Brief

The moral law in the Old Testament is rooted in the moral character of God. Why should one do or not do this or that? The simple answer is, "Because I am God." Why do covenant partners with God act as they do? Because of the holy, distinctive character of the covenant Lord. God created the universe of goodness and beauty and righteousness. Therefore, actions of any other kind are evil, anti-God. We find this confession in the prayer of Psalm 51. "Against You, You only, have I sinned and done what is evil in Your sight." In other words, I acted in ways other than God would have acted.

There is a divine "election," chosen people, and also a divine "rejection" if the elect choose not to walk in the ways consistent with who God is. The rule is this. Be holy *even as I am holy*. Holiness is not primarily loyalty to a religious establishment or an ethical code or doctrinal system. It's the integrity of a required relationship with a Person, the creating and reaching and loving God.

Deuteronomy is one of the Old Testament books most frequently quoted in the New Testament. Jesus is seen as the new Moses who will lead an even greater exodus from the bondage of sin into the freedom of life in the Spirit of God, the greatest of all promised lands. To be holy, then, is to hear God's voice and obey his commands as the Spirit directs and enables.

Christians are to look back to the giving of God's Law, be aware that its particulars have been revised in various settings over the centuries, and look forward as Jesus focuses best the revealed mind of God for today's people of God. Salvation from death in Egypt should lead to a new life in Canaan that's accompanied by thanksgiving and constant obedience. This new life must be protected from the deterioration witnessed by the prophet Micah, and it must not neglect its social obligations like "justice for all." The details may vary, but not the essence. God's character never changes even if strategies and particulars do.

4. The Present Challenge

The prophet Isaiah is a prominent biblical model of holiness displayed in public. He was encountered dramatically by the holy God, had his lips cleansed with hot coals from above (chap. 6), and soon was a spokesperson in the courts of kings on behalf of justice in local and international affairs. Public officials must be cautioned that the "gods" of the powerful often are little more than projections of their own greed and ambition, even if wrapped in popular religious language.

Christian communities are in danger when either isolating themselves from the corruptions of politics in the name of remaining pure or forcing their will into the public arena, seeking to limit the dissenting right of all unbelieving opponents. They also are at fault when insisting on favored ways of worshipping and serving, as though one size fits all and holiness is to be defined as we have in our denominational manual.

5. Response from the Heart

My Growth Need: Doing the things God would do.
Ezek. 38:23; Amos 5:14; Rom. 12:1; Phil. 4:8; 1 Pet. 1:14-16.

The Law of God is centered in loving God and neighbor. The Hebrew prophets focused on loving God by reflecting God-like ways in our family and social actions. Theirs was the call to justice, kindness, and fairness. Micah's key question "What does the Lord require of you?" sounds the call for justice and humility. This message anticipated the teaching of Jesus which features an inner holiness based on love and caring for others. God's question, "Whom shall I send?" prompted Isaiah's reply, "Here am I; send me." Is that your reply also? Are you ready to do what you've come to understand the Lord God requires?

> Jesus calls us o'er the tumult
> of our life's wild restless sea,
> Day by day I hear him saying,
> "Christian, come and follow me."
>
> Jesus calls us by Thy mercies,
> Savior, may we hear Thy call,
> Give our hearts to Thine obedience,
> Serve and love Thee best of all.
> —Cecil Frances Alexander

Personal Prayer: O God, may I have sensitive ears to hear your call and a humble heart to recognize its specific meaning for my life. May I have an obedient spirit that says "Yes" to You in ways that allow others to better hear your call for themselves. Caution me from making premature decisions about the specifics of how others should act in circumstances different from mine. Enrich my personal relationship with you in ways that make increasingly possible my being actively holy as you are holy. Spirit of God, I so need you to enable me to lead a truly "spiritual" life.

**My Spiritual Growth Need:
Shining as God's light in the darkness.
Ezek. 38:23; Amos 5:14; Rom. 12:1;
Phil. 4:8; 1 Pet. 1:14-16.**

Reading 24

YOU SHALL BE HOLY--#3

It's hard to be "holy" even when you really want to be. How can an individual or whole people exist in this troubled world as agents of loving redemption? How can we exist as a distinctive people truly reflecting God rather than our own selfish selves or the world around us? How can people get to be "Godly" and no longer "worldly"? It's clearly expected of Christians. It's also the largest challenge we face. Of course, we will remain human with all its limitations even when being holy. At what points, then, should we exceed the "fallen" aspects of humanity and in the process not alienate ourselves from those people we are called to love?

1. The Big Picture Verse.

1 Peter 2:9. The Context: The Books of Ezra and Nehemiah.

But you are a chosen people, a royal priesthood, a holy nation, God's own people, in order that you may proclaim the excellence of him who called you out of darkness into his marvelous light.

2. A Bit of Background

Memory of the Exodus was the formative force shaping the Old Testament people of God. It had made them a freed people with a promised land and the potential of a great future as God's treasured possession (Ex. 19:5-6). But so much changed over the generations. They yielded to "other gods," including the lure of surviving only by becoming like the nations, with a king and all that came with that way of being patriotic and powerful. Disaster finally came, as the prophets had warned, and in the fifty years of Exile in Babylon the people had to grapple with the biggest of all questions.

Was God truly superior to the "gods" of the Babylonians? Was the loss of their government, their beloved capital city of Jerusalem and its great Temple really their fault after all? Once they got home again, as now they were in Ezra and Nehemiah's time, what should they do, who should they be this time?

The Judaism seen in the New Testament has its roots in this rebuilding time following the Exile. The supremacy of the Torah, the professionalized authority of the priesthood, the rigid legalism and ceremonial precision all emerged from the post-Exilic new way of trying to be God's people. Circumcision, Sabbath observance, and a range of dietary laws became almost fetishes, ways of showing that God's people are distinctive and faithful. Holiness now meant following numerous particulars of behavior under the watchful eye of the dominant clergy.

Ezra 1:1-10:44 chronicles the return of Jewish exiles from Babylon, especially his own coming with authority and a large gift for the Temple from the king of Persia. He is shocked by the sight of Jews not part of the Exile being married to non-Jewish women (Ez. 9:1-15). His righteous indignation brings them all to a large assembly where they agree to a mass divorce and disowning of the "mixed" children. Ezra reads the Law to the people as their rule of life. They were to be a unique people staying free of the outside contaminations that had brought ruin to their forebears. They were to be "separated from all strangers" (Neh. 9:2). Covenant faithfulness now was understood as less the principles of justice, humility, and mercy stressed by the prophets and more the keeping of racial exclusiveness and ceremonial obligations.

While isolationist and quite mechanical, the people at least recognized that they were to be God's special treasure. But how can a people be holy and also an attractive light to the nations? By seeking to keep themselves unspotted from the world, the Jews became more a harsh and intolerant pariah among the nations, a people shunned rather than emulated. If they weren't so self-protective, however, would they survive at all as a distinctive people, a holy nation? This is a serious question for all "holiness" people.

3. The Message in Brief

Does being the "holy nation" as intended by God mean building walls around the faithful and resisting all outside tempters? That way, holiness easily becomes a haughtiness hated by outsiders. It would take Jesus to demonstrate how to be both totally true to God and always reaching out in love to others, all others. Holiness somehow is to be distinctive without being divisive, a difficult challenge in any age.

The post-Exilic Jews did what they thought was necessary to be God's real people in a terribly fallen world. They didn't get it quite right, as believers often fail to do, but they sincerely tried. As would be learned later, being holy involves becoming whole, filled with new life in the Spirit of Jesus. It must avoid a long list of do's and don'ts that may be more culturally than religiously based. Christian holiness hardly means being super-patriotic to any nationalistic identity, at whatever cost to "foreign" neighbors.

4. The Present Challenge

The United States of the 2020s is much like Israel after the Exile. The world scene had changed so much. Multi-ethnic realities were eating away the traditional identity of God's people. The old body politic had given way to a refreshed "body ecclesiastic." In other words, to be her intended self, Israel now thought she had to be a faith-based people so unlike her disastrous trip into the chaotic world of "being like the nations," having a king and military power. In the past, that hadn't worked out well at all. The prophets had cried out against its compromises and the Exile had been a bitter lesson of divine judgment.

Today's American church is in about the same position. It has lost much ground as a recognized and respected foundation of the nation's heritage and values. It's scrambling to define its identity and grieve its loss of influence. What shall be its new identity in the culture? On what does its integrity depend? How can it be a holy people of God in a radically secularized new world?

5. Response from the Heart

My Growth Need: Shining as God's light in the darkness.
Ezek. 38:23; Amos 5:14; Rom. 12:1; Phil. 4:8; 1 Pet. 1:14-16.

It's not a simple thing to hear and understand God's call to be holy. Peter describes the church as chosen, a royal priesthood, fully God's own (1 Pet. 2:9). To be God's own is certainly not to consider ourselves more highly than we ought. The irony of this is that the higher we think of our own holiness the less holy we actually are. Spirituality is an inner reality, creating and recreating the spirit of kindness, goodness, patience, and love.

We believers must become priests to each other, forgiving each other, not lifting ourselves up but honoring the work of God in those around us. We must be the light of God to the world, anything but more of its darkness.

> Take time to be holy, speak often with God,
> Find rest in Him always and feed on his Word.
> Make friends of God's children, help those who are weak,
> Forgetting in nothing his blessing to seek.
>
> Take time to be holy, the world rushes on;
> Spend much time in secret with Jesus alone.
> By looking to Jesus, like him you shall be,
> Your friends in your conduct His likeness will see.
>
> —William Longstaff

Personal Prayer. O Lord, will I ever know if I'm living like you? Help me forget about constantly weighing myself spiritually. Help me keep my eyes on Jesus as my example, and guide and help me to love with a love that always looks to give, never take, judge, or condemn. Only then can I begin to fulfill the goal, being like Jesus, actually shining the light of Jesus to all around me. And it's not just me as an individual believer. How can we as the church be your representatives, Holy God, when we are so human, so wrapped up in our ways and needs? If our exile really is over, you must show us the way home or we'll get lost again!

Reading 25

YOU SHALL BE HOLY--#4

The church is in a definitional crisis and an expectancy drought. What is Christian holiness and is it possible for it to be present and function in the realities of our present lives? The church must develop practices designed to assist people in their spiritual discipline, and thus itself be a practical means of sanctifying grace. Congregations, among many other things, must be a holiness training school. Spiritual growth isn't automatic. Before we go, we must grow. Christian growing is centered in the blowing of the Spirit.

1. The Big Picture Verses.
Acts 2:1-2 and Philippians 1:6. The Context: The Acts of the Apostles and Philippians.

When the day of Pentecost had come, suddenly from heaven there came a sound like the rush of a violent wind. All of them were filled with the Holy Spirit. The One who began this good work in you will continue to complete it.

2. A Bit of Background

The second volume of Luke's New Testament writing is called the "Acts of the Apostles." Ironically, much of what is delivered in this writing involves only a little about Peter and much about Paul, leaving out most of the original apostles. Therefore, it seems that the real theological aim of Luke is to demonstrate that the dramatic expansion of the early Christian church is the story of the power of the Risen Christ in action. Luke's Gospel tells what Jesus *began* to do; Luke's "Acts" reports what Jesus *continued* to do as his Spirit worked with and through a range of faithful disciples.

This second volume of Luke, therefore, really is more the *Acts of the Holy Spirit*. Disciples were instructed to wait on the Spirit, who came dramatically on Pentecost (Acts 2). Then it is the Spirit who is shown instructing, guiding, and enabling Christianity to grow in widening circles, from Jerusalem toward the ends of the earth, concluding in Rome, the political and military center of the world known to Luke.

One act of the early apostles was to write letters of warning and encouragement to the young churches. Paul was especially prolific. His most informal and affectionate letter was sent not to a problem church like Corinth or to fickle ones like those in Galatia but to one that had just sent him a love offering to ease his imprisonment in Rome. He reassures his dear friends in Philippi of his gratitude and pleasure that being in jail had not impeded his evangelistic calling. Jesus indeed is Lord, even when imprisoned in the Empire's capital city.

Christian life is to be patterned after Christ who shed his divine status for that of a servant and lived and died in perfect obedience to God. Believers in Jesus are to be "holy," that is, "of the same mind, having the same love" (2:2). We are to press on, knowing that "it is God who is at work in us, enabling us both to will and to work for his good pleasure" (2:13).

3. The Message in Brief

The One who began the good holiness work in us will complete it (Phil. 1:6). Forming us into the image of Jesus can be achieved in a moment so far as our decision to have it so is concerned. Completion of this divine work, however, takes time, discipline, and more and more divine grace. A helpful image of this process is the mustard seed (Lk. 13:18-19).

How does the kingdom of God take shape within us? We have to walk the entire journey of the life of faith. The mustard seed starts small and keeps growing. Eventually there are many branches, so that at the end of one's life it is possible to say, "God has done it!" Such a testimony is not one of pride of accomplishment but of pure joy and gratitude. Prayer isn't so much something we are to *do*, practicing the world of words, as it is something we now *are*, practicing the presence of God as one truly set apart, holy.

Paul tells us that, if we really wish to be "wise" as believers, we must become "fools for Christ's sake (1 Cor. 3:18). Such wisdom is closely associated with Christian "holiness." Being a "holy fool" is a late stage of the Christian's journey of faith. A believer by then knows well his or her dignity in Christ and has no further need of polishing or protecting it before the public. Holiness is when the believer really has met God, matured in that relationship, and is functioning comfortably as a child of God without hypocrisy or apology.

Such holy believers are best equipped to proclaim the reign of God because they have truly accepted it for themselves, come to understand it, and are daring to really live it out to the glory of Christ. This new life in Christ moves from self-preoccupation to a God-focus that frees one to be truly *for others* in the love of Christ. Mature Christian faith such as this brings an inward purification by God's gracious power.

4. The Present Challenge

The meaning of "being holy" is anything but clear these days in our churches. Whatever it is, it's more than mechanical obedience to any set of religious life rules. As Paul's letters to the Romans and Galatians make abundantly clear, "law" can give correct information but cannot bring the personal transformation needed. Our human egos are too bloated and twisted. There has to be a "dying to self" that releases our true self to its purest loving potential. "Sin" isn't simply something we *do* but more fundamentally something we *are*, something we somehow must stop being. Victory over sin may never be total in our lifetimes, but its power to overwhelm and defeat us must and can be defeated through the gracious ministry of God's sanctifying Spirit.

Holiness is intentionally living in the presence of God, regularly being aware of that presence, and being fully willing to represent that presence in daily living. It's being engaged with the Spirit in God's ministry. It's being an available servant of Jesus Christ (Phil. 1:1), cooperating with the Spirit who is continuing the good work already begun within (1:6). It's encouraging the love of God to overflow into us more and more with knowledge and insight (1:9). The more this happens to its members, the more the church will be alive in the Spirit and successful in its mission.

The cry for Christian holiness reaches out to us in this prayer from Paul: "May your love overflow more and more with knowledge and full insight to help you determine what really matters, so that you may be pure and blameless, producing a harvest of righteousness" (Phil. 1:9).

5. Response from the Heart

My Growth Need: Learning to keep growing as I go and do.
1 Chron. 16:29-34; Ps. 19:9-10; Ps. 25:4; 1 Cor. 3:17-21; Col. 3:16; Phil. 1:6.

Here's a poetic exercise in seaside sanctification, an intentional continuing to complete the good work God has begun (Phil. 1:6). Each of us has certain ideas, memories, and self-images so strong that they tend to define and control us. My father was a drunkard—never trust a man. The kid in the next seat was smarter than me—I'll never be smart. What she did to me years ago hurt so much I'll never forgive her or trust anyone. God's probably out to get me like everybody else. Talk of healing is only fantasy.

Picture yourself sitting by the seaside watching ships go by. Put names on them, like "I'll Never Be Smart" and "Healing's Only Fantasy." Watch your ships get smaller and smaller as they go to their unknown destinations. Now try separating yourself from these ideas and self-images as they go toward the horizon and soon slip out of sight. Reach toward Jesus and hear him say, "Give me that hurtful self-image. Let go of that idea. I'll help you be released, freed from old bondages and open to new possibilities. Seaside sanctification!

The life of holiness doesn't happen instantaneously. It's a process made possible by the Spirit of God. The key person in the early church was not any of the disciples. It was the Holy Spirit who blended the disciples together and made them a holy people. The Spirit who lived within Peter, Paul, Priscilla, James, and Timothy wants to be alive today in you and me.

Oh Master, let me walk with Thee
in lowly paths of service free,
Tell me Thy secret–help me bear
the strain of toil, the fret of care.
Teach me Thy patience: still with Thee
in closer, dearer company,
In work that keeps faith sweet and strong,
in trust that triumphs over wrong.
—Washington Gladden

Personal Prayer. O Lord, I know you cry and laugh with me, for you are with me in all things, every day. Words often fail me. Help me rest in the silence of your Spirit with growing trust and gratitude for your presence with me. Free me from old bondages; complete in me the good work you have begun. Take me to the seaside and help the ships take my chains with them as they go. Assure me, precious Lord, that you will complete in me what you have begun. Keep my faith sweet and strong until in trust it begins to triumph over wrong.

**My Spiritual Growth Need:
Submitting to God's will deep within.
Ps. 40:8; Matt. 6:10; Rom. 12:2;
Eph. 1:3-4; I Thess. 5:23.**

Reading 26

YOU SHALL BE HOLY--#5

Being adequately "holy" is less a perfect *waiting* for the Lord's return and much more a perfect *loving* and active *serving* in the meantime. The Thessalonians had end-time questions, and so do we. However, they must not render us passive as believers, people waiting for just the right circumstances. Mission never has paths forward without obstacles in the way. Sitting out the present is an intolerable and unholy stance. Holiness is love in action. God's promises are sure, although the timing often is unclear. While Jesus will return, his Spirit already has come. Therefore, what is very clear is the call to go on God's mission *now*! True saints don't sit and wait but are filled with the already-present Spirit who goes and serves.

1. The Big Picture Verses.
1 Thessalonians 4:3-6. The Context: 1 and 2 Thessalonians.

For this is the will of God, your sanctification: that you abstain from sexual immorality; that each one of you knows how to control your own body in holiness and honor, not with lustful passion, that no one wrong or exploit a brother or sister in this matter. For God did not call us to impurity but in holiness.

2. A Bit of Background

Paul's earlier three weeks in Thessalonica had been productive but also chaotic. He and his friends were accused of being revolutionaries and had been run out of town. There now was a threat to the holiness of life in the congregation. The believers were only one step away from the paganism in which they had grown up, and this threat was compounded by an apparent misunderstanding of the second coming of Christ. They were worrying about the well-being of those already dead. Further, their main motive for maintaining personal purity seems to have been the hope that they would be found faultless when the Lord suddenly returned (3:13, 5:1-8, 5:23).

While certainly there is nothing wrong with being faultless, these misguided believers were allowing their dramatic expectation of the second coming to disrupt their daily responsibilities. For some, this had gone to the extent of watching the skies and turning into hysterical and idle busybodies. To this Paul says a firm "no!" When the Lord does come, it's best that his children be found actively expressing holiness by doing the Lord's will in love. While Christians do have a rich future ahead, there is no better way to prepare for that future than make the best of *the importance of today*. We who are expecting are nonetheless to be faithful workers of love, not neglectful idlers. Holiness is love in action.

3. The Message in Brief

Christians are now living in the *between* times. We experience the uneasy tension of serving lovingly in God's present while awaiting God's brilliant someday. While waiting, we are to be experiencing and expressing the first fruits of what soon will be. Christian holiness has an obvious moral dimension to be experienced and then expressed. It calls us to conduct life in honor, in part by avoiding sexual perversions. It also has a particular relation to the second coming of Jesus, one that easily gets confused.

Will God one day return to claim his own and bring justice for all? Yes, indeed! The question is how believers are to conduct themselves *in the meantime*. Paul speaks of the resurrection as a personal transformation that he expects to experience while still alive. True Christian identity and church membership are to be rooted in Christian experience. Essential is an experience of being transformed into the image of Christ by the action of the Spirit. Affiliation with a church body apart from new life in Christ is false church membership and poor theology. True belief is to be experienced and practiced, not merely intellectualized and verbalized.

First Corinthians 7:25–31 draws practical conclusions about the desirability of not concentrating on the conviction that the world is about to end. Instead, we are to remain free to pursue the mission of the kingdom of God, and do so *now* and not merely *then*. Romans 8:18-25 interprets the present suffering of Christians as a necessary prelude to our future glory. Shall we sit on the world's sidelines and wait for the sky to break open? No, we are to continue pursuing the holiness of ourselves and the fallen world around us, being faithful *in the meantime*.

4. The Present Challenge

We must learn that we don't so much think ourselves into a new way of living as live ourselves into a new way of thinking. Christians shouldn't over-think the second coming of Jesus and the details of the coming heaven. Instead, we are to live the faith now into a new way of presently being, Christian holiness. World events always have been tragic, causing people to speculate about their meaning for the immediate future. Today is no exception. It's good to be informed; it's not good to be absorbed by a favorite news feed to the point of failing to be the hands and feet of Jesus today, regardless of what tomorrow apparently will bring.

There are unanswered questions about the final tomorrow. Here's the best answer to them all for now. Relax! Focus on becoming and behaving in holiness. God will care justly and lovingly about all things we don't yet understand. Meanwhile, we are to get up and dressed. The ancient psalmist gazed into the skies and saw the "glory" of God (Ps. 19). To the Old Testament person, "glory" was the obvious clothing of God. It was attire revealing God's true person in his gracious actions. Disciples of Jesus will discover their intended identity together as the church only when we begin to reflect the Holy One's presence and guidance for *now*.

The church is called to be one people in Christ by the power of his Spirit. We are to put on the clothing of God in order to reveal to others God's true essence, his shared glory. We must be holy as God is holy. Such involves this life focus: "May I never rest till I have the witness of the Spirit that my heart is the temple of the indwelling God and I have the full confidence that Christ reigns supreme on the throne of my affections, bringing every thought into obedience with himself."[1]

5. Response from the Heart

My Growth Need: Submitting to God's will deep within.
Ps. 40:8; Matt. 6:10; Rom. 12:2; Eph. 1:3-4; I Thess. 5:23.

The spiritual goal of modern Christians must go beyond relief from the guilt of sin. It must dip into a new stream of life, a genuine "conversion" to the *True Self*, with God received and allowed to reshape the inner life. The True Self is no longer ego-centered but God-centered and directed. It's a Christian life "with life's vantage-point switched from looking *at God* to looking out *from God*."[2]

Although we cannot see God, we nonetheless can come to love and trust God. We increasingly can rejoice in the Spirit's presence and provisions. We can adore the glory of God and long to fulfill the will of God. We can gladly receive and anxiously exercise the fruit of the Spirit (Gal. 5).

> I am pressing on the upward way,
> New heights I'm gaining every day;
> Still praying as I'm onward bound,
> Lord, plant my feet on higher ground.
>
> I want to scale the utmost height,
> And catch a gleam of glory bright;
> But still I'll pray till heav'n I've found,
> Lord, lead me on to higher ground.
> —Johnson Oatman, Jr.

Personal Prayer. Oh Lord, holiness seems necessary and yet elusive. Help me see that I cannot attain it in my own, but must trust that you will provide all I need to grow and overcome temptation, even as you overcame your temptations in the wilderness when beginning your ministry. Live in me, Lord, and may you receive all

---

[1] Phoebe Palmer, *The Way of Holiness*.
[2] Richard Rohr, *Immortal Diamond*.

the praise and honor. Clothe me with your glory and feed me with the fruit of your Spirit. I realize that the more I submit the more your image emerges in my heart. I can find myself "sanctified," truly set apart *to* you and *for* you. Let it be. Praise God!

"ORDINARY" TIMES--PREFACE

Christian lectionaries (Bible reading plans) often use the word "Ordinary" for many weeks of the Christian Year. The reference is to the extended time between Easter and the return of Advent and the eventual coming of Christ. It's thought of as the church's time of focusing on the present arrival of the reign of God in the full range of human life. Given the reality of the Risen Christ, all time now is to be "sanctified," that is, the ordinary days of life are to be brought into the orbit of resurrection life, infused with the ministry of the Spirit of Christ in everyday affairs.

Christian life is supposed to be what we routinely say and do because we have come to believe in the resurrected Messiah and opened ourselves to his ministering Spirit. These words of Gloria Gaither are to be our daily prayer:

> I then shall live as one who's been forgiven.
> I'll walk with joy to know my debts are paid....
> I then shall live as one who's learned compassion.
> I've been so loved, that I'll risk *loving too*....
> Your Kingdom come around and through and in me;
> Your power and glory, let them shine *through me*.

Experienced holiness must become *expressed* holiness in the everyday affairs of ordinary life. The resurrection of Jesus is now the inspiration and power of our resurrection living in every circumstance, with the New Testament our particular guide.

Granted, the New Testament does not present a single systematic theology or address specifically every unquestion that complicates our way. What it does present is a fundamental story that always sends us in the right direction. That story might be summarized as follows.

God has acted to rescue this lost and broken world. The rescue is through the death and resurrection of Jesus and now through a new community, the church. It's empowered by the Holy Spirit to reenact the loving obedience of Jesus Christ as a sign of God's redemptive purposes for the world.

While different New Testament writers emphasize different aspects of this story, all affirm it and seek in different ways and settings to faithfully report and actively advance it. We who belong to Jesus are now to be models and agents of this story, guided as we go by the author of the story, the Spirit of God.

The Cycle of Personal and Church Life

Human life, with its sins forgiven and the spiritual journey now launched by the Spirit, consists of three distinct phases:

> The season of *well-being,* the life orientation that evokes gratitude
> for the constancy of blessing;
> The season of *suffering and death,* the disorientation that
> evokes resentment, self-pity, and fear; and
> The season of *surprise* when we are reoriented by new gifts of
> God causing joy to break out as the darkness is dispersed.

These seasons are all reflected dramatically in the Book of Psalms, the prayerbook of the ancient Jewish people. They mark the paths walked by all Christian believers today.

All seasons are seen in the life of Jesus himself: "Though he was in the form of God. He emptied himself. Therefore, God has highly exalted him" (Phil. 2:5-11). We believers in Jesus were created as the pinnacle of God's intention, have known the depths of sin's destruction, and now are offered the joys and responsibilities of renewed life, eternal life in the Spirit of the Christ.

One biblical scholar has called these spiritual seasons *Orientation* (stability), *Disorientation* (disarray), and *Reorientation* (surprising newness).[1] We will follow this pattern as we keep reading through

---

[1] Walter Brueggemann, *The Message of the Psalms.*

the remainder of the Bible, exploring who God is, what God has done, and especially what we as his people should be and do now as individuals and together as the church. We begin with "Orientation," readings about foundational Christian beginnings, what God has done to address our gone-wrongness. This sets the stage for a reorientation of the people and mission of God in our present world in dramatic disarray.

The story of the life and ministry of Jesus was recorded for the use of all coming generations of disciples. Four "Gospels" emerged and became widely accepted as inspired by God as accurate and compelling records of God's dramatic coming to us in the man Jesus. While they rely on each other in part, Mark being first, they are differing accounts of the same story told by authors for different audiences. Their combined wisdom prepares contemporary believers for maturing in Christ and facing a range of ordinary and challenging times.

We begin our final set of Readings with the written Gospels. John Mark came first in Rome about 65 A.D., relying in part on his close association with Peter and having to deal with Emperor Nero's savage attack on Christians. In the following few years, three other accounts of the life and teachings of Jesus followed, two quite dependent on Mark. We know them now as prepared by Matthew and Luke, with John a more independent writing.

Together, these four "Gospels," Readings 28-31, share the greatest story ever told, the foundation for Christians who now live in many settings. Readings 32-33 trace the early church's initial expansion, the acts of the Holy Spirit through amazingly faithful apostles and pastors.

Why are Readings 34-45 necessarily presented under the negative caption "Disorientation"? Weren't the Christian beginnings the wonderful fulfillment of Jewish longings and expectations, the "new covenant" envisioned by Jeremiah, a turning upside down for Christ of the Roman world? One would think that the "Songs of the Day" would not be burdened by another medley of "Songs of the Night." But even the earliest of Christian churches faced evil enemies, as the people of God always have and will.

Since God always is faithful, the final group of Readings, 46-52, complete the year and come under the welcome caption "Reorientation." Although evil keeps having its day, even in the church, its time is limited and fresh "Songs of the New Morning" already are being heard as the New Testament comes to a close. The biblical revelation rounds out with clarity about church mission, important advice to church leaders, and a jubilant celebration of the God who never dies and always loves.

Reading 27

SONGS OF THE DAY

Believers can sing with joy because God is, has, and one day will do all necessary for our well-being. This is the keynote of the biblical psalms and the bedrock of Christian faith. Whatever happens, all is secure. God is the spiritual springtime who is our shield for today and the seed of our better tomorrow. Praise God that the morning light is sure to come! Live today as the Lord directs and do not be disabled by constant wars and rumors of wars.

1. The Big Picture Verses.
Psalms 1:1, 28:1. The Context: Psalms 1, 8, 14, 33, 104 (read them all!).

O Lord, our Sovereign, how majestic is your name in all the earth! Happy are those who do not follow the advice of the wicked, or take the path the sinners tread, or sit in the seat of scoffers, but their delight is in the law of the Lord, and on his law they meditate day and night.

2. A Bit of Background

The Book of Psalms may be thought of as the hymnbook of the Jewish heritage. Called the "Psalter," it's sung exclusively in Christian worship among a few Christian traditions today. It's a prayerbook and devotional handbook, the bursts of praise and the cries of the ancient Jew in the negative circumstances of life. The 150 psalms are grouped variously. Psalms 1-72 seem to concentrate on the earliest period of the formation of the nation and the great days of David and Solomon, whereas Psalms 73-150 reflect the later period of Israel's experience of God's steadfast love. Some are joyous, some somber, all relevant for today.

Since the psalms cover the full range of spiritual experience, Walter Brueggemann divides them into orientation, disorientation, and re-orientation. We sing and pray in joy about God's good creation, in shock and sorrow about the awful injustices and tragedies of our world, and finally in our recoveries as we freshly rejoice over God's undeserved saving grace and restorative actions.

The value of the psalms for today comes in part because this inspired prayer poetry gives expression to all phases of spiritual experience, and often in frank and dramatic form. The book begins in obedience (Psalm 1) and ends in boundless joy (Psalm 150). Like the actual experience of God's people told at length in the Old Testament, almost everything imaginable comes between 1 and 150.

3. The Message in Brief

The basic truth about the meaning of divine grace is that God has acted *first*. God already has saved his people before they could cry to him for salvation. Grace comes before repentance. What the psalmist often does is seek forgiveness for sinful rebellion. This is done while remembering what God already has done on our behalf. Those very human psalm writers discovered that the sacrifices of bulls and goats could only educate to the true meaning of sacrifice, which must be an act of the heart and the will. Despite human life needing to be lived in a world of disease, earthquake, and war, "the Lord is my shepherd; *I shall not want*" (Ps. 23:1).

The dominant note of the Book of Psalms is the praise of God for the loving kindness that chose Israel and delivered her from many enemies, including her wayward self. There are numerous promises of a greater deliverance yet to come and reports of God's holiness that brings sinners to their knees in humility and obedience. While most of the Old Testament offers little hope of anything much beyond this present life, Psalm seems an exception. True communion with God cannot be broken, even by the event of death (Ps. 73:23–28). In the New Testament we find this: "I am convinced that neither death, nor life, nor angels, nor rulers, nor things present, nor things to come will be able to separate us from the love of God in Christ Jesus our Lord" (Rom. 8:38–39).

4. The Present Challenge

A consistent tension existed in Israel between meticulous obedience to the Temple and its rituals (sometimes almost cult-like) and the spiritual lives of the people away from Jerusalem and its watchdog priesthood. The Hebrew prophets and psalms thunder against a lack of worship integrity (Ps. 51:16–17). Memory is crucial. The psalms are filled with fresh realizations that God has been at work throughout the people's history, despite the many failures. God has guided the people's destiny from the days of Moses to the present and promises even better for the future. The faithful must keep their eyes on God and not get caught up in themselves and their rigid religious traditions.

The church of Jesus exists not for itself but to be a humble instrument of God conveying the story of divine love to all the world. What a story that is! "Bless the Lord, O my soul. O Lord my God, you are very great!" (Ps. 104:1). If believers meet and experience God's grace together, the end always will be an experience of joy and praise. The English word "hallelujah" simply means "praise the Lord." "Jah" is the shortened form of "Yahweh," the Hebrew name for God.

Psalm 146 begins and ends with "Praise the Lord!" Such a positive message of joy and praise, when humbly shared with true excitement and gratitude, will be a powerful witness to many who live in despair. In the world's darkness, here is a song of the day!

5. Response from the Heart

My Growth Need: Tuned by joy in all circumstances.
Ps. 9:1-2; Acts 16:25-26; Eph. 5:18-21; Col. 3:16-17; 1 Thess. 5:16-18.

One of the great ways to celebrate and increase faith is to sing. The psalms gave the people of God that opportunity. It was their way of rehearsing the faith, remembering the story, and celebrating life in God. The majesty of worship can be seen in a congregation singing together, especially in harmony. The spirit is lifted and the heart made glad.

The creation of songs by believers ranges from oratorios and cantatas to simple verses and melodies. Worshippers join their voices, praising God and receiving great joy in return. Are you joining some great chorus of voices? Is there darkness in your present experience? The life of faith can and should be filled with songs of the day!

> *Joyful, joyful, we adore Thee,*
> *God of glory, Lord of love;*
> *Hearts unfold like flow'rs before Thee,*
> *Op'ning to the sun above.*
> *Melt the clouds of sin and sadness,*
> *Drive the dark of doubt away;*
> *Giver of immortal gladness,*
> *Fill us with the light of day!*
> —Henry Van Dyk

Personal Prayer. I may not have a great singing voice, but no matter. Lord, give me a singing heart and a grateful people with whom to sing. May the clarity of my vision of you, O God, and my understanding of your work grow each day within my life. May the expression of my faith, especially in singing, be a sweet sound to You, and may joy spread across my soul and the whole body of worshippers. Whatever the darkness that clouds life, when I sing in faith the day comes! How I pray that you, Lord of love, will unfold like flowers before me, filling me with the light of day!

Reading 28

HE'S REALLY THE GOD-MAN!

Why address first the Gospel of Mark? Because that's how the four Gospel writings originally came about. We need to be sure of who Jesus really was (and is) before we attempt to teach and seek to convince others about him. Mark gives us the basic story of Jesus before Matthew, Luke, and John then elaborate on that story in different ways for different readerships. All four agree on the most important thing. Jesus actually was God with us!

1. The Big Picture Verses.

Mark 1:11, 8:29, 14:62. The Context: The Gospel of Mark.

A voice came from the heavens, "You are my Son, the Beloved; with you I am well pleased." Jesus later would ask Peter, "But who do you say that I am?" The answer, "You are the Messiah!" Still later, the high priest would ask if Jesus claimed this divine status. The answer, "I am."

2. A Bit of Background

The generations of Jews living just before the time of Jesus formed a small but proud people who so hoped for better times as one foreign power after another grabbed their throats. The number of beggars, mentally ill, and diseased people who appear around Jesus is evidence of a deeply troubled people. The ministry of Jesus caused a resurgence of hope that the Messiah finally had come. Even though soon executed for supposed blasphemy, hope was kept alive among many because of the news of the resurrection of Jesus and the ongoing and passionate preaching of his followers.

In 64–65 A.D. the awful Roman emperor Nero unintentionally served Christians of all times. He apparently set fire to his own capital city, Rome, and blamed it on the local Christians, turning on them in fury, with Peter and Paul two of the executed martyrs. A fellow Christian, John Mark, began writing the story of Jesus. The initial eyewitnesses to his crucifixion and resurrection now were dying and Christians needed fresh encouragement as they faced severe persecution. Rome may have burned, but the greatest of all stories now burned in Mark's heart. Peter once called Mark "my son" (1 Pet. 5:13). He had been a young missionary who traveled with Paul and in whose house in Jerusalem early Christians had met (Acts 12:12). He was in an ideal position to write an account of Jesus.

Mark's Gospel uses the word "immediately" forty-one times as he gallops from one event to another, anxious to tell this story quickly and with excitement. He reaches a highpoint when Jesus asks Peter who he thinks he really was. The dramatic response, "You are the Christ, the Messiah!" (8:29). That's exactly what Mark's story is all about, a real man who had come from God, in fact was God with us so that even the grave soon would not be able to hold him! (16:6).

Mark tells this Jesus story for the small Christian community in Rome shocked by the brutal loss of its beloved leaders. Soon three other "life stories" of Jesus would appear, with Matthew and Luke heavily dependent on Mark while adding other material chosen for their differing readers. John's writing also would appear, quite different in focus and giving no evidence of being directly dependent on Mark. Even so, John and the others seek to spread the great news. Jesus has come to be God with us!

3. The Message in Brief

Since memory easily enhances reality, some modern skeptics have speculated that the "Jesus of history" and the "Christ of faith" aren't really the same person. Mark, however, begins by refuting such a distortion of the truth. He writes of the good news of "Jesus Christ," the man Jesus and the Christ of God *in the same person*. John the Baptist met Jesus at the Jordan River where the heavens announced dramatically, "You are my Son, the Beloved" (1:11). The story of Jesus told my Mark is nothing less than the story of *God with us!* The "kingdom of heaven," God's sovereign reign, had drawn very near. It was time to repent, receive, and proclaim the good news to others.

Who exactly is Jesus? He is no less than God's Messiah (8:27–29), the One come from heaven to bring salvation to all who believe, the One who chose the way of the Suffering Servant foretold in Isaiah 53. Mark's account is realistic, frank, and action-oriented, showing that this heavenly one was also a real human being, God come *in the flesh*, the infinite God who somehow for a time was also finite, with us and for us but not *from* us.

4. The Present Challenge

While the Gospel of Mark is clear about the humanness of Jesus, with this clarity always is an awe and astonishment about his fuller identity (1:22, 27; 4:41; 10:26). Amazingly, Jesus is one of us *and* God with us. Mark is called the "essential" Gospel, the one on which two others rely heavily. His writing is a direct echo of the eyewitness accounts and preaching of Peter. The challenge for us power-driven "moderns" is to humbly accept this story as the greatest one ever told, and then dare to orient our own realities around it. Jesus was "meek" not weak. Meek means power under control. Jesus could have called on thousands of angels to save him, but chose to die on our behalf.

The people who really know Jesus are humble people awed by the gentle graciousness of a sacrificing God. Jesus came to be in this living and dying business *with* us because he was *for* us. From the ugly cross he teaches the beautiful way to win in life by losing, following the victorious and yet suffering Sovereign. Christians are to represent this Jesus who willingly gave up everything for us. The people who stand out in his life, and are set for a wonderful life to come, are the people who don't flaunt who and what they are doing since they know all is really the Spirit's working in and through them. It's who Jesus is and what his Spirit now does that really matters.

5. Response from the Heart

My Growth Need: Excited by the real Jesus.
Matt. 28:18-19; Mk. 6:3; Lk. 5:20-21; Jn. 3:1-2; Jn. 7:40; Heb. 1:1-2.

How did all the stories about Jesus get their start? No doubt the disciples shared their memories orally for as long as they were alive. You and I should be thankful that John Mark, who traveled with both Peter and Paul, took the initiative to write his account and filled it with truth and urgency. The urgency is for us to keep spreading the good news now. "Go into all the world and proclaim the gospel" (16:15). Having met Jesus face-to-face, we can never be the same or comfortably keep quiet.

Have you really met Jesus? Do you know who he really is? Are you making it your business to tell others? Is this your testimony?

> Fairest Lord Jesus,
> Ruler of all nature,
> O thou of God and man the Son;
> Thee will I cherish,
> Thee will I honor,
> Thou, my soul's glory, joy, and crown.
> —(unknown)

> Turn your eyes upon Jesus,
>   look full in His wonderful face
> And the things of earth will grow strangely dim
>   in the light of His glory and grace.
> —Helen Lemmel

Personal Prayer. Lord, may I meet Jesus anew each day, really meet him. Help me see him clearly, respond in love, and follow him daily in my work and actions. May somehow I be able to help others see Christ and allow this life-changing good news to enter their lives. Thank you, Lord, for John Mark, early teller of the story. His testimony long ago enables mine this very day. I realize that knowing who Jesus is makes all the difference. He is one with me as a real man, although without sin, thus really understanding me. He also is one with God and thus able to transform me into his own image. Oh, the wonderful light of his glory and grace!

My Growth Need:
Taught by the Master himself.
Matt. 4:23, 5:2, 7:29; Jn. 1:14, 38;
Rom. 1:4; Col. 1:15-20.

Reading 29

THE JEWISH MESSIAH

Leaning on but greatly expanding the writing of Mark, here's the heart of Matthew's account of Jesus. Jesus is the expected One, the center of Jewish belief and teaching, and now the subject of Christian proclamation to all the earth. In the Christian's faith curriculum, Jesus is the center of all biblical revelation and the hope and future judge of all humanity. He is both the refinement of his Jewish heritage and its fulfillment. He is the greatest of teachers and the highpoint of his own teaching. He explains for us the way to the Father, and *he is that way*!

1. The Big Picture Verses.

Matthew 5:1-16. The Context: Gospel of Matthew.

When Jesus saw the crowds, he went up to the mountain, his disciples came to him, and he began to speak, saying: "Blessed are . . ." and "You are . . . ."

2. A Bit of Background

Matthew has been described as the great teacher sent from God. The Gospel he composed has a superb teaching structure. Famous are his chapters 5-7, a collection of the teachings of Jesus known as the Sermon on the Mount. Actually, this is only one of five teaching units in this Gospel, something of a mirror of the five books of Moses (Genesis through Deuteronomy). Matthew's purpose is not to repudiate but to fulfill the earlier Jewish teaching, and certainly to convey a passionate concern for Christian mission to the whole world.

About twenty years after Mark's Gospel appeared in the West (Rome), Matthew's appeared in the East (Syria). This new story of Jesus relies heavily on Mark, reproducing nearly all of Mark's verses. Matthew adds especially the teachings of Jesus and numerous attempts to show that he fulfilled the prominent prophecies of the Jews, linking Jesus to the Law and the Prophets. Matthew's intended audience obviously is the Jewish and Jewish-Christian communities. His message? "Here is your expected Messiah!" The Old Testament background dominates this Gospel. The Jewish-Christian writer begins with a detailed genealogy of Jesus, son of David, rooted deeply in the whole Abrahamic tradition (not back to Adam as in the Gospel of Luke). God has one purpose that runs through both Testaments, a purpose foreshadowed in the first and fulfilled in the second.

The nature and role of the new Christian fellowship is clearly of concern to Matthew. He adds much of the teachings of Jesus to undergird the worship, discipline, and mission of the new church. He groups things in threes and sevens to ease memorizing and repeating. Echoing Moses giving the old Law to the people at Mt. Sinai, the "Sermon on the Mount" (chaps. 5-7) is Matthew's core curriculum of Jesus for the new people of God, preparing them for their task of world evangelism (28:19-20). For instance, the seven parables in chapter 13 describe the nature of God's kingdom and the essential guidelines for the church's life.

3. The Message in Brief

The tendency over time always is to encrust God's revelation with many "traditions of the elders," making religion unnecessarily burdensome, archaic, and a process of obeying mechanically a mass of life rules. While Jesus shows high regard for the Law of his people, he announces a "new" law of love. It features the personal inwardness of God's expectations of us, putting a new focus on issues like murder (5:21–26) and adultery (5:27–32). The "righteousness" of the Christian must exceed that of the Scribes and Pharisees, not by neglecting the Law but by fulfilling its real intent. This approach points toward inward "holiness" rather than the outward mechanics of the spiritual life. Be as your Heavenly Father is (5:48).[1]

Matthew highlights the presence of Christ when believers gather (18:20-22) and our readiness to forgive since we have been forgiven so much (18:23-35), both key components of an internal state of Christian holiness. Externally, Matthew ends his story of Jesus with a clear call to the church's missionary vocation, her marching orders to go everywhere telling the story, teaching and baptizing (28:16-20). Here is the heart of Matthew's Gospel message. Jesus is the Christ, the Son of God. He came not to destroy the law of Moses but to fulfill it by teaching a more excellent way of life as members of a new faith community, the Christian church, the new holy nation destined to embrace all humankind.

4. The Present Challenge

The Gospel of Matthew tells the story of the true identity of Jesus. It's an extension of the story of God's preparation for Christ in the history of the Jewish people. Matthew begins with a Jewish genealogy that leads to Jesus, who then is presented as Israel's new David, the fulfillment of God's history with his people Israel. Jesus, in fact, is the true Israel, God's agent of good news in this world, a full embodiment of the divine being and intention.

Mathew's Gospel may come from the first century but it's equally relevant for the twenty-first. It bridges old and new, joining their hands and teachings, valuing the Old Testament as essential to understanding the New, but clearly facing the fresh future with Jesus. All the divine promises to the former people are said to be fulfilled in the true Israel, Jesus. Something greater than the Temple is here (12:6) and you have heard *but I tell you . . .*" (5:17, 21, 27, etc.). We must hear this ongoing telling and accomplish the worldwide mission envisioned by Matthew (28:18-20). All are to be at home with Jesus, who is none other than God intentionally with us all for our salvation.

---

[1] For a fresh presentation of this important Christian teaching and mission, see Barry L. Callen, *Christian Holiness* (Aldersgate and Emeth Presses, 2023).

> To an open house in the evening,
> Home shall men come,
> To an older place than Eden,
> and a taller town than Rome.
> To the end of the way of the wandering star,
> To the things that cannot be and that are,
> To the place where God was homeless,
> and all men are at home.

Matthew would have said a hearty "Amen!" to these prophetic words of G. K. Chesterton. Jesus was born among us, alienated by us, and yet is our eternal home.

5. Response from the Heart

My Growth Need: Taught by the Master himself.
Matt. 4:23, 5:2, 7:29; Jn. 1:14, 38; Rom. 1:4; Col. 1:15-20.

Not every person who welcomes the good news in Christ is called to be a preacher. Many are called to teach the meaning of the story, and certainly to live it out before others. Matthew, as one of the primary Christian links with the Jewish people, has provided the teaching Gospel. He clarifies and redirects the pronouncements given by key Jewish teachers, showing how Jesus is the Christ who fulfills and makes plain the new life of God provided to the believer. Matthew's beautiful structure and language draw people to embrace it. Thus, it's listed first in the collection of the Gospels. From the past of the Jewish heritage emerged Jesus to bridge the ancient with the most modern.

> Teach me Thy way Lord, teach me Thy way,
> Thy guiding grace afford. Teach me Thy way.
> Help me to walk aright, more by faith, less by sight,
> Lead me with heav'nly light. Teach me thy way.
> When doubts and fears arise, teach me Thy way.
> When storms o'erspread the skies, teach me Thy way.
> Shine through the cloud and rain, through sorrow, toil and pain; Make Thou my pathway plain, teach me Thy way.
> —B. Mansell Ramsey

Personal Prayer. Lord, I don't want to be a shallow follower of Jesus. Teach me, shape me within to the message and Spirit of Jesus. Let Matthew's story teach me how to follow true love and discern how I can and should be like you. I want to be part of the true Israel. Show me the way that honors the past of your chosen people and also places me in the center of your present will. May I honor the "Elders" of the faith in the Old Testament and be well instructed in the New Testament way to the Father through Rabbi Jesus who was indeed the Messiah.

My Growth Need:
Healed by the greatest doctor.
Ps. 34:18; Isa. 41:10; Lk. 6:19; Jn. 14:27;
Acts 1:8, 4:12, 13:47; Phil. 4:19; Rev. 21:4.

Reading 30

THE DOCTOR'S STORY

The symbol of Luke's Gospel is a calf, the animal of sacrifice. Jesus is pictured as the sacrifice for all the world, breaking down the barriers between Jew and Gentile, sinner and saint. To know Jesus is to be full of compassion. Luke was a doctor, seen in some of his language and attitudes. Jesus is the great healer of all humanity.

1. The Big Picture Verses.
Luke 2:10, 19:10. The Context: Gospel of Luke and the Book of Acts

Announced the angel: "I am bringing you good news of great joy for all the people; to you is born this day in the city of David a Savior, who is the Messiah, the Lord." The Son of Man came to seek out and to save the lost.

2. A Bit of Background

Luke's extensive writing, Luke-Acts, is the centerpiece of the whole New Testament. This doctor provides us with a two-volume work telling the stories of both Jesus and the early church. He is a skilled writer in the Greek language, the beloved doctor referred to in Paul's letters. Likely he was a Greek living in Antioch, the first center of Gentile Christianity.

Like Matthew, Luke relies on Mark's earlier Gospel for the story of Jesus but goes well beyond Mark with literary artistry and much new material. Dr. Luke addresses the educated person, intending to give a full account of Christian beginnings for the benefit of a pagan convert, Theophilus (1:3). He makes the case to him that Christianity isn't an obscure sect of Judaism but potentially a world faith, anything but a disruptive force in society as the Romans often charged.

Luke's writing is a beautiful portrayal of a boundary-breaking faith moving across frontiers in the power of God's Spirit. In the Gospel portion of his work there appear the classic stories of the Prodigal Son and Good Samaritan, as well as pictures of reconciliation between Jew and Samaritan, Jew and Gentile. Jesus is shown reaching to the black sheep of society, including women and the poor, and focusing on prayer and meditation used often by Jesus to sustain himself in his frantic schedule and against significant opposition. There is a note of good news and joy dominating Luke's entire work. Joining it is a universal element. Luke traces the descent of Jesus from Adam, founder of the human race, not merely to Abraham, founder of the Jewish people as does Matthew.

Compared to the other Gospels, Luke shows little theological interest. He's more pragmatic, a sensitive doctor constantly focusing on the practicalities of human hurting and healing, always pointing to Jesus, the great Friend, Healer, and Savior. He reports Jesus in Nazareth announcing his mission "to bring good news to the poor, to proclaim release to the captives and recovery of sight to the blind, to set free those who are oppressed" (4:18).

3. The Message in Brief

The Christian church of all times should reflect the major emphases of Dr. Luke. Jesus is presented at his most beautiful and the gospel at its widest reach. His is a Gospel of prayer, Jesus being shown praying at each great moment of his life, and of women, with many occasions told from a woman's point of view. Throughout this Gospel is the note of praise, as in the *Magnificat* (1:46–55), the *Benedictus* (1:68–79), and Simeon's song *Nunc Dimittis* (2:29–32) in which he hails the infant Jesus as "a light for revelation to the Gentiles."

As it was for Jesus and his early followers, the Christian faith always should be reaching in love to all people without distinction, and doing so with the dignity of a Luke who tells the sweet story of the love of God come in Jesus for all people. The people loved Jesus because he obviously loved them and spoke directly and healingly to their greatest hurts and desperations. So goes the story as told by Luke.

4. The Present Challenge

We find in this third Gospel the careful research and writing of a great soul. Luke's concerns, reflecting those of Jesus, include strong opposition to pious pretentions and self-righteousness (the Pharisee), callousness to human suffering (the priest who passed the injured man on the other side), vindictiveness to repentant sinners (the elder brother), greed at the expense others (the rich fool), and racial pride (distain of the Samaritans).

These serious human failures unfortunately are perennial, still seen all around us. Religion must not be relegated to finding personal comfort and gaining sin's forgiveness. Jesus focused his attention of healing love for the least of humanity around him, the sick, lost, hopeless, rejected. This way of life is difficult and even dangerous. Jesus never told his disciples there would be no yoke to wear, only that he would see that it was light enough to bear. Are you ready to accept this self-giving way of life? It's called being a real Christian.

5. Response from the Heart

My Growth Need: Healed by the greatest doctor.
Ps. 34:18; Isa. 41:10; Lk. 6:19; Jn. 14:27; Acts 1:8, 4:12, 13:47; Phil. 4:19; Rev. 21:4

I am impressed with the doctor's way of telling the story with such beautiful language and carefully written accounts. I like how he instructs his believing confidant, Theophilus, to go deeply into the life and teachings of Jesus. Some of us need this kind of instruction. That's where one finds real joy and rich ministry.

The keyword representing the writing of Luke/Acts is "witness," a person who has both experienced and actively tells the Jesus story. Luke must have interviewed many about their time with Jesus, gathering remembrances of his teaching, suffering, death and resurrection, and his appearances and message of repentance and forgiveness. Where does all that leave you?

Lord, I want to be a Christian in my heart.
Lord, I want to be more loving in my heart.
Lord, I want to be more holy in my heart.
Lord, I want to be like Jesus in my heart.
—African-American spiritual

Something beautiful, something good,
all my confusion he understood;
All I had to offer him was brokenness and strife,
but he made something beautiful of my life.
—Gloria Gaither

Personal Prayer. Thank you, Lord, for the Gospel of Luke and his connected stories of the early church. What a treasure for the church of all times. Lord, make my life so transparent that my experience of Jesus and his good news for all will be crystal clear to others. Let me reveal with excitement that I longer belong to myself but to You, the one who has remade me from within. May the Spirit of the risen Christ live, breathe, and love in each of us, beginning with me!

Reading 31

ECHOES OF GENESIS

The emblem sometimes associated with John's Gospel is the eagle, the bird flying higher than any other. This fourth Gospel has thoughts that fly as high as human thought can go. Christian truth is so simple and yet so profound. His name is Jesus, and the writer is John. The opening lines take human thought about the divine as deep as we can manage. They soar so high that we are transported to the very throne of God. Genesis begins with God acting in the very beginning. John begins with Jesus joining God then, and with God always in loving action.

1. The Big Picture Verse.
John 1:1-5, 3:16. The Context: The Gospel of John.

In the beginning was the Word, and the Word was with God, and the Word was God. He was in the beginning with God. All things came into being through him. The light shines in the darkness and the darkness did not overtake it. God so loved the world that he gave his only Son so that everyone who believes in him may not perish but have eternal life.

2. A Bit of Background

This Gospel writer is said to be the disciple whom Jesus loved (21:20, 24). John's account of Jesus stands out in responding love with its profound insight into the significance of the person and work of Christ. John's writing is not one of the "Synoptics," the first three Gospels "seen together" because of their sharing much of Mark's Gospel. John presents the same Jesus, but in a range of dramatic and differing ways. He is the true Vine, the Bread of life, the Light of the world. Rather than "Messiah," a Jewish concept unknown to the larger world, John highlights the identity of Jesus in other and sometimes non-Hebrew philosophic terms (1:1–18). Jesus didn't begin as a baby in Bethlehem but *always was* as the *Logos*, the Word, the eternal expression of the creative God now made flesh for our human salvation.

This Gospel reverts to the first words of Genesis that identify the divine energy originally bringing order out of chaos, an act of creative love. There is stress on the pre-existence of Jesus. "Before Abraham was, *I am*" (8:58). John speaks of the glory Jesus had with the Father before the world was made (17:5). This pre-existence, however, is not understood at the expense of his true humanity, assumed voluntarily and sacrificially for our human benefit. Writing in Ephesus where "Messiah" and "Son of David" would have had no meaning except to a few Jews, John moves from the expansive heights of Genesis, pre-dating Israel, to philosophic concepts with rich Greek heritages.

John is the "symbolic" Gospel, seeing certain earthly events as moving images of eternity. Note the series of "signs" in chapters 2-12. The opening prologue (1:1-5) might be paraphrased: "The Cosmic Force responsible for initiating the existence of all is also the secret of victorious human living. This Force, actually a Person, has made possible an intimate availability of itself to us fallen humans through the man Jesus. When we open ourselves to his coming and experience his overflowing love, the transforming reality of the creating and redeeming God becomes ever clearer and makes us truly new in the divine image."

3. The Message in Brief

The Word, the eternal Wisdom who is God, has become flesh in the man Jesus. To see the Son is to see the Father. Jesus is our source of truth and grace, the sharing on our human scene of the very mind of the eternal Father. John provides seven miracles or "signs" that illumine aspects of God's Self-revelation in Jesus. He ends his Gospel admitting that any human record of the person of

Jesus has necessary limitations (21:18-25). This Gospel is so simple that its salvation message can be grasped by anyone (3:16), and yet it's so profound that living with it for a lifetime will not plumb its depths.

Jesus Christ has come into the world, but people have loved darkness rather than light. All who do evil do not come to the light to avoid their deeds being exposed. But some come to the light so that it may be more clearly seen (3:19-21). Jesus is the Light of the world. John's Gospel was written so that you and I might believe and thus have life through the person of Jesus. As we believe, we know that the Spirit of truth is coming to us to guide into all truth. The Spirit is that of Jesus himself, and thus will glorify Jesus and declare to us what is his (20:31, 16:13-14). John's twin goals in his writing are that each of us be converted to this truth and then grow deeply in its limitless riches.

4. The Present Challenge

Ours is an age of spiritual hungering and searching, one that readily sheds old traditionalisms and religious institutions while grasping for something personal and authentic. How will such people come to know the real and amazing identity of Jesus?

It may have to be as Albert Schweitzer suggested back in 1906:

> He comes to us as one unknown, without a name, as of old by the lakeside. To those who obey him, whether they be wise or simple, he will reveal himself in the toils, the conflicts, and the sufferings which they shall pass through in his fellowship and, as an ineffable mystery, they shall learn in their own experience who he is.

Are "moderns" patient enough to linger by the lakeside for as long as it takes? Are we so practical that we want only what works for us quickly and obviously, without any complex philosophy or theology attached, and certainly with no confining religious trappings or necessary pattern of Jewish fulfillments? John presents Jesus relatively free of any religious establishment. He just is, always was, and in the end will yet be!

5. Response from the Heart

My Growth Need: Inspired by the Word made flesh.
Josh. 1:9; Ps. 27:1; Jn. 8:12-16, 9:5; 1 Thess. 2:13; Heb. 10:24-25; 1 Jn. 1:5-7

I love to tell and re-tell the stories of Jesus as reported in the Synoptic Gospels (Matthew, Mark, and Luke.) The Fourth Gospel approaches the telling of these stories in John's own unique way, reminiscent of the biblical beginning in Genesis. God as the Son is sustaining life through the Spirit and enfleshing that reality in the world. In his Gospel's prologue (1:1-18), John draws on the Jewish history of the encounter of Moses with the great "I AM." He expresses the truth of God in Christ using Greek thought, the divine "Logos" or Word. However the story is told, rejoice in its magnificent truth!

> I love to tell the story of unseen things above,
> of Jesus and His glory, of Jesus and His love;
> I love to tell the story because I know 'tis true,
> It satisfies my longings as nothing else can do.
>
> I love to tell the story for those who know it best
> seem hungering and thirsting to hear it like the rest;
> And when in scenes of glory I sing the new, new song,
> 'Twill be the old, old story that I have loved so long.
> —Karherine Hankey

Personal Prayer. Lord, I and most people I know are not well versed in Jewish history and theology. Trying to explain Jesus in that context just doesn't get very far. But then there's your beloved John. His explanations really make sense. Lord, thank you for who you are, what you came to do, and what your servant John has written. To think that the One who was at the beginning and will be when time is no more knows and cares *about me*! May the reality of your forgiveness set me free to live life to the full! May the amazing words of John 3:16 fill my brain and fire my very soul.

Reading 32

THE GOSPEL TAKES ROOT

Was Christianity to be just another sect of Judaism? No. The good news is that Jesus is Lord *of all!* The commission was going to all the world with the good news and Luke, the writer of Luke-Acts, is anxious to show the challenges and successes of beginning this extended mission. Early disciples of Jesus are encouraged to consider it all joy when they encountered various trials (James 1:2). They could embrace suffering as a kind of glory and even sing in the darkness (Acts 16:25). *Joy to the World* should be more than a popular Christmas carol. It's really the Christian's theme song! The joy belongs to the *whole world.*

1. The Big Picture Verses.
Acts 1:8, 10:34-36. The Context: The Book of Acts, chapters 3-12

I (Peter) understand that God shows no partiality. Anyone who fears God and practices righteousness is acceptable to him. Jesus Christ is Lord of all. You will receive power when the Holy Spirit has come upon you and you will be my witnesses to the end of the earth.

2. A Bit of Background

This second volume of Dr. Luke's New Testament writing gives us a major look at the first days of the Christian church. He recalls that the Lord had given the first disciples a general plan of action before his departure, as Moses once had done for the old Israel. Now Luke records a selection of key events of the church's early expansion, including its demanding birth pains. He did so with at least three aims in mind.

First, since it already was a time of persecution of the church, Luke seeks to show that this new faith is politically innocent and morally blameless (18:14, 19:37, 23:29, 25:25). Second, Luke takes the evangelistic command of the Risen Christ (1:8) and shows its spread in ever-widening circles. Third, his theological intent is to make clear that this dramatic expansion is not the result of mere human activity. Decisions are made by believers *in the Spirit* (6:3), then accomplished with the guidance and gifting of the Spirit (13:2, 15:28, 16:6-7).

The beginning of the gospel outreach was on Jewish soil. A key issue to be sorted out immediately was the degree to which the new Jesus faith was, in effect, just another sect of Judaism. It quickly is shown to be something founded in but no longer restricted by the specifics of its ancient Israelite roots. The dramatic Pentecost event was a big lesson learned by Peter's experience (chap. 10). Then came Stephen's bold speech that brought Jewish wrath and his stoning execution that drew new lines of separation.

The pivotal event was Judaism's chief persecutor of the "Christians," Saul being converted in Damascus to a new believer in Jesus. What now? Saul (Paul) sees the bigger picture of God's intent—no limits to God's mission of good news. The Jerusalem Council convenes to decide on what basis Gentiles (non-Jews) could be admitted to the new church. Paul's mission to the Gentiles begins in earnest with multiple journeys in multiple countries. The barriers came down, with the worldwide mission of the Jesus people in full swing.

3. The Message in Brief

Judging from the three great missionary sermons of Paul that Luke summarizes (13:26-41, 14:15-17, 17:22-31), we conclude that the following was the basic Christian message first spread across the world. What had gone before in Judaism, nature, and even paganism was leading up to Jesus Christ where all would find their climax. History is the arena of God's activity. In Jesus, a new age had dawned and all Jewish prophecies fulfilled (2:14-21). The unjustified murder of Jesus somehow served the redemptive purpose of God (2:23). It soon yielded to the dramatic resurrection of Jesus and then to the coming of the Spirit who began to send witnesses everywhere.

The forgiveness by God, made universally possible by all these dramatic events, provides the gifts and power needed for the future. The hour had come when humans must respond to this blessedness with a "yes" of faith and glorious new life or a "no" of rejection and resulting judgment. The invitation was extended to all humans, Jew and Gentile alike. Luke reports that in his Gospel he had dealt with all that Jesus *began* to do and teach (Acts 1:1). Turning to the end of the Book of Acts, one encounters its deliberately unfinished character. The ministries of those first Apostles was only *the end of the beginning*!

4. The Present Challenge

The first Christians did not think of Jesus primarily as a person located in past history. For them, the paramount miracle was not the Jesus of yesterday but Christ the Lord now very present with them through the Spirit's dramatic working. Following Christ meant living in a new fellowship, the company of those in whom the living Christ was moving and working across the world. Christianity is never to become just another of the many organized religious establishments in this world. It's to be a living faith functioning around the belief that Jesus lives and reigns and that, through his Holy Spirit, is helping present believers in all the changing settings and seasons of life.

As Peter announced his key new vision (Acts 10), we too must dare to see the world mission of the church, with the grace of God in Christ freed of national barriers and cultural preferences. Like John Wesley, we should "look upon the world has my parish."[1] The gospel of Christ's love fits in no human box defined by our organizations, ethnicities, nationalities, or economic circumstances. The church expansion seen in the Book of Acts is not the story of a growing religious organization or institution. It's the story of hearts warmed by God, in fellowship with the Spirit, and on common mission together.

---

[1] John Wesley, *Journal*, June 11, 1739.

How inclined we are now to reduce God to level and consider ourselves the key actors in the church's work? The primary mover in Christian evangelism is the Holy Spirit who prompts, leads, convicts, teaches, and transforms. The primary practice of a Christian evangelist, oddly enough, is not to evangelize but to pray for openness to the principal evangelist, the Holy Spirit.[2]

> Like a mighty army
> Moves to church of God;
> Brothers [and Sisters], we are treading
> Where the Saints have trod.
> —Sabine Baring-Gould

5. Response from the Heart

My Growth Need: Inflamed by the arriving Spirit.
Ex. 19:18; Lk. 3:16, 4:18-19; Rom. 8:26-27, 12:9-13; 1 Cor.12:13

Luke, the most prolific of all the writers of the New Testament, opens his Book of Acts with powerful good news to the world. The gospel of Jesus had outgrown its Jewish beginnings. Believers of many backgrounds were overcoming their fears, prejudices, and narrow Jewish thinking. God grace shows no partiality for the Jews and grants full acceptance of non-Jews. This was a great turning point in telling the story of Jesus.

What caused the faith community of Jesus to grow so quickly in the first centuries after the resurrection of Jesus? In reading Luke's story, we see the powerful, effective proclamation to love each other, even a willingness to lay down life for the message and for other believers.

> Spirit of God, descend upon my heart;
> Wean it from Earth through all its pulses move;
> Stoop to my weakness, mighty as Thou art,
> And make me love Thee as I ought to love.
>
> Teach me to love Thee as Thine angels love,

---

[8] See Priscilla Pope-Levison, *Models of Evangelism*.

One holy passion filling all my frame;
The baptism of the heaven descended Dove,
My heart an altar and Thy love the flame.
—George Croly

Personal Prayer. I am moved, Lord, by the powerful witness of the first-century church, especially how they loved each other and expressed willingness to lay down their lives for the cause of Christ. May I express in my life that same commitment. Give me, Lord, the courage and love that is willing to give freely and share the good news of Jesus widely. May my heart be aflame with Thy love. Thank you for Dr. Luke's sharing of the pivotal Christian past. Now it's my turn to share. Help me Lord!

My Growth Need:
Commissioned as an apostle of Christ.
Mt. 28:19-20; Luke 6:13; Acts 2:1-42, 5:12-16;
1 Cor. 12:27-31; Phil. 1:27-28.

Reading 33

JOURNEYS WITH JESUS

Really belonging to Jesus involves much more than a brief meeting and repenting of past sin. It's also a journey through life and into the troubled world, taking the good news of Jesus and accepting the risks involved. Jesus is only well known as our lives are given to him, lived with him, and sent by him. Real knowing comes in the going and serving by the Master's side. His commission is for all of life and into all he world. The Book of Acts quickly informs us that going must not be alone or it surely will fail. The Spirit must be our companion and guide. Even if not alone, there are costs to be paid.

1. The Big Picture Verse.
Book of Acts 1:8. The Context: The Book of Acts, chapters 13-28.

But you will receive power when the Holy Spirit has come upon you, and you will be my witnesses in Jerusalem and in all Judea and Samaria, and to the ends of the earth.

2. A Bit of Background

Dr. Luke introduces Stephen as the first to publicly make a clear distinction between Judaism and the new fellowship of Jesus. He also was the first of the Christian martyrs (6:1-8:40), the high cost he paid. In the process of his execution, Luke introduces one of the leading persecutors, Saul, soon to be a convert to Jesus (9:1-30) and thereafter known as Paul, early leader of the Christian expansion internationally. Luke organizes that expansion story around the journeys of Paul, basically three of them, with a fourth being his imprisonment and deportation to Rome. These are detailed in chapters 13-15, 15-18, 18-21, and 21-28.

During these journeys, Paul and various named colleagues founded churches and sometimes were the victims of severe Jewish opposition, shipwrecks, and much more. It's the stuff of today's action-packed movies. The new churches struggled to take root and grow, often being troubled from outside by violent resistance and from inside by deviations from the faith Paul preached. The challenges were practical and theological, sometimes gross and often more subtle, all threatening to derail the whole missionary enterprise.

Paul wrote a series of letters to these churches from various locations, attempting to protect the integrity of the faith and the health of the new congregations. The last were from prison in Rome. These letters soon came to comprise a significant portion of the New Testament and still are providing guidance for the churches today.

3. The Message in Brief

Explains Luke, I will attempt to tell all that Jesus began to do and teach (Acts 1:1). This historian's writing in his Gospel and in Acts has an unfinished character because the mighty doings of Jesus and his people are *still in progress*. Like a mighty army moves the church of God. We now are treading where the saints have trod! Luke's story of Christian beginnings traces the church from its initial religious center in Jerusalem to the very heart of the Roman Empire, Rome, and spiritually from a virtual Nazarene sect of Judaism to a truly universal fellowship of Jesus believers.

Many names appear, although the two men most featured are Peter and Paul, leader of the original twelve apostles and point man of the thrust outward to the Gentile world. The dynamic of this amazing expansion story, however, is not human but the Spirit-filled church, the body of Christ. The larger truth is that this church spread by the ministry of God's Spirit functioning through obedient servants of Christ. Luke's second book could be called the *Acts of the Spirit*.

4. The Present Challenge

Luke ends his early church history quite abruptly, leaving Paul in his Rome prison waiting the outcome of his appeal to Caesar. Apparently, more important to this historian than rounding out his story with full resolution of Paul's ministry was his showing how the young church successfully expanded from Jerusalem to Rome. Luke's Book of Acts has 28 chapters, leading many readers today to conclude wisely that what's really important is that the story continue.

It's the intent of God's Spirit that we now be the ones to continue the book's real purpose, inspiring us to become the instruments of the Spirit in forming *chapter 29* and beyond. To do this, we Jesus people must be less enamored of building religious institutions and more committed to forming communities of the Spirit that are intentionally on mission, journeying with Jesus to the ends of the earth and to the end of time.

5. Response from the Heart

My Growth Need: Commissioned as an apostle of Christ.
Mt. 28:19-20; Luke 6:13; Acts 2:1-42, 5:12-16; 1 Cor. 12:27-31; Phil. 1:27-28

We might owe in part the conversion of Paul to the prayer of Stephen. This prayer ("Lord, do not hold this sin against them") was perhaps on Saul's mind as he journeyed to Damascus. The sudden appearance to him of the risen Christ was a dramatic experience that changed him forever. Who really is this Jesus and am I really forgiven?

What happens when we meet Jesus? We experience a measure of compassion not known before. How can we be the same after such an encounter with none other than Jesus himself? Saul had not met Jesus in the flesh, nor have we. Who Saul was after Jesus appeared and confronted him soon was a powerful testimony to the young Christian community. Jesus had changed his heart, his desires, his values, his vision, his very life.

What a wonderful change in my life has been wrought,
Since Jesus came into my heart!
I have light in my soul for which long I had sought,
Since Jesus came into my heart!
                    —Rufus Henry McDaniel

Lose your shyness, find your tongue,
tell the world what God has done;
God in Christ has come to stay,
live tomorrow's life today.
                    —Brian Wren

Personal Prayer. Lord, I am captured by what happened to Saul and now long to be changed by my own meeting of Jesus. I want each new day, each new adventure to come from following Jesus. May the bright light of Jesus' appearance shine on each of us and illuminate a new path for us to take. May life now be defined as journeying with Jesus, continuing the grand story of the Book of Acts (of the Holy Spirit). What a change there will be, my Lord, when you come into my heart! As chapter 29 of Luke's original work is written, may my life be privileged to be a verse or two!

Reading 34

SONGS OF THE NIGHT

The journey of faith in this world will encounter darkness. As did Jesus, we risk some dangerous roads. Unlike him, we too often will fall into paths of sinfulness and life's disorientation. How we must rely on God's steadfast love that seeks to save and redeem. It's a hard fact. The spiritual songs of the day sometimes stumble into darkness and become songs of the night. Have mercy on us, O God!

1. The Big Picture Verses.
Psalm 51:1-2, 7. The Context: Psalms 51, 79, 80, 81, 88
(read them all!)

Have mercy on me, O God, according to your steadfast love. Wash me thoroughly from my iniquity, cleanse me from my sin and I shall be whiter than snow.

2. A Bit of Background

The history of God's people is littered with instances of enemies invading. Alien and arrogant outsiders have mocked the chosen and tricked them into complicity with evil agendas. The faithful have found themselves being used as instruments of the state for purposes that have sickened God. Words like slavery, holocaust, and crusades bring shame right to Christian church altars. Barbarians have made God's servants carrion for birds of prey. The psalmist asks God how long he will put up with the abuse and failures of his people. There are limits to divine patience.

How long will God's people so easily permit anti-God forces to draw them into complicity with outright evil? Those representing God in this world must be shrewd, finding ways to maintain their integrity in the face of opposition. Cries the psalmist, "You have put me in the depths of the Pit, in the regions dark and deep. I am shut in so that I cannot escape. I suffer your terrors. I'm desperate!" (Ps. 88:6, 8, 15). "How long, O Lord? Will you be angry forever? Let your compassion come speedily for we are brought very low" (Ps. 79:5, 8). "Stir up your might and come and save us!" (Ps. 80:2).

Only mentioning the names of Bathsheba and her murdered husband Uriah highlights the depth to which King David once fell. When bottom had been reached, he finally cried out to God, a lost little lamb longing for his shepherd and the home fold. No more games, no more hiding. He admitted the awful truth. A humbled human king asked God to soak him in a cleansing process until he came out truly clean again. "Don't throw me out with the trash or fail to breath holiness in me. Unbutton my lips, dear God, and I'll let loose with your praise." David was cleansed, unbuttoned, and let loose! Because God is God, there always is hope.

3. The Message in Brief

God's thunder once rumbled over Mt. Sinai. Oddly, the people only wanted God to listen to their complaints. Instead, the heavenly thunder insisted on taking the floor. God announced that once he had shouldered the burdens of the people and set them free from Egyptian bondage. But they had taken advantage of that freedom and soon found themselves left to the serious consequences of their selfish error. The voice of God was speaking harsh words indeed. "I had set before you life and you chose your own way, death. Drink your fill of living your own way. The taste will be bitter indeed!"

Psalm 80 is a community complaint. Why the complaining of God's own people? Because their home place, the beloved Jerusalem, was in ashes, the walls broken down and vandals were sorting through the rubble for whatever they could take away. "Restore us, O Lord!" was the pleading of the people. Now in real trouble, they realized the extent of their terrible situation. "We have no insurance to cover all this destruction. Aren't we your special people? How can you, our God, be so distant from us when we need you most?"

The big problem was that the destruction was the people's own fault. They had thrown into the fire God's known will for them, and then they had turned around and tried to blame the awful result on God's inaction. They had no real repentance for their selfish agendas, only complaint. We are being warned about the consequences of making idols of our nations, group traditions, private desires, and even our most treasured of religious beliefs and practices.

4. The Present Challenge

God is presented in Psalm 81 as frustrated and even a little sarcastic. "My people didn't listen, paid no attention." So what does God do? God lets go the reins of his people and tells them, "Run! Do it your own way. Crash and burn!" (vs. 12). What had the people done during their time of not listening to God? They'd gone after the latest in local gods, opting for religious fashion and presumed utility instead of ultimate reality. That might have been stupid, but at least they thought they had found excitement for a short time. Then came the disaster, the crashing and burning.

If only these were reports of yesterday, not threats facing God's people still today! Faith can be so fickle and self-serving. Pointing fingers isn't the thing to do—who of us is guiltless? We must be a "confessing" church, confirming our beliefs and also repenting of our sins, individual and corporate. Forgive us, O God, and bring us up out of the pit, much of which we have dug ourselves.

5. Response from the Heart

My Growth Need: Encouraged in the darkest of life.
2 Chron. 7:14; Ps. 37; Matt. 6:31-34; Jn. 16:33; Rom. 8:28; Phil. 4:6-7; Col. 3:13

Songs go into the dark corners of our hearts to illumine the most difficult and the need for redemption in each of us. This was certainly true for David who confessed, "Your hand was heavy upon me. My strength was sapped as in the heat of summer. Then I acknowledged my sin to you. I did not cover up my iniquity. I said, 'I will confess my transgressions to the Lord,' and You forgave the guilt of my sin" (Ps. 32). Repentance resulted in forgiveness. For those who make such confession, life begins anew.

> And can it be that I should gain
> An int'rest in the Savior's blood?
> Died He for me, who caused His pain?
> For me, who Him to death pursued?
> Amazing love! how can it be
> That Thou, my God, should die for me?
> He left His Father's throne above,
> So free, so infinite His grace;
> Emptied Himself of all but love,
> And bled for Adam's helpless race;
> 'Tis mercy all, immense and free;
> For, O my God, it found out me.
> —Charles Wesley

> Depth of mercy! Can there be
> mercy still reserved for me?
> Can my God His wrath forbear,
> me, the chief of sinners, spare?
> Now incline me to repent,
> let me now my sins lament,
> Now my foul revolt deplore,
> weep, believe, and sin no more.
> —Charles Wesley

Personal Prayer. Create in me a pure heart, O God, and renew a steadfast spirit within me. Do not cast me away but sustain me (Ps. 51). Be light in my darkness so that I can shine your light to the world. I finally have come to the point of admitting my guilt, hidden for so long. I understand your judgment, Lord, fully deserved. Now I long to experience your great love, wholly undeserved and yet flowing from your generous heart. Return the music in my soul from a song of the night to a song of joy in the morning!

Reading 35

YOU WANT AN EARTHLY "KING"?

Is there need to be "like the nations" to survive as God's people in this kind of world? What power structures are absolutely necessary and what are disastrous compromises? Who is king of the church? Can two masters be served at once, ever? God's people are caught between heaven and earth, belonging to one and operating in another. One carries heavenly expectations and the other earthly obligations. Often the people called by God fear for their survival and opt for means of proceeding that seem quite opposite to what God would choose for them. Integrity somehow must be maintained while practical necessity is pursued.

1. The Big Picture Verse.

Zechariah 4:6. The Context: 1 and 2 Samuel, 1 and 2 Kings.

This is the word of the Lord: "Not by might nor by power, but by my Spirit" says the Lord of hosts.

2. A Bit of Background

My college course on the history of England involved a flurry of royal names and the complex webs of intrigue around them. It sounds little different in the history of God's people as found in the Old Testament. Samuel was the great transitional figure, the last of the "Judges" and first of the Prophets. He received from the people a request that they have a king "like the other nations" (8:5, 20).

This had an ominous ring because it could turn out that in effect they were wanting to set up a pharaoh, with the Jews again slaves now under their own political establishment.

Samuel warned that such a direction could be received by God as a rejection of his rule over the people (8:7). Nonetheless, they insisted and Saul was chosen as the first king. As feared, things turned out badly. Eventually God rejected the kingship (15:26), with even the beloved King David shown to be profoundly flawed (the Bathsheba affair), even while being "a man after God's own heart" (1 Sam. 13:14).

A power establishment grew over time among the Jews and was centralized in Jerusalem, with the Temple built by David's son Solomon. Soon there is much taxation, religious compromise, and a division of the kingdom into north and south, Israel and Judah. Dynastic continuity was assured, but only if there would be obedience to the Lord (1 Kings 9:4–5). With the many faulty kings reported over time, however, the northern kingdom fell and the southern kingdom lasted only 136 years longer, both judged harshly by the prophets as doomed religious failures.

God's people had experienced an upsurge in nationalistic feelings under Saul, the dream of establishment and expansion under David, and the influence of greatly expanded commercial enterprise under Solomon. Jewish kings made international alliances, coming to rely on earthly weapons and national allies more than on God. They soon learned that human politics carries within it the seeds of self-destruction for God's people.

3. The Message in Brief

When God's people neglect their divine call and covenant with God, inevitably they come to grief. God seeks to teach through their folly and failures, although finally will judge them severely. When the church plays at power politics as its way of survival and dominance in a culture, the dangers are great and the price generally high. The fulfillment of God's mission, as shown so clearly by Jesus Christ, is hardly the political and military paths of the ancient Jews. He said that his kingdom was not of this world. One must give to any Caesar only what truly belongs to him.

There is a prominent paradox. The church clearly is *in* this world and has a mission of redemption *for* it, but somehow that mission has to be accomplished without the church being perverted and overwhelmed *by* the world. Moses laid the foundation for Israel, David built the essential structure, but eventually Jesus fulfilled the dream. David's commonwealth may have been thought of as Israel's "golden age," but Jesus would radically redefine it and one day will bring it to total fulfillment by his Spirit, not by human kings and armies.

4. The Present Challenge

Today's church in North America and Western Europe is in significant decline. Its previous influence had been sustained in large part by its alliances with the kings of nations and empires. Its expansion often had been assisted by the political colonization of its allied secular powers. With that rarely the case any longer, the church is scrambling to find its integrity and the means of its ongoing survival, let alone its evangelistic mission across the globe. A key guide must be the long experience of God's people found in the biblical records. Many cautions are found there.

The long experience of the church in North America is surely a prime test case. American history has tended to affirm that what was originally founded was a "Christian America," with the nation's identity, law, morals, and national vision all heavily informed by the Christian tradition. Moving to the twenty-first century featuring its individualism and secularism, a virtual culture war has been on. The church's influence, security, and special privilege are becoming things of the past. Political slogans like "Make America Great Again" are emotional and divisive. What should the church of today be seeking? Does it desire a Christian king? Would having one be an advance or retreat from God really wants for his people?

5. Response from the Heart

My Growth Need: Humbled instead of seeking worldly power.
Mt. 6:24; Gal. 5:22-25; Eph. 2:2-7; Phil. 4:13; 1 Tim. 1:7; Jam. 4:6

The sense of insecurity runs deep within the human psyche. In a world in which brute force rules, people long for some way to feel safe, usually through military might. Strong leaders are sought, even in the church. Do you really believe that love is more powerful than bombs and armies? The church somehow is to be a cross-formed community, a servant people relying on the power of the Spirit.

The inability to live "in the Spirit" was very true for the ancient Hebrews, and still is for nations and churches. The challenge for the church is to open our hearts to allow God's Spirit to live within and direct our thinking, decision-making, and manner of life. This has never been easy and certainly isn't now.

> Come, Holy Spirit, I need You;
> Come, sweet Spirit, I pray;
> Come in Your strength and your power,
> Come in Your own gentle way.
> —Gloria and Bill Gaither

Personal Prayer. Will there ever be church business meetings where numbers of members and effectiveness of ministry programs aren't the only measures of "success"? Will be ever get past thinking that "our church" is the one that should prevail in the larger Christian community since we have our theology straighter than the rest? O Lord, Spirit of love and gentleness, teach me and my congregation that your manner of life is adequately "powerful" in all ways that you intend. It's power under the control of love that's able to bring change in *the Jesus way*. Teach me how Your gentleness can live in and bring peace through my life. Keep my selfish ego, my king-wanting, from trying to run things.

Reading 36

A RELIGION OF RACIAL PURITY?

Patriotism is admirable and also potentially dangerous when dominating religious faith. God indeed did call and love Israel, which turns out now to be more than any particular country or race of people. God wants a purity of heart, not of a solidarity of nationalism or uniformity of DNA. Love is to be more prominent than self-pride and self-defense. The purity that's divinely desired resides in the heart, not in the color of skin, language spoken, or passport carried. The church has a fatal tendency to turn inward, build walls, and corner the divine Spirit, who nonetheless remains determined to move freely across the globe.

1. The Big Picture Verses.
Jonah 4:11; Joel 2:28. The Context: The Books of Jonah, Ruth, and Joel.

God said to Jonah, and then to Joel: "Should I not be concerned about Nineveh, that great city in which there are more than 120,000 persons?" "I will pour out my spirit on all flesh."

2. A Bit of Background

After the blood and thunder of the Book of Judges and the brutality of the hated Assyrian Empire, something very different appears in the Bible. It's the lovely international tale of Ruth and the shocking attitude of God toward Nineveh, one that God's prophet Jonah found totally unacceptable.

There was a period under Ezra and Nehemiah when racial purity became something of a fetish in Israel. Loyalty to God meant resisting "outsiders" and the compromises they bring. Such prejudice certainly is seen in Joel where non-Jews (Gentiles) by definition are viewed as actual enemies of God. Therefore, often the question comes up. Should loving God unreservedly result in hating or at least keeping apart from those who clearly do not?

Alongside all insistence on the purity of all people whom we judge acceptable is the countering biblical belief that God's mercy is wider than all the rigid laws of the Jewish Scribes, and that Gentiles (outsiders) also have a place within the scope of God's love.

Telling indeed is the concluding fact encountered in the Book of Ruth. Obed, son of Boaz and Ruth, would be the father of Jesse, who in turn would be the father of David. Here is an immigrant being in a direct line of the beloved king. Maybe purity adjusts to however it's perceived. Shocking is the similar conclusion of Jonah. The Assyrian capital city, the ultimate of detested outsiders, repents of its great sins and is forgiven by God, leaving God's prophet sulking—he'd rather the disgusting non-Jews be destroyed. We see here an unexpected and unwelcome forgiveness, unwelcome at least by God's own prophet.

The story of Ruth is a shining light. It happens mostly in a lovely barley field during harvest time. The female protagonists are the immigrant Moabite Ruth and her Israelite mother-in-law Naomi. Both are widows making their way through loss, famine, and socio-economic insecurity. They manage somehow and life finally turns good. Why? Because God is good, all the time, and to *everyone,* even a Moabite!

3. The Message in Brief

Openness, love, and forgiveness need to prevail in a world filled with exclusiveness, discrimination, hatred, and revenge. The heroine in the Book of Ruth was not a pure Israelite but a native of Moab. The Assyrians, guilty as they were, still were beloved by God, the prophet Jonah notwithstanding. The mission of God's people is to be a messenger of good news to all the world, a light set on a hill that shines across all human boundaries and prejudices. The treasured possession of God's people is to be a gift to the world, not something to be hoarded as a private possession of only the "pure" ones.

Love is more basic than ethnicity. The church's circle is to be widening to take more people in, not tightening to keep all the supposed wrong people out. Denominational divisions may have begun with good intentions but must not be continued to protect a narrow institutionalism within the body of Christ. Eugene Peterson's biographer explains that eventually Eugene had to get rid of the "sectarian ghetto" of his boyhood in order to mature into a spokesman of Christ to all of God's people.[1] The same Christian tradition can be richly wide and sickly narrow.

The world today is full of refugees, orphans, and other struggling persons. People are experiencing life as aliens and strangers. Biblical revelation is not intended as more condemnation of those already suffering, but as love extended and true family offered. Peter writes to "God's elect, strangers in the world who have been chosen and given a new birth and an inheritance that can never perish" (1 Pet. 1:1–4). We all were strangers to God by our sinful choice and now, only by God's grace, are we strangers to the world by its choice. How wonderful that God loves and chooses strangers!

4. The Present Challenge

So little has changed. Recent wars in Vietnam, Iraq, Afghanistan, and Ukraine reek of continuing nationalism, racial purity, and narrow religious dogma. Millions of people have been displaced and wealthy nations struggle over whether to allow the fleeing immigrants in or wall them out. Will the church follow the vengeful Jonah and the harsh nationalistic Joel? Will it dare the more difficult path of the lovely story of Ruth and the preferred Samaritan who paid the price of stopping and being compassionate regardless of who was in the gutter? How much better it is to live the expansive faith of a loving God than to clutch it tightly as a personal treasure to be protected from all who are different.

Recent generations were cursed by a Nazi fixation on racial purity, often quoting Christian sources supposedly supporting such a

---

[1] Winn Collier, *A Burning in My Bones*.

perverted view. Nationalism and religion usually are a toxic mix. We must see the Christian meaning of Joel's prophecy of the Spirit's outpouring (Acts 2:14-18). Paul points to it (Gal. 5:22) and Luke speaks of it often in the Book of Acts. God's blessings are said to be available to all persons regardless of ethnicity or nationality (2:21, 39; 10:45, etc.). May the church reach in love and allow God to be judge of the purity of others.

The church needs to evidence to the surrounding world a great mystery. It's that God's people are not captive to culture, nationality, race, or class. Samuel Hines opposed "the creation of white churches or black churches. There is nothing mysterious about a church made up of people who look alike and act like. Such a church says nothing significant to the world beyond the typical service club. There must be something in the church that cannot be explained except by the fact that *God lives in his people.*"[2] The church must evidence a vision of its essential oneness while also being enriched by its obvious manyness.

5. Response from the Heart

My Growth Need: Cautioned about failing to love.
Deut. 10:17-19; Mt. 5:43-48; Mk. 12:31; John 3:16;
Acts 10:34-36; Eph. 6:9

> There's a wideness in God's mercy,
> Like the wideness of the sea;
> There's a kindness in his justice
> which is more than liberty.
>
> For the love of God is broader
> Than the measure of one's mind;
> And the heart of the Eternal
> Is most wonderfully kind.
> "There's a Wideness in God's Mercy,"
> —Frederick W. Faber

---

[2] As quoted in Barry Callen in *The Wisdom of the Saints*.

The Book of Jonah is included among the Hebrew prophets, but who in the book is the true prophet? It hardly could be the man named Jonah who certainly didn't behave like one. When the hated king and people accepted the good-news story, Jonah said bitterly to God, "I was afraid that's what you would do!" To him, the Assyrians had no right to benefit from God's love. Will you and I ever learn this powerful message of the true nature of God? Will we lay aside our prejudices and allow the Spirit to open our hearts to all persons?

> Just as I am Thy love unknown
> Hath broken *every* barrier down;
> Now to be Thine, yes Thine alone,
> O Lamb of God, I come, I come.
> —Charlotte Elliott

Personal Prayer. O Lord, your love includes me, long an outsider to you. How wonderfully gracious you are! Now is my turn, generous Spirit of forgiving love. Especially knowing Jesus, I realize that you include everyone within your grace. Please give me the same wideness of spirit that Jesus himself demonstrated. Because of your great love, draw the circle of my caring so wide that it includes everyone, barring none. Come freshly to my heart and break every barrier down. Stop me from sulking like Jonah and rather be the good Samaritan in all places you direct.

**My Growth Need:
Determined to be fair to all.
Deut. 32:4-5; Ps. 82:2-4; Isa. 1:16-17;
Micah 6:8; Lk. 11:42-44.**

Reading 37

WHERE'S THE JUSTICE?

Who gets to decide what's just and who will benefit? Policy makers tend to write the rules in their own favor. My wife and I just wrote a new script for our church's Christmas Eve service. Joseph and Mary arrive in town needing a little help. The local hospital turns them away because they have no proof of insurance and all charity spots are used. The local hotel was fully booked because of a convention in town and only advance reservations were being honored.

The Social Security office announced to the desperate couple that no security was found in the official rules for undocumented immigrants, even if they claimed the government had ordered them to come to this town. Some kind soul finally pointed them to the homeless community huddled in an isolated grove of trees. There they were offered an old tent and a few bottles of decent drinking water—no proof of identity or social status required. What happens to faith when there's no justice to be found?

1. The Big Picture Verses.
Amos 2:4-5; Micah 6:6-8. The Context:
The Books of Amos and Micah.

I will send a fire on Judah, and it shall devour the strongholds of Jerusalem.... What does the lord require of you, but to do justice, and to love kindness, and to walk humbly with your God.

2. A Bit of Background

We see throughout the Old Testament that Israel was urged to realize that the justice of God has a "preferential option for the poor." This option becomes a requirement for Israel because it's rooted in God's very nature and loving activity. The practice of justice is really the process of imitating God. We are told in Deuteronomy 10:18-19 that God "executes justice for the orphan and the widow and loves the strangers, providing them food and clothing. You shall also love the stranger for once you were strangers in the land of Egypt."

In 1981 two large volumes of mine were translated into Japanese, with my permission and pleasure. That caused me to reflect on my father's World War II generation when the word "Jap" was a common vulgarity in the United States. Later, a Russian translation of a Bible stories book by a church colleague was translated and imported into that country and used widely in schools to teach morality to young children, when such Bible instruction wasn't allowed in public schools in the United States. Now, as I write these lines, Russia has invaded Ukraine and American goods are being banned in the invaders marketplace.

How times and sensitivities and world circumstances change! Such change is seen repeatedly in the Old Testament, often creating social chaos and fresh need for justice among impoverished and even enslaved peoples. Israel once had been enslaved and now was to be especially sensitive to the needs of such abused people. Where is the intended justice? Harsh songs of pain are heard in the night.

3. The Message in Brief

The Protestant reformer Martin Luther is quoted as seeing the biblical message this way. "There are those who seek to see God by penetrating the immensities. One ought rather to sink into the depths and seek to find God among the suffering, erring, and the downtrodden. Then the heart is free from pride and able to see God." Richard Foster has spoken sharply as a modern prophet like Amos:

> Social justice gives relevance and bite to the language of Christian love. Too often our talk about love is sentimental and soft. It needs to be toughened by the hard realities of absentee landlords and

prostitute rings and drug smugglers and industrial spies. We cannot speak with integrity of loving our neighbor until we are prepared to face the structural violence that is built into many of our policies and institutions.[1]

None should claim complete innocence. Being God-like is especially hard today because injustice is built into many social systems within which we all live. Beyond what we say about believing in God, justice comes only when we as God's people *act like God* toward those in most need.

4. The Present Challenge

A celebrated Old Testament scholar, when examining Psalm 146, asks about the source of the great concern for the oppressed, hungry, imprisoned, orphaned, etc. He concludes that it comes from the psalmist having actually met God. Meeting God tends to turn one from being inward-oriented to lovingly reaching outward, becoming concerned for others as much as for oneself.

He concludes with this observation: "Do you know how badly we have corrupted that? What does "to be born again" mean to the typical American evangelical? Doesn't it mean how to get my soul saved, get me safely to heaven? I think that is an absolute perversion of biblical truth."[2] To be born anew may indeed head one toward heaven, but first it means being headed toward the well-being of others! Walk humbly and do justly.

E. Stanley Jones probably was the best known of the thousands of Anglo-Saxon missionaries active in India in modern times. An 1938 *Time* magazine issue called him "the world's greatest missionary evangelist." While in India, Jones experienced a major reorientation of his Christian theological stance, one that released him to his unusually productive ministry there. At first his theology had been defensive and judgmental of Indian religious extremes. But he came to place the securities of his faith on the altar and became free to explore and appropriate any good or truth found anywhere. This allowed him to love rather than pity India. He could treat all people

---

[1] Richard Foster, *Streams of Living Water*.
[2] Dennis Kinlaw, *Lectures in Old Testament Theology*.

encountered with justice and mercy, their religious deviance from Christian beliefs notwithstanding.

Today dramatic religious and cultural diversity is all around us. Do we respond by listening openly and loving truly, or are we quick to judge the unchristian differences in ways that are unjust and fail to reflect mercy? The latter approach quickly undercuts the potential of Christian impact of the Jesus kind.

5. Response from the Heart

My Growth Need: Determined to be fair to all.
Deut. 32:4-5; Ps. 82:2-4; Isa. 1:16-17; Micah 6:8; Lk. 11:42-44.

A prophet is a person especially called by God to speak with a clear and penetrating voice, challenging us to live justly as God shows the way. Who are the prophets of today? Amos and Micah spoke for God in the eighth century before Christ, a time in Israel of ease and plenty for many people, with the wealthy enriching themselves at the expense of the desperate poor. Amos thundered, "I hate, I despise your religious feasts; I cannot stand your assemblies. Away with the noise of your songs. Let justice roll on like a river, righteousness like a never-failing stream!"

Micah added this. "Will the Lord be pleased with thousands of rams, ten thousand rivers of oil? Shall I offer my first-born for my transgression, the fruit of my body for the sin of my soul? No! Instead, act justly; love mercy; walk humbly with God." We must enlarge the number of those believers called to be prophets. That role is not the exclusive privilege of monks, priests, preachers, or a few of the most heroic lay persons. God calls everyone who will listen and obey. Let justice roll! Justice is never easy nor ever optional.

> God of grace and God of glory,
> on thy people pour thy power;
> crown thine ancient church's story,
> bring her bud to glorious flower.
> Grant us wisdom, grant us courage,
> for the facing of this hour.
>
> —Harry Emerson Fosdick

Personal Prayer. O Lord, am I in the company of the called, your chosen, your representatives in this world? Since by your grace I know I am, please help me to not miss your voice or tap on my shoulder or needed scolding or offer of needed courage. I realize that you are standing before me pointing the way. Jesus demonstrated how to live and love. He is the way, cross and all. He was treated so unjustly and yet never turned on others for his own benefit. Give me both the willingness and ability to hear the higher calling and follow in the way of Jesus. Being just involves personal cost and yet great reward. Lord, I am ready to pay!

My Growth Need:
Specified, not just theoretical.
Psalms 82:3; Prov. 1:2-7; Isa. 1:17; Micah 6:8;
Lk. 11:42. Phil. 1:9.

Reading 38

LET'S GET PRACTICAL

It's actually quite easy to use language to distract from the immediate and practical. We like to deal in theory, letting others figure out how to apply our high-sounding words—especially our religious ones that supposedly operate in some "spiritual" realm. The Hebrew language of much of the Old Testament, however, is quite graphic and immediate, concrete and action-oriented. So is the Jewish-Christian tradition in general. God is said to be known best by his practical actions in this world on our behalf. So are followers of Jesus supposed to be known. Faith must go well beyond pleasant language. We are and we really believe only what we *actually do*.

1. The Big Picture Verses.
Proverbs 1:2-7; Philemon 1:9. The Context:
The Books of Proverbs and Philemon.

I, Paul, prefer to appeal to you on the basis of love, and I do this as an old man, and now also as a prisoner of Christ Jesus.... The fear of the Lord is the beginning of knowledge.

2. A Bit of Background

Theology can deteriorate into speculative explorations about highly abstract theories, leaving ordinary people amused at such apparent uselessness. One definition of the outcome of a doctoral dissertation is the student having learned more and more about less and less until finally knowing everything about almost nothing. Similarly, religion can be awkwardly isolated from real life. Proverbs and Philemon are rarely read because they seem to deal with no lofty theological topics. They are right down to earth where life is really lived.

After the high drama of the Egyptian exodus and the lofty Law received on Mount Sinai, the book of Proverbs brings us down from the heights to the humdrum of everyday conduct. A wise man translates general moral principles into particular life guidelines. The "fool" idols away life, gathers dishonestly, and is prey to personal lust. By contrast, reverence for God is the basis of practical wisdom (1:7). Deep religious conviction should mix with practical common sense.

Proverbs is structured around a "son" who begins at home his learning of life lessons at his father's knee. He then moves into the wider world where such wisdom is tested amid a mind-boggling number of scenarios. Moving to the New Testament, we find a very practical matter addressed. The Book of Philemon is a private note to a dear friend of Paul's about a personal matter. Philemon was a well-to-do citizen of Colossae who had been robbed by a former slave who had run off to Rome, sorrowed over his sin, somehow contacted Paul, and become a new man in Christ. This slave, Onesimus, is now on his way back to Colossae with an associate of Paul. They are delivering area letters, one from Paul to Philemon about Onesimus.

Paul, himself once a murderous outcast from the Christian community, pleads the young man's case, asking for mercy. Apparently it worked, Onesimus gratefully preserving the Pauline letter for us to learn the delicate practice human reconciliation. Why no direct condemnation of human slavery in the letter? One answer is "progressive revelation." In Paul's setting, slavery was so accepted that it was not on his list of priorities. He did recognize a common kinship among all believers for whom Christ had died. This grand vision already was leading to unusually practical social results, and one day would come to condemn slavery itself. But for now, Paul prepares the way by thanking Philemon for his great love and loyalty to the Lord and then asking that he receive back his slave *as a brother*—maybe even send him back to Rome to continue helping prisoner Paul.

3. The Message in Brief

The love of Christ must spill over into gracious acts of love that when necessary can transcend accepted social conventions. Christian faith is far more than a set of truthful religious concepts. It is new spiritual life and a new community of brothers and sisters who love and care for each other in very practical ways. To become *like* Christ must involve *being* Christ to others in real human relationships. And exactly how are we to *be* in order to become *like* Christ to others?

The challenge calls us to a life stance of simplicity, vulnerability, dialogue, voluntary powerlessness, and humility. This is how Jesus interacted with real people long ago. This also is how disciples of Jesus are to interact with real people in the present. Paul did it gently but firmly with a converted slave and his cheated master, appealing to him to do the right "on the basis of love." Jesus challenges us to consider anyone in need as a "neighbor," someone to be loved in very practical ways. My wife goes to our local church pantry several days each week. She jokes with the needy "neighbors," listens to their hurts and complaints, and passes out free food. She is a true daughter of the Lord.

4. The Present Challenge

Sharing and living Christian faith is done well by following the pattern of John Wesley. Rather than seeking to be a theoretical theologian, his concern always was to communicate well the good news in Jesus with the people. His theological ideas are now gleaned mostly from his "practical" works--sermons and letters--written to address the specific life situations of his followers. These persons came from every social class in English society, requiring him to "labor to avoid all words which are not used in common life." He intended to "speak the plain truth for plain people." That may be theology at its best.

Professional theologians typically write for fellow theologians, creating material that the average person would not fully understand or have the patience to try. There's a place for sophisticated language, but hardly in the pulpit or on the street. "And God said," "Do this in remembrance," and "Jesus fed the multitude." Actions, specifics, human needs, concrete realities, the real substance of the faith's ministry. God came to us as a child, not as an elaborate theological creed. We had to be able to see, touch, watch, and then mimic.

We must learn how to "test the spirits." How do we find the right one? We are to believe the one that confesses Jesus Christ as God come in the flesh (1 Jn. 4:2). That Spirit, the Spirit of Jesus, will sort truth from error (1 Jn. 4:6) and get us past being plagued by fear (1 Jn. 4:18). How do we know we are children of God? When we find ourselves loving God with our whole hearts and gladly obeying his commandments (1 Jn. 5:2-3). Are you at that practical, self-giving, loving point?

5. Response from the Heart

My Growth Need: Specified, not just theoretical.
Psalms 82:3; Prov. 1:2-7; Isa. 1:17; Micah 6:8; Lk. 11:42. Phil. 1:9

We all want to be wise and a major section of the Hebrew Scriptures is known as the Wisdom Literature. A good example of this wisdom is the Book of Proverbs, practical everyday life and understanding in light of God's ways in the world. God wants us to apply our faith to practicalities, even minor details. Wisdom is available to all, but not all partake of it.

The name Onesimus means "useful." Scholars tend to assume that Paul's letters were first collected in the city of Ephesus. There was in that city a bishop in the late first century whose name was Onesimus. Is it possible that this runaway slave whom Paul befriended could have been responsible for the collection of Paul's letters now being available to us in the New Testament? Indeed, it is. If true, he certainly would have been useful to Paul and all of us as well. Small actions can have large consequences beyond our imagining!

> Savior, teach me, day by day, love's sweet lesson to obey:
> Sweeter lesson cannot be, loving Him who first loved me.
> With a childlike heart of love, at Thy bidding may I move,
> Prompt to serve and follow Thee, loving Him who first loved me.
> Teach me all Thy steps to trace, strong to follow in Thy grace,
> Learning how to love from Thee, loving Him who first loved me.
> —Jane E. Leeson

Pay attention and listen to the sayings of the wise; apply your heart to what I teach. For it is pleasing when you keep them in your heart and have all of them ready on your lips (Prov. 22:17-19).

Personal Prayer. Lord, I admit to having read many books, even written some. I want to be wise and useful in very practical ways to you and all those you call. Teach me to listen in humility so that I may become wise and useful. Help me hear with care, knowing which voice is yours and what action will be the doing of your actual will. When I serve, whatever my role in life, may I be a willing instrument of your Spirit, open to the Spirit's guidance in all circumstances. May I appeal to others "on the basis of love" with a child-like heart. My brain should be allowed to function fully, of course, but never at the expense of the practical work of my hands and feet in your service.

**My Growth Need:
Compromise is unacceptable.
Josh. 24:14-15; Lk. 10:25-28; John 14:15-17;
James 4:17; Rev. 14:12-13.**

Reading 39

NO COMPROMISE!

When justice is absent and threats abound, when the heat is on and our songs are all bitter ones in the night, is it time to make a deal with the devil? The temptation to yield is great, even though the cost would be disastrous. The history of God's people has been troubled by numerous instances of compromise, trying to have things both ways, serving two masters as a way to survive and get ahead in the face of trouble. While tempting, such a path never works. The stakes are too high to risk a loss of the faith's very integrity. Whatever the threat, no compromise!

1. The Big Picture Verse.

Daniel 12:12. The Context: The Books of Daniel and Esther.

Happy are those who persevere. Go your way and rest; you shall rise for your reward at the end of the days.

2. A Bit of Background

Daniel is as difficult a book to interpret as it is dramatic and important. It's written in Hebrew and Aramaic, switching back and forth between the languages. It contains both "prophetic" and "apocalyptic" sections, making it demanding for a non-specialist to know how to interpret various passages. Actually, well-informed scholars are hardly in agreement themselves. The generations immediately preceding the coming of Jesus is the most likely original setting, although even that is disputed.

The central issue in the books of Daniel and Esther is clear enough. How should God's people function in alien political, cultural, and especially religious environments? What should happen when it appears that God has completely forgotten or at least abandoned his people? The biblical answer is, "Stand firm, being fortified by memories of past times of no-compromise and with a vision of God finally acting dramatically to change everything for the right and good. Joseph had been a slave in Egypt, Daniel now was an exile in Babylon, and Esther was a Jewess in the Persian royal court. Alien rulers are pictured as beasts waging war against the holy ones until "the Ancient One came" (Dan. 7:22).

Following the Exile of the Jews in Babylon, there came fresh hope for a new day of freedom. Sadly, what came over the centuries ate away at that hope. The little Jewish community was burdened by one brutal foreign occupation after another, including Persia where Esther became Queen by winning a beauty contest and suddenly was in position to save her people (5:1-8, 7:1-4). In the generations immediately before the coming of Jesus, hope was nearly gone. A paralyzing pessimism had taken root because culture was being brutally "Hellenized," forced into Greek channels alien to the Hebrew faith tradition.

If anything was ever to put things right, apparently it would have to be God dramatically breaking in, crushing the evil, and birthing a new world. In Esther we watch a Persian ruler in action. In Daniel, with Babylon in the background, it's now a Syrian ruler determined to spread Greek culture at the complete expense of the Jewish heritage, including forcing the Temple in Jerusalem to be a place for the worship of Zeus, the "abomination of desolation." Now what? The easiest path was compromise. Drop standards, look the other way, give in and just go on.

3. The Message in Brief

There are times when this fallen world seeks to destroy the people of faith. God calls on the faithful to resist, not compromise, to stand tall like the heroes of yesterday who faced fiery furnaces that only purified their faith. One day soon God will cause righteousness to reign and the faithful to rejoice. God is sovereign even over powerful secular rulers who despise God and for a time manage to persecute his people. As is made clear in the Bible's final pages, God is Alpha and Omega, the beginning of all things and the One who outlasts all things. Compromise is unacceptable. The triumph of God is on the way. Stay true!

The terrible Antiochus Epiphanes of Daniel's time was followed by the ugly Roman emperors Caligula, Nero, and Domitian in the time of the early Christian church. More recent names could be added to the list, of course. The self-serving and godless rulers of this world are capable of the worst, including executing Jesus himself. The faithful, however, should be looking at another list. The heroes of our faith must be remembered and be our guides. The Christian's annual calendar includes "All Saints Day." Don't forget to celebrate it as one way to stand firm and go on with faith unspoiled.

4. The Present Challenge

There is indeed a "cloud of witnesses," Christian saints and martyrs of yesterday who must be remembered if the threats to the faith are to be survived today. Discouragement is understandable, but pessimism and compromise are unacceptable for the faithful. God has been and again will be faithful and loving, finally preserving his people and vindicating the right. Rather than be shocked by the morning headlines, the call is to be emboldened by confidence in the conquering God. Dispel the dark clouds with shouts of joy and songs of the morning, even when the sunrise is not yet seen peeking over the horizon.

Christianity has enjoyed cultural dominance in the Western world for centuries. That now is changing rapidly, causing the church to rethink its nature and role in "foreign" territory. Dare it be merely a defensive operation, always fearing failure and disgrace and being crudely aggressive? Dare it seek to regain influence by dominating unbelievers, forcing them to compromise what they truly believe—which could be nothing beyond themselves? We may be living now much as the earliest church had to live, in very foreign cultures. It did more than survive. It prospered by the strength of its belief and the joy of its loving witness. May we do the same!

5. Response from the Heart

My Growth Need: Compromise is unacceptable.
Josh. 24:14-15; Lk. 10:25-28; John 14:15-17; James 4:17; Rev. 14:12-13.

> Other refuge have I none, Hangs my helpless soul on Thee;
> Leave, O leave me not alone, Still support and comfort me.
> All my trust on Thee is stayed, All my help from Thee I bring;
> Cover my defenseless head with the shadow of Thy wing.
> "Jesus, Lover of my Soul"
> —Charles Wesley

The Book of Daniel, called "prophetic," is both historical (chaps. 1-6) and "apocalyptic" (chaps. 7-12.) Apocalyptic writing is intentionally difficult to understand, meant to fortify the faithful and confuse the persecutors. It highlights heroism, including the three Hebrew youth who persisted in their faith only to be thrown into a fiery furnace. They're named Shadrach, Meshach, and Abednego, although I remembered them when young as "My Shack, Your Shack, and Bungalow." Their faith in God was rewarded with a miraculous rescue, a great message to the Jews who were under attack from Antiochus Epiphanes IV. God would save them as he had previously. The Book of Daniel, as well as Esther, promises God's protection for those who are faithful. It may not come today, but when it does it will last for eternity.

> Children of the heavenly Father, safely in his bosom gather;
> Nestling bird nor star in heaven, such a refuge e'er was given.
> Though God giveth or he taketh, God his children ne'er forsaketh;
> His the loving purpose solely, to preserve them pure and holy.
> —Carolina Sandel Berg

Personal Prayer. Lord, I believe, but still I need your help for my unbelief. I trust you and I'm willing to rest my life in your hands. Whether I live or die, I know I'm yours. Thank you for your great promise to care for all your children, even in the worst of circumstances. If I'm in such circumstances because of my own earlier compromises, forgive and restore me. Convince me of the greatest of all truths that I need right now, that nothing can ever separate me from the love of God known in Christ Jesus, my Lord. I shall not be moved!

My Growth Need:
Endurance for the whole journey.
1 Chron. 16:11-15; Ps. 86:11-13; Rom. 5:3-5;

Gal. 6:9-10; Heb. 12:1-2; James 1:2-4.

Reading 40

WHEN CHRISTIANS GET "WEARY"

What is *faith*? It's the substance of things not yet seen (Heb. 11:1), holding on with confidence to that which is not yet. There is risk, of course, and also great reward, especially when confidence is placed in the reality of Jesus Christ as the redeeming God with us now and always. The very practice of faith can quietly begin to draw benefit from that which it affirms and on which it relies. While it's the opposite of cynicism and negativity, persons with faith still can get weary and be tempted to give up. Their doubts and questions can begin to overwhelm their affirmations. This must never happen to Jesus people who by faith have hold of the greatest truth in all creation!

1. The Big Picture Verses.
Hebrews 12:1-2. The Context: The Book of Hebrews.

Let us run with perseverance the race that is set before us, looking to Jesus, the pioneer and perfector of faith, who for sake of the joy that was set before him endured the cross, disregarding its shame, and has taken his seat at the right hand of the throne of God.

2. A Bit of Background

"Apostasy," giving up, falling back, perverting, is a major concern of the writer to the Hebrews (10:32). Some Christians obviously were becoming "weary" (12:12-17) and wandering away. This biblical writer addresses the seeming irrelevance of the old Jewish rituals and animal sacrifices. Isn't they like flogging a dead horse?

Is the whole Old Testament "old" and thus irrelevant for Christians? In a way it is, but certainly not altogether.

This inspired book is addressed to Christians who once were Jews and now were being persecuted and inclined to turn back to previously comforting certainties. This is understandable, of course, but seen by the writer as wholly unacceptable. Some were reluctant to sever ties with their ancestral Jewish faith which had some advantages at the time. Judaism enjoyed some protection of Roman law and young Christianity did not. Even so, the writer insists that believers have everything to gain by pressing on and everything to lose by falling back.

The call is to accept the living Christ as the central certainty of Christian faith and let go of the old Jewish legalism now only a superficial shadow from yesterday (10:1).[1] The only sure bridge between humans and God is the man Jesus who was God with us. The old priesthood and sacrificial system pointed in this right direction, yes, but proved incapable of being the needed bridge to it. The religion of the Old Testament was only questing while the faith of the New Testament proclaims the actual truth. Nonetheless, much still holds the testaments together, with the Old still basic for understanding the New.

Where is Christian faith to focus, on a religious system of another day or on the man Jesus who is "the pioneer and perfector of our faith" and who is "the same yesterday and today and forever"? (12:1–2, 13:8). Jesus is the only sure way to ultimate reality, to God. In fact, he is God with us. One must never weary of this basic truth and revert to anything else, for there is nothing else in any way comparable.

3. The Message in Brief

Jesus Christ, now our eternal contemporary, must be seen as constant and fully adequate for the present and future. Jesus is the same yesterday, today, and forever. Yesterday is when he laid down his life on behalf of his people and became their unparalleled High

---

[1] See the excellent commentary by James Earl Massey titled *Preaching from Hebrews*.

Priest. Today he is risen and exalted at God's right hand as our sole intercessor.

In Jesus Christ we have access to the true tabernacle which God pitched among humans (8:2). In him we take hold of the things that cannot be shaken (12:27) and have access to the city whose maker and builder is God (11:10). The whole of Hebrews is written to encourage us to "draw near" to Jesus Christ (10:22). It establishes his full and singular supremacy. He is greater than the prophets (1:1–3), Moses (3:1–6), and the old Jewish priesthood. Jesus is the perfect High Priest, the absolute mediator between humans and God.

Therefore, "Let us then with confidence draw near to the throne of grace that we may receive mercy and find grace to help in time of need" (4:16). During difficult times, we are to follow the advice of Paul, looking for signs of God's coming reign in Christ and being partners in planting signs of God's reign through how we live in Christ. Said Paul, "Do not be weary in doing what is right" (2 Thess. 3:13). Jesus is active now, claiming the whole world for himself. Believers must dare to join this expansive enterprise (13:13).

4. The Present Challenge

We live in a world where the old landmarks are fast disappearing. Unparalleled change tempts us to retreat to old and outmoded ways of defining and defending our faith. We Christians dare not choose isolation, sitting tight in our old camps. We need the ministry of the unchanging but ever-onward Christ. While we belong to a kingdom which cannot be shaken (12:28), we must remember that the revelation we have in Christ is both final and *dynamic*, summoning us to new dimensions of inspired Christian thought and action. The gospel of Christ requires that we both *affirm* all that Rabbi Jesus has accomplished and *serve* the present age in his name.

Some of today's social analysts are saying that "secularism" is nearly dead. "There is genuine interest in the supernatural and a mounting desire for sanctity. People are longing to encounter the sacred and searching high and low for the holy."[2] Much land yet

---

[2] Jason E. Vickers, *Minding the Good Ground*. See Barry L. Callen, *The Living Dead* and *Christian Holiness*.

remains to be possessed in the name of Christ. We followers of Jesus must not revert backwards, get distracted, become weary and retreat. We are called to go forward, on to the end of the road, on to the waiting City of God. We must allow God "to make us complete in everything good so that we may do his will, working in us that which is pleasing in his sight" (Heb. 13:20-21). Are you prepared to go on, weary or not?

5. Response from the Heart

My Growth Need: Endurance for the whole journey.
1 Chron. 16:11-15; Ps. 86:11-13; Rom. 5:3-5; Gal. 6:9-10; Heb. 12:1-2; James 1:2-4

Hebrews urges believers to persevere in the face of difficulty and even persecution. The one who is both the great high priest and the sacrificial Lamb is the Christ. We are pointed to the Jewish celebration of Yom Kippur, the Day of Atonement, highlighting God's forgiveness. There is no limit to the expansive and restoring love of God. The provision of mercy and strength is to all!

> My heart is fixed on Jesus, the Sun of all my thought;
> What wondrous work of grace his love within my soul hath wrought!
> He found me poor and helpless, by every sin oppressed,
> And died that I might be redeemed and have eternal rest.
>
> My heart is fixed on Jesus, since I to him belong;
> For every day He gives me hope, for every night a song.
> Through trial and deep water His promises are sweet,
> And sheltered 'neath the wings of love, I find a safe retreat.
> —Lavinia E. Brauff

Personal Prayer. O Lord, I find the message of Hebrews both comforting and strengthening. It's a book of wisdom as well as one of God's love. I'm glad that I keep reading it and exploring the depths of its message when I find myself persecuted or just plain tired and tempted to give up. You come to me, Lord, as I ponder its pages. Through the wisdom of this writer I find strength to go on. Keep me from going back to old ways that have proven inadequate. At the same time, my dear Savior, never let me forget the spiritual giants of the past who pioneered my faith. I'm so grateful that, despite all, my faith holds!

My Growth Need:
Integrity is really everything.
Prov. 11:3, 28:6; Jn. 14:6; 1 Cor. 8:21;
Phil. 4:8-9; Heb. 13:17-18.

Reading 41

PROTECTING THE FAITH'S INTEGRITY

Of course God doesn't need any protecting, but apparently his people do, and often they act like God does also. How is the Christian faith to be lived with integrity and shared credibly and persuasively if there is no clarity about what it actually is? Do some believers in Jesus have special insight into faith's meaning? Is there one Christian tradition that's got it all right and should be mimicked by the others? Or does the integrity of the faith lie more in the relational arena of love than in intellectual precision and mechanical obedience to set religious laws and creeds? Whatever the answers, this much is clear. Belief that's confused and not properly grounded will be unable to share effectively the good news in Jesus Christ.

1. The Big Picture Verses.
1 John 4:7-8. The Context: The Letters of 1, 2, and 3 John.

Let us love one another because love is from God. Whoever does not love does not know God, for God is love.

2. A Bit of Background

There had developed quickly in the early Christian community some "variations" on the faith as taught by the first Apostles and Gospel writers. These new teachers and their wandering thoughts were thought to present a danger so great that those faithful to the original teachings reacted vigorously. They dared to call the variations "a lie" and point out that these "heretics" were wholly unacceptable faith instructors. The name "Gnostic" was attached to some of the deviances. These had a misleading "mystical" tinge and a non-biblical philosophic focus. This caused the three letters of John to strongly insist on a *loving fellowship* as the central sign of true Christian integrity.

The misleading truth alternatives tended to question the direct relation of the human Jesus to the divine Christ. One prominent Gnostic argued that, since human flesh is evil, the divine *Logos* entered the earthly Jesus only at his baptism and was a second spirit within him until just before the crucifixion. Then the divine *Logos* quickly departed from Jesus. This thinking was judged by the biblical teachers to be a direct threat to true Christian teaching. It insists that the real Jesus was fully identified with us humans, and yet always God with us, so without sin. Some Gnostics went even further, insisting that the divine Christ could never have inhabited evil flesh. Therefore, Jesus was some kind of earthly ghost, the divine only appearing to be one of us humans. Insists biblical writers like John, there is no integrity in that kind of heretical thinking.

3. The Message in Brief

Christian believing that has integrity will never be merely a religious theory or be reduced to an abstract idea. Christian faith is the testimony of eternal life that now has been revealed concretely in the human-divine person Jesus, something we have been privileged to see with our eyes and touch with our hands (1 Jn. 1:1). This direct contact has caused us to admit our sin, and it makes possible our claiming and spreading the light of God shining in Christ. We must love, not in mere words but in actual deeds (1 Jn. 3:18). Love is the place where integrity resides.

We must recognize that there are clever deceivers right in the church, so we must learn to "test the spirits" (1 Jn. 4:1). Some will claim to have special knowledge and will carry that claim with spiritual arrogance, raising mystical experience above moral living as the sign of legitimacy. They may even segregate the human Jesus from the divine Christ, crumbling the very heart of the faith. In response, we must believe in God's Son, Jesus Christ, and express the integrity of our belief by loving one another. This can be done well only by allowing the Spirit of Christ to live in and through us (1 Jn. 3:24). In Jesus, God was with us. In the Spirit of Jesus, we are to become God's true representatives in the world.

4. The Present Challenge

Here are the three gems of Christian truth, with their colors blending beautifully as they shine forth in the world. They are true spiritual life, true divine light, both necessarily infused with true eternal love. The light of love is life indeed. Only walking that way is to remain on the narrow path with Jesus. Centuries of church institutionalism now have accumulated considerable wreckage around the life of us Jesus people. We both need religious structures and are in danger of being overwhelmed by them.

As our philosophic explorations and detailed mission strategies proceed, how we need to not lose focus on the *divine love* that is to form, infuse, and define the community of faith, the church. Only here do we find the integrity of faith that we are to protect, nurture, and reflect to the world. Otherwise, the church tends to be seen as just another social service organization that seeks to comfort its members and do some good for others. Such are worthy, of course, but lack any dramatic good news from heaven!

5. Response from the Heart

My Growth Need: Integrity is really everything.
Prov. 11:3, 28:6; Jn. 14:6; 1 Cor. 8:21; Phil. 4:8-9;
Heb. 13:17-18.

John's writings have a way of drawing us close to the heart of God. He affirms explicitly what most of the Bible says at least implicitly. The very nature of God is love. The life of Jesus is the clear expression of that love in action. Jesus was moved with compassion when he saw human suffering and he gave his life for our salvation. No attempt to counterfeit this love can be tolerated. As a follower of Jesus, We are called to be living examples of God's love to those in our lives. We are to clothe ourselves with humility and let love be seen in our daily actions.

> He left His Father's throne above
> So free, so infinite His grace—
> Emptied Himself of all but love,
> And bled for Adam's helpless race.
> 'Tis mercy all, immense and free,
> For O my God, it found out me!
> 'Tis mercy all, immense and free,
> For O my God, it found out me!
> —Charles Wesley

Personal Prayer. O Lord, I find it hard to sort among the spirits trying to capture my attention. Give me eyes can see through this fog. Like anyone else, I like to be in charge, thought right, and able to make the church system work for me. But it your church, Lord! Keep me amazed at your love and help me embrace the humblest act so that love may be made real and obvious in my life. Help me see that every person is worthy of being served, and only in serving with love am I being your child. My precious Father, you emptied yourself of all but love to come to me. May I do the same as I go to others. Convince me every day that protecting your faith properly is done only by loving one another because love is from God.

Reading 42

TROUBLE IN THE SANCTUARY!

And you think your church has problems! Surely nothing beats the mess Paul found in Corinth. Infighting, court-going, spiritual bragging, and worship chaos are a few ugly places to start. How can there be diversity without division in the church? What's the only workable and "excellent" way to be God's people in God's way? Though we tend to idealize the "good old days," they may come more from our imaginations than real history. When there is trouble right in the sanctuary of Christian churches, what's the solution? It's certainly helpful to trace the steps Paul took in helping the Corinthians. The central solution he offered them is clearly as relevant now.

1. The Big Picture Verses.

First Corinthians 13:1-2. The Context: 1 Corinthians.

If I speak in the tongues of humans and of angels but do not have love, I am a noisy gong or a clanging cymbal; and if I have prophetic powers and understand all mysteries and all knowledge, and if I have all faith so as to remove mountains but do not have love, I am nothing.

2. A Bit of Background

Early Christianity was venturing into a world where some religious communities actually promoted drunkenness and sexual promiscuity as acceptable means of achieving mystic communion with God. Some of this perverse thinking had seeped into the early church, promoting "free thought and love" and threatening the integrity of Christian life. Believers tempted in this way had misunderstood Paul's call to an alternative to strict legalism. It's not an "anything goes" mentality! The gospel of Jesus presents a unique liberty *in Christ* to be expressed graciously through the *fruit of his Spirit* (Gal. 5:13, 16–17), not through the lusts of the flesh.

The city of Corinth was a moral sinkhole. Being true Christians there, "called to be saints," presented challenges rarely paralleled even today. Opposition to true life in Christ surrounded the Christian community and obviously had invaded the sanctuary with its chaos. Paul saw the church there standing on the edge of total collapse. Many of its members were persons with a history in one of the local pagan cults. Corinth was a geographic crossroads of the Mediterranean, home to all nationalities, religions, and cultures. It was known unashamedly as the most profligate of cities in the Roman Empire. On a rock towering high above the edge of the city stood a gold-gilded temple dedicated to the goddess Aphrodite and housing some 1,000 prostitutes, key to its worship practices.

Would this most "secular" of settings eventually swallow the Christian community? The congregation had split three ways around differing honored personalities. Some members were arrogant about their superior Christian knowledge and virtue, while others were taking fellow believers to the civil courts. There was considerable confusion about what the Christian faith taught regarding marriage and sexual relations, and many were confused about whether or not to eat meat bought in the public markets after being offered to local idols.

With the prominence of very "forward" women in the city, it wasn't clear how women were to function in the congregation. When the Lord's Supper was celebrated, there was obvious drunkenness and gluttony. Public services often were disorderly because some who were engaging in meaningless ecstatic speaking aloud. What more could go wrong? More importantly, what could save this sorry situation?

3. The Message in Brief

The center of this letter of Paul to the Corinthian believers seems to be 1:18-2:5. The message of the cross, while foolishness and weakness in the world's eyes, is in fact the wisdom and power of God. Since Jesus was crucified and rose again, believers in him need to undergo personal deaths to their old ways and rise to new lives in Jesus. They must be new persons forming a new kind of community. When Christians wander away from Christ, the pagan world of corruption and competition destroys their fellowship and they begin to behave like pagans. The only solution is a vital union with Christ that brings a new kind of Christ-centered life, one of genuine Christian love.

Division in the church is a scandal that can't be tolerated. Let any who boast do so only about the Lord who alone is worthy (1:31). There can be diversity without division since there is a variety of gifts from God, but there is only one Spirit. All believers are given spiritual gifts, and all for the common good (1:4–7). What about sexual perversion? We were bought with a price and our very bodies are temples of the Holy Spirit in which God should be glorified (6:19-20). What is the key to a healthy Christian fellowship? It's *love*, the greatest of all God's gifts (chap. 13).

4. The Present Challenge

Our present time seems to have advanced very little from the moral perversions seen in old Corinth. Electronic devices now bring such perversions graphically to us personally wherever we are, no matter how young we are or how religious our homes might be. Violence is common, schools aren't safe to attend as children, and illegal drugs are everywhere and lethal. Have Christians grown so used to all this that they are numbed by it, even drawn into some of it? How believers today need each other for instruction and support. How they need to be public examples of what love and moral purity really is.

Today Christian families and whole denominations are splitting because of sharp disagreements over what marriage is and how human gender is to be defined. What range of diversity should be affirmed as acceptable within the Christian community? These

Corinth-like question is ancient and difficult indeed! Paul's instruction to the Corinthian believers remains relevant. It's more than relevant. It's urgent!

5. Response from the Heart

My Growth Need: Love that forgives others despite all.
Lk. 6:31-36; Jn. 13:34-35; Acts 2:44-47; Eph. 3:17-19; 1 Jn. 4:18-19.

Corinth was a beautiful city located on the Corinthian Gulf across the water from the monuments at Delphi, the center of worship for ancient Greece. The people of Corinth brought their chaotic religions into Christian worship, creating a toxic situation. How careful we must be with our supposed divine gifts.

> Though I may speak with bravest fire,
> and have the gift to all inspire,
> and have not love, my words are vain
> as sounding brass and hopeless gain.
>
> Come, Spirit, come our hearts control,
> our spirits long to be made whole.
> Let inward love guide every deed,
> by this we worship and are freed.
> —Hal Hopson

Personal Prayer. Oh Lord, many of us have walked what's left of the streets of ancient Corinth as modern tourists. We've thought of the chaotic events that took place there, of the people who longed for wholeness, a correct understanding of spirituality, and an experience of the reality of God. I'm grateful that the gospel penetrated their spirits and brought them to new life. Thank you for now being with me as you were with them. Teach me love as you taught them. Bring loving peace to the sanctuary in which I worship. May we be witnesses to the world and not just more of it!

Reading 43

BUILD YOURSELVES UP

The faithless and immature believer never will withstand the onslaught of this world. We who are "saved" must pursue "holiness," being truly set apart, God-like, growing up into Christ. Otherwise we will fail the test of Christian life in the world. To avoid the poison that permeates society, Jesus people must progressively come to share in the very life of God. God is able; are we willing? Called to become like God is a high calling indeed. Will you listen with care to this call and be open to real growth in this holy direction?

1. The Big Picture Verses.
Jude 24-25; 2 Peter 1:2. The Context: The Books of Jude and 2 Peter.

May grace and peace be yours in abundance in the knowledge of God and of Jesus our Lord.... Now to him who is able to keep you from falling, and to make you stand without blemish in the presence of his glory with rejoicing, to the only God our Savior, through Jesus Christ our Lord, be glory, majesty, power, and authority, before all time and now and forever. Amen.

2. A Bit of Background

Jude, maybe a brother of Jesus (Matt. 13:55; Mark 6:3), identifies himself only as the brother of James and a servant of Jesus Christ. Regardless of who he was, his compassionate concern is felt immediately in his brief biblical writing. The early Christian church was being threatened. Outside propagandists were bent on poisoning the purity of church life and the good name of the Jesus communities. They were suggesting that morals and religion are separate things. Get religion right and traditional morals become optional.

It was being said often, "Believe rightly and then do as you please." Thinking straight supposedly freed one to do whatever seemed and even felt right. Jude reacts vigorously. Peter then seems to lift lines right out of Jude to repeat the concern and point to the same solution. Words of denunciation aren't pleasant to read but are essential for the church's integrity and the effectiveness of its witness. These New Testament writers aren't inclined to mince words. Christian liberty must not be allowed to collapse into immoral license!

Freedom from practicing strict adherence to the Jewish law was tempting some Gentile Christians to believe that being free in Christ liberates one from all moral anchors. The truth? The faithful are "to contend for the faith that once and for all was handed down to the saints." Believers always must remember the time of the Exodus when many were punished for their sins by death (Num. 14:29, 37) and even angels fell from grace (Gen. 6:1–4). Jude's concluding verses are a powerful "benediction" intended to fortify the faithful in dangerous times. God is able and his children are to be faithful.

3. The Message in Brief

Unfortunately, those trying to be faithful to Jesus always are in danger of falling back into the perversions of the old life of sin. There are false teachers and constant temptations to please oneself instead of serving the Lord. Peter and Jude join in pointing to the best way to fight against such evil that's always seeking to infiltrate the church. The way is twofold. "Snatch some from the fire" and encourage the rescued believers to build up each other in the true faith.

How is the needed spiritual maturing to occur? Jude advises remembering the teaching of the original apostles, keeping in close touch with the love of God, and praying regularly as enabled by the Holy Spirit. Peter insists that God's divine power "has given us everything needed for life and godliness" (2 Pet. 1:3). We must grow up into the great privileges we have and never assume that God's free grace releases us from moral restraint. Temptations always remain just around the corner. The duty of Christians is to be firmly grounded in the faith and always growing in the knowledge of Jesus Christ (2 Pet. 3:17-18).

4. The Present Challenge

The culture of secular societies tends to infiltrate church life and slowly degrade its integrity. Our electronic devices get the world's news and its values to us constantly and everywhere. The frequently sad result is obvious. When observing Christian behavior in everyday life, the general population often sees little difference between Christians and non-believers. The church's best response is not to stiffen into a defensive posture, but to lean heavily on confidence in God's provision, as Jude concludes in verses 24 and 25. To do this, believers must mature in the faith and together build up the church so that it has the wisdom and strength to resist all evil incursions into its life.

The immoral poison of today's secular society requires a careful Christian guarding of the line between liberty and license. Believers must champion the fundamental reality of new life in Jesus Christ. We must become actual "participants of the divine nature" (2 Pet. 2:4). What must be built up in us is our active communing with God "so as to dwell in God and God in you."[1] We must be clear about who Christians are. Jude says we are those called by God, beloved by God, and kept by Jesus Christ. Paul says we are called to be "saints" (Rom. 1:7; 1 Cor. 1:2), believers with a difference who do not live by the standards of this world. We are to be "holy" as God is holy.[2]

5. Response from the Heart

My Growth Need: Strength to withstand all that comes. Ex. 15:1-4; Ps. 46:1-3; 2 Cor. 12:9-10; Phil.4:12-14; II Tim. 2:1-5.

---

[1] John Wesley, *Notes*, 1:3.

[2] For current explorations of the several dimensions and implications of Christian holiness, see Barry L. Callen, *Christian Holiness* (2023).

Peter and Jude recognize the human capacity, even inclination to do wrong, sometimes very hurtful wrong to others. How does God respond to us? The response is a call to deepen our relationships with the divine Spirit who will show and enable the better way. We are encouraged to focus patiently and positively on the good that God wants *for* us and then *from* us on behalf of others.

True knowledge of God is experiencing the awesome nearness of the Spirit and living daily by employing the fruit of that life-changing nearness. Jesus teaches us how to be more and more God-like, actually reflecting traits of the divine character by participating actively in the presence of the divine Spirit and in the divine mission.

> Come, Thou Fount of every blessing,
> Tune my heart to sing Thy grace;
> Prone to wander, Lord, I feel it, Prone to leave the God I love:
> Here's my heart, O take and seal it, Seal it for Thy courts above.
> —Robert Robinson

> O to be like Thee! Blessed Redeemer,
> This is my constant longing and prayer.
> —Thomas O. Chisholm

Personal Prayer: Thank you, Lord, for coming to me through your servants Jude and Peter. They are offering crucial words of warning and benediction, the blessing of peace and the good life offered in Christ. The next time I'm tempted to wander or turn to my weaknesses, my I find strength from your divine presence within. Continually re-shape me through life in your Spirit, Jesus. May others around me see your life in action on their behalf. May the peace and love of God flow freely through me to all around me. That's what I understand "holiness" to mean. Keep teaching me, Lord, as I walk your way.

Reading 44

DEALING WITH STRAYING CHURCHES

Churches should be and can be outposts of heaven in this troubled world, but they also can go very wrong. Individual life can be a reflection of God alive within or sad evidence of quite the opposite. The conclusion of the biblical material includes a review of how a series of local congregations in the early church were doing. The finding is complex and mostly discouraging. They were to be divine candlesticks shining to the world. In fact, they were flames of divine light struggling to stay burning or already having gone out! The Bible draws to a close in this tension of delivered good news in Christ and awareness that its appointed messengers may fail in their holy task. It need not be so! God is near, forever alive, and holding the keys to the future.

1. The Big Picture Verses.
Revelation 1:3, 17-18. The Context: Revelation 1-3.

Blessed are those who hear and keep what is written here, for the time is near! God says, "Do not be afraid; I am the First and the Last, the Living One. I was dead, and see, I am alive forever and ever, and I have the keys of death and of Hades."

2. A Bit of Background

We are given a glance of the condition of the early church in John's time as it faced persecution and its own internal issues. Ephesus was courageous but lacked enthusiasm. Smyrna was being harassed and seemingly at the mercy of its enemies. Pergamum was too ready to compromise, while Thyatira was too tolerant of unwholesome influences in its own ranks. Sardis seemed to be spiritually dead, Philadelphia was small but faithful, and Laodicea was complacent and half-hearted, in danger of being spit out of God's mouth altogether. What a report of God's faithfulness and human frailties!

The Book of Revelation is strange form of "apocalyptic" writing designed to give a glimpse ahead at the coming drama of the ending of all things. How can we survive the process and coming judgment? How should we prepare? The answers involve our proper relationship to the Spirit of God. The final biblical book is structured around four "in the Spirits" (1:10; 4:2; 17:3; 21:10). Readers are urged to share this experience of faithful human-divine relationship which alone will allow a proper understanding of John's writing and enable our rising to the fullness of our worship of the glorious God.

The highlighted cluster of seven Christian congregations were in what now is Turkey. They are addressed individually by the voice of God through John the inspired writer. What must they do to be ready for what's to come shortly? What failures demand immediate correction? They are identified as beloved candlesticks among whom the Risen Christ walks. He analyzes, judges, and directs needed reform. This direction is still so relevant!

3. The Message in Brief

Beyond being Lord of history and of the future as well, Jesus Christ is to be Lord of the church *now,* and obviously so. John writes to seven local churches of his time in various stages of strength and weakness. He reassures them that, whatever happens here on earth, their destiny can be safely in the Lord's hands if they will only be faithful. Churches are to repent and reform as needed while time remains. They are to listen carefully to the wind of God's Spirit and respond accordingly (3:22). With the faithful, Christ will share his triumph when he comes. But, in the meantime, we must know that the Bible provides two critical perspectives on God's future for the creation.

First, the Bible gives divine foundations, impulses, intents, and assurances, but *not* calendars and detailed political schemes with contemporary nametags. Second, holy lives of meaningful service prior to Christ's return are being enabled and must be engaged in the meantime. At Pentecost, the Spirit of Jesus *already has come to us* in order to move *through us* as ministering agents of love in a broken world.

> Spirit of God, descend upon my heart;
> Wean it from earth, through all its pulses move;
> Stoop to my weakness, mighty as Thou art,
> And make me love Thee as I ought to love.
> —George Croly

4. The Present Challenge

If we update the locations of the congregations named by John, the same church problems still appear today. Sardis, for example, is a warning to churches of all times. It gave the appearance of being spiritually alive, while in fact it was dangerously dead. Churches of today must know, and be acting like they know, that the future age already is invading the present evil age. Christians are not to wait until the second coming of Christ to experience the resurrection potential of "last things."

Christians have been living in "the last days" since the first-century inauguration of the reign of God through the Christ-Pentecost events recorded in the Book of Acts, chapter two. The *dunamis* (dynamic power) of God's Spirit is the main thing the church has going for it. The church must never think that impressive buildings, budgets, staff, or volume of members necessarily represent or enable the power of God's Spirit. That kind of misunderstanding is the menu for church disaster. The adequacy of the church in any age is this announcement of the resurrected Jesus:

> Do not be afraid; I am the First and the Last, the Living One. I was dead, and see, I am alive forever and ever, and I have the keys of death and of Hades (Rev. 1:17-18).

5. Response from the Heart

My Growth Need: Listening to God speaking to the church.
2 Chron. 7:14-16; Ps. 51:8-13; Mt. 24:9-14; Eph. 5:14-17;
1 Jn. 1:9; Jam. 4:6-8.

The book of Revelation is written to the churches of Asia with the intention of warning and encouraging the Jesus followers in difficult times. It's a call to holiness and faithfulness. We need to learn to be patient with each other and aware of the temptations of the backward pull as well as the nearness of the coming future of God. The key is to keep our eyes on Jesus and alive in his Spirit.

> Our task on earth unfinished till threats of war shall cease,
> Our voice must raise a protest where greed still robs our peace.
> One fellowship Christ called for of every class and race,
> The church must live the vision that's shown in Jesus's face.
> —S. Ralph Harlow

Personal Prayer. O Lord, may I be given the gift of discernment to be able to recognize the good from the bad, the alive from the dead, especially when evil begins to seep quietly into my life or that of my church. Give me insight to see, courage to speak, and commitment to work with fellow believers so that we can encourage each other to be patient and steadfast, holding on to the gospel of Christ, our only lifeline to God's future. I sense the tension of living in "the last days." Make me faithful to your call *in the meantime*!

Reading 45

BEASTS AND GOLDEN STREETS

It's hard to be sure about the details of heaven when none of us has been there and the biblical revelation is short on description. At least one thing is clear. Rather than get carried away with images of golden streets and angelic choirs, we should focus on the One who sits on the divine throne and is in charge of the future. Whatever heaven turns out to be, it will be wonderful beyond description. This we know because Jesus Christ will be there on the throne and we already know him. Tears will be gone and the water of life will be flowing freely. Let us look ahead with thanksgiving, and without neglecting our mission responsibilities now.

1. The Big Picture Verses.
Revelation 7:17. The Context: Revelation 4-22.

The lamb is at the center of the throne and will be our shepherd, and he will guide us to springs of the water of life, and God will wipe away every tear from our eyes.

2. A Bit of Background

These final chapters of the book of Revelation have suffered the fate of two opposite kinds. Either they have been abandoned as completely unintelligible or they've been turned into the happy hunting ground of religious eccentrics building personal timetables of events to come. In fact, to the original readers they were quite understandable, a comforting tract for their troubled times, and now for ours. Revelation chapters 4-22 form the epilogue of Bible, balancing the prologue of Genesis chapters 1-11. They complete the bookends of God before the beginning and after the ending of human times.

The Book of Revelation is an *apocalypse*, an "unveiling" book, picturing the day when God will intervene dramatically to end the sordid situations created by humankind. Such unusual writing is especially hard to understand, in part because it's trying to describe the indescribable and report what no eye has ever seen before. It's an underground resistance literature, secretly defying the present evil powers and keynoting the coming of God's better times.

The comforting message is simply this. There will be an end of the lifetime of the whole creation and all its evil, an end fully in control of the loving and Almighty God. Revelation 4-22 is a call for the people of Jesus to resist to the death if necessary the demand of the Roman emperor to be called God. Only the God made known in the Lamb, Jesus, is God, the God of all history and of all time that stretches even beyond time. "Armageddon" is pictured as the ultimate clash of good and evil, with the good finally the glorious victor. With the triumph of Christ, the sovereignty of God over the whole of creation is assured forever (11:14-19).

3. The Message in Brief

Here is a "tract for bad times" that lifts the veil and intends to nerve the faithful for survival in the present. All the current suffering of God's people must be endured without compromise. The faithful must live in expectation of the soon-coming of Christ to welcome home his Bride (the church) and bring judgment where needed.

For the church, the threatening beasts of today will be gone and remaining will be the golden streets of tomorrow. We live in a planned universe, not a mad and meaningless chaos. One day God will be all in all. The glory of God will illumine all and the Lamb, the Risen Jesus, will reign over all forever and ever.

So ends the message of the Bible to us who yet struggle in this fallen world. God is to be the absolute Lord of the church today (Rev. 1-3) and also will be the Lord of the future in the dramatic tomorrow of grace-full bliss. Beyond the troubled cities and congregations of us humans, there indeed will be the City of God. It isn't far away and is being readied for us! There will be no more pain, tears, or death because all these will have passed away (Rev. 21:2-4). We who are faithful finally will be able to see clearly what for now remains only a dim hope.

> Our Father's wondrous works we see
> In the earth and sea and sky;
> He rules o'er all in majesty
> From His royal throne on high.
> —Clara M. Brooks

4. The Present Challenge

The book of Daniel pictures the Greek Antiochus Epiphanes as a blasphemous parity of true religion. In the Bible's final book, John sees the Roman Empire as a beast from the realms of darkness. We are presented with an updated application of the leviathan of Psalm 74:14. Now it's the agent of the Dragon with its heads being successive emperors persecuting Christians and martyrs (Rev. 17:6).

What's the main point being made? The Roman Empire, and all others to follow, finally will give way to the inevitable victory of the Everlasting One, the crucified and risen Christ, the final Overcomer, the Lamb of God who bids us follow him to victory and eternal life. The essence of this divine "prophecy" is not to tell us in detail what is going to happen tomorrow. Instead, it's to turn us from our evil ways and encourage us to realize who God is so that we might become right with him, which guarantees our future. Rather than predicting the future's detail, the Revelation of John points us in the right future direction and hopes to prepare us for its soon coming.

The beastly picture of the present is described well as diabolical power, arrogance, and injustice being practiced in totalitarian and war-like nations of the 1st and 21st century. What are we who believe in Jesus to do? We are to be faithful in the meantime! The Spirit of Christ enables patience and trust and a stubborn hope. The enduring hope is that the sovereign God, whose heart we now have seen beating in the coming of Jesus, soon will show his might and bring his judgment. It will be the dramatic return of the One who is all in all, before and beyond all time, the Alpha and Omega, our Risen Lord.

To prepare for that dramatic and glorious day, we now are to concentrate on relating to this coming One and participating in his mission in advance of that final day. Once *informed* of God's true sovereignty, we are to be *re-formed* into the image of Christ and engaged with him prior to his coming again. We are to seek and embody "holiness," living in the image of the coming Christ himself.

5. Response from the Heart

My Growth Need: Confidence that all will be well.
Ps. 27:3; Isa. 32:17, 57:15; Jn. 11:21; Phil. 1:6; Heb. 10:35-36; Rev. 22:1-5.

Saint Augustine lived in a frightening time (354-430 A.D.). Rome was sacked in 410, signaling that the mighty Roman Empire was on the point of collapse. He proceeded to write one of the great Christian books of all time, *The City of God*, center of the kingdom that cannot fall. Dietrich Bonhoeffer lived in a different time of social calamity, World War II when German churches too easily accommodated themselves to the awful circumstance created by Hitler, including Bonhoeffer being martyred. Even so, as with the Roman Empire centuries before, the monstrous Third Reich was short-lived and collapsed. This is the eventual fate of all human empires that function counter to the will of God.

The last word always is the Lord's. The evil that could not defeat Jesus on the cross will enable the church to carry its cross successfully into the world. Regardless of what happens, one day the faithful will be granted a glorious resurrection to life eternal.

> Crown Him with many crowns, the Lamb upon the throne.
> Hark, how the heavenly anthem drowns all music but its own.
> Awake, my soul, and sing, of Him who died for thee,
> And hail Him as the matchless King, through all eternity.
>
> —Matthew Bridges

Personal Prayer. May Christ ever be lifted up by me as the Lord of heaven and earth, the Lamb that was slain to express God's love, my Shepherd and Guide and Friend. May we recognize, O Lord, Your Presence ever in our midst. Our hearts belong to You. *My* heart belongs to you. Let me thrill at what is coming and not despair at the troubles to be endured in the meantime. Help me in each of my days to honor your reign even when it isn't yet obvious to all. Come, my Lord, to my heart and to all the world!

My Growth Need:
Light blazing over my dark horizon.
Ps. 16:7-11; 30:4-5; Lam. 3:22-25;
Jn. 15:10-11; Rom. 15:13; Phil. 4:4-7.

Reading 46

SONGS OF THE NEW MORNING

The Bible records many psalms of the morning, new-day songs of gain and joyous restoration because of God's pure grace. The night of evil may have been deep and dark, but now come songs of a new morning. They may be unexpected and undeserved, but divine grace abounds and flows from God's heart. God is active, loving, and victorious. Hope shines brightly again. Praise God!

1. The Big Picture Verses: Psalm 40:1-3.

The Context: Psalms 30, 40, 65, 124, 125, 126 (read them all!).

I waited patiently for the Lord; he heard my cry, drew me up from the desolate pit, out of my miry bog, and set my feet up on a rock, making my steps secure. He put a new song in my mouth, a song of praise to our God.

2. A Bit of Background

Determining the identity of God's people has been a long challenge, seen in stages through the centuries narrated in the biblical record. The coming of Jesus brought needed light on the subject. The church was born, rooted in the Jewish heritage but also much expanded to encompass potentially the whole of humanity. This expansion was a new truth song of great joy!

God's true people are the ones who see and celebrate the new morning of God's saving grace. As Psalm 40 puts it, "Here I am, Lord. I delight to do your will. Oh my God, your law is within my heart. Let your steadfast love keep me safe forever" (40:7-8, 11).

God's people are the ones who recognize that the earth itself is God's creation and is to be honored and cared for. "You make the gateways of the morning and the evenings shout for joy. You visit the earth and water it; you greatly enrich it. You provide the people with grain" (Ps. 65:8-9).

As the unknown future is faced, God's people remember his gracious actions of yesterday and thus have good reason to hope for whatever tomorrow may bring. "Those who trust in the Lord are like Mount Zion, which cannot be moved but abides forever. As the mountains surround Jerusalem, so the Lord surrounds his people from this time on and forevermore. Our help is in the name of the Lord who made heaven and earth" (Ps. 125 1-2, 124:8).

One caution must not be missed. We are to remember God's actions yesterday, but then proceed as necessary *to forget*. That is, we must not allow looking back to block our openness to seeing God acting in fresh and amazing ways today and tomorrow. Yesterday has wisdom to share, but that wisdom can sour if we get stuck in reverse and lose connection with fresh possibilities. Going back in grateful memory should be a resource and not a hindrance to going forward.

The first verses of Psalm 126 look to the past, while the final verses look with expectancy to the future. Looking to the past must not be our way of hoping for a restoration of all the "old ways." That's mere nostalgia. The hope is finding how to live into God's new way of being, a way always relevant for the changing circumstances of today and tomorrow.

3. The Message in Brief

Psalm 30 is a song of celebration because of a dramatic overnight turn. What God does in the dark is turn us from sadness to joy, distress to well-being. The result is that "joy comes in the morning" (30:5). Paul knew the tortured memories of having been an early persecutor of the Jesus people. The morning joy was his entry into a very new identity and vocation. It came by his abrupt embrace of the reality of the resurrection of Jesus. In this marvelous fresh day of faith, Paul could write, "May the God of hope fill you with all joy" (Rom. 15:13). His heart was now full and bubbling over.

The last lesson Jesus taught his disciples was that God has eminent domain in all things. There is only one God and he has all possibilities and no competitors. "My soul thirsts for God, for the living God." I am lost without God. I am created to be in relationship with God. Here's the amazing fact that speaks so wonderfully to our lostness and great thirst and empty hearts. God loves, comes, and seeks full restoration of relationship with us!

One meaning of the doctrine of the divine "Trinity" is that God is by very nature a rich *relational* being. Even though God is complete within himself, God is so full of relational love that he reaches out for us. He sent his Son to enable us relationally starved humans to join in the divine richness of relational fulfillment. My soul surely thirsts for being found by that lovingly relational God!

Who's a "saint" in God's eyes? It's someone who has become an extension of God's *hesed* (loving faithfulness). By God's grace, Christian saints are members of the covenant community of Christ, believers experiencing God's relational restoration and loving care. The holy ones are those who have gratefully become active in passing on to others this *hesed*, this opportunity to experience God's faithfulness that brings belonging and joy.

4. The Present Challenge

In moments of pain, confusion, and unanswered questions, so much depends on the Christian believer having available a powerful memory of God's past actions—a key reason for careful Bible reading. Such memory gives assurance and guidance to the present. What God wants now will be in line with what God has done in the past and intends for the future. Hymns such as "Great Is Thy Faithfulness" and "God of the Ages, Whose Almighty Hand" will inspire faith in new possibilities despite any present circumstances.

What about when there is no clear memory of what to do in a novel set of circumstances? What should happen when a decision must be made and there is no map, only wilderness and an open road with no divine GPS? The psalmist answers, "I bless the Lord who gives me counsel" (vs. 7). We are to praise and practice the presence of God, relishing holy love and being open to the present ministry of God's Spirit. Remaining close to the Shepherd is the way to find home.

Some words of Gloria Gaither sound the proper note. In her blog (Oct. 3, 2022) she reflects on the fall season of the year. It's the time for departing, she says. The seasons of planting crops, nurturing the fields, and finally harvesting are over. In the arriving chill we must let go, survive, prepare to start over, dare to look ahead. Her final words dance with hope for God's tomorrow yet unseen. Here's the tenacity of a biblical faith. Picturing a bag of harvested grain, "we sift the kernels through our hands and sing, to find them pregnant with the spring!" God provides songs of a new morning!

5. Response from the Heart

My Growth Need: Light blazing over my dark horizon.
Ps, 16:7-11; 30:4-5; Lam. 3:22-25; Jn. 15:10-11; Rom. 15:13; Phil. 4:4-7.

My memory of God in my life brings me great joy. When I needed comfort or peace or being loved or guidance and hope, God was there and active in my private experience. God has been with me in good times and bad, and I'm so grateful for that presence. Yet, as wonderful as such memories are, better yet is the belief that God will be with me in each new day. God's mercies are new every morning (Lam. 3.) There's always a freshness about God's presence. That's the reason we write new songs, celebrating the contemporaneity of our life with God.

As the "mirror of the human soul," the biblical psalms reflect the great diversity of human experience. Standing tall among all these songs are the ones of praise and thanksgiving, lifting the singers into the very presence of God.

> God of the ages, history's Maker,
> planning our pathway, holding us fast,
> Shaping in mercy all that concerns us;
> Father, we praise you *Lord of the past*.

God of this morning, gladly your children
worship before you, trustingly bow;
Teach us to know You always among us,
quietly sovereign *Lord of our now*.

Lord of past ages, Lord of this morning,
Lord of the future, help us we pray:
Teach us to trust You, love and obey You,
crown You each moment, *Lord of today*.
—Margaret Clarkson

Sing praise to God who reigns above, the God of all creation,
The God of power, the God of love, the God of our salvation.
With healing balm my soul He fills, and every murmur stills,
To God all praise and glory.
—Johann Jay Schutz

Personal Prayer. How can I praise You, Lord, except in my creaturely little way? You are far beyond my comprehension and yet in your compassion you come so very near. I long to come near to you daily, to be made whole in your presence and an active instrument of your peace. Make it so, dear Father! Help me always to remember that you are history's maker and in full control of the eventual future. You reign above. You are the maker of gracious new mornings. To you be all praise and glory!

My Growth Need:
Gladness that God has included me!
Matt. 16:18; Acts 2:42-47; 1 Cor. 13:8-13;
Eph. 2:19-20; Gal. 2:7-9; 1 Jn. 1:3, 7.

Reading 47

EXACTLY WHO ARE GOD'S PEOPLE?

Exactly who are eligible to be members of the church of Jesus Christ? Jews only, Christians only, the sinless only, everybody, and according to whose standards? Can we manage to achieve church membership with our good works? Who are the carriers of the good news of the arriving kingdom of God? Where is the real church of God? Am I extending its borders as God would wish or trying to limit its membership according to my private preferences? These are hard questions!

1. The Big Picture Verses.
Romans 8:1-2, 12:1-2. The Context: The Book of Romans.

There is no condemnation for those who are in Christ Jesus. For the law of the Spirit of life in Christ Jesus has set you free from the law of sin and death. Present your bodies as a living sacrifice, holy and acceptable to God. Do not be conformed to this age but be transformed by the renewing of the mind.

2. A Bit of Background

Throughout the Book of Acts Luke lays the groundwork for a dramatic new definition of the "people of God." Then in his letter to the Romans Paul probes the theology and implications of this dramatic redefinition. Rome was the center of the Roman Empire that dominated the days of Luke and Paul. Although Paul had not been there prior to his writing to these believers, he hoped to use this church as a base of future ministry opportunities. Naturally he was anxious to introduce himself to the Roman church and share with them his years of matured thinking about the nature and meaning of the Christian faith, including the widened borders of the church, the new Israel.

This letter to Rome is Paul's most "systematic" theological presentation. The church of Jesus is said to be comprised of all those who are "in Christ" and prepared to be "living sacrifices" in service of the good news of God's saving presence with us in Jesus. In Adam all have sinned. We sinners are helpless, except that God in Christ has entered the picture on our behalf. The terrible crisis in Adam—in us all--can be reversed by faith in and solidarity with Jesus Christ (5:15-21). This is a blessed possibility for anyone prepared to repent and receive from the Father's good hand. Here's a classic testimony of the widening reach of the saving grace of God.

> In the evening I went very unwillingly to a society in Aldersgate Street [London, England] where one was reading Martin Luther's *Preface to the Epistle to the Romans*. About a quarter before nine, while he was describing the change which God works in the heart through faith in Christ, I felt my heart *strangely warmed*. I felt I did trust in Christ, Christ alone for salvation, and an assurance was given me that God had taken away *my* sins, even *mine*, and saved *me* from the law of sin and death.[1]

Who can be counted among the members of Christ's church? Those who gratefully share such a testimony.

3. The Message in Brief

Only what God has done in Jesus Christ can lift us humans to the heights where God dwells. Only when properly related to Jesus Christ through his Spirit can we find true fulfillment as members of the divine family. Anyone can move from death to life because of God's Son (3:21-31), and faith in the saving mystery and power

---

[1] John Wesley, *Journal*, 1738.

of his cross is the only way (1:17). The obedience of Jesus unto death has become the promise of our eternal life. We are saved *by faith alone*, not by frantically trying to comply with any set of moral standards or self-achievement (9:6-18). Being graciously counted among God's people by mercy and grace alone inspires lives of gratitude, love, and joyous obedience.

We must not seek to control the boundaries of God's church by human standards. Peter is a good example. He gladly sat and ate with Gentiles in Antioch until a Jewish faction arrived and convinced him that it was more prudent to sit only with these Jews—public hypocrisy! Peter suddenly had given more importance to his cultural and racial origin than to common relationship with Jesus which transcends such human distinctions. Even in the church of our Lord, peer pressure frequently splits us into factions that spawn hurt and even hate instead of rejoicing and serving together. Let's keep hearing Charles Wesley's classic report about God's universal love:

> Come, sinners, to the gospel feast,
> Let *every soul* be Jesus' guest;
> There need not be one left behind,
> For God has bidden *all mankind*.

John, brother of Charles, made clear that "orthodoxy," straight thinking about theological matters, is part of the faith, but not *the substance*, which is holy love reigning in the heart. The substance is actually walking sacrificially on the path of cross and resurrection in the power of God's loving Spirit.

4. The Present Challenge

The book of Romans has served as a theological compass enabling significant Christian leaders over the centuries to re-orient themselves and their theologies more closely to the original Christian message. Included have been no less than Saint Augustine, Martin Luther, John Wesley, and Karl Barth. When joined to God's people by faith in Jesus Christ, nothing in this life or the next can separate us from Christ's love (8:28). What a message of hope for our modern world that's full of division and despair!

Who exactly are God's people? Only Jews, only Jewish-Christians, or others also? Here's the good news for a large portion of today's humanity. The chosen of God are not limited to a privileged few of a particular race or land or religious affiliation. They are the many who choose to respond in faith to the good news revealed in Jesus Christ. Even those who never hear the name of Jesus are subjects of God's love and of the Spirit's redemptive ministry. We who are privileged to be fully aware of the work of God in Jesus must avoid arrogance and judgment about those less privileged through no fault of their own.

Membership in the choir of heaven appears open even to those who can't carry a tune and never saw the sheet music of Jesus in this world. Psalm 96 draws the worshiper's attention to the greatness of God's glory in comparison to the "gods" of Israel's neighbors. It's a song of expansive praise of the universal God who reigns over all and loves all. "All the earth" is urged to join in the song of thanksgiving, and all nations are potentially included in the choir's membership. Any narrow defining of "the chosen" likely is not equal to God's generous boundaries of who's necessarily in and who's definitely out.

5. Response from the Heart

My Growth Need: Gladness that God has included me!
Matt. 16:18; Acts 2:42-47; 1 Cor. 13:8-13; Eph. 2:19-20;
Gal. 2:7-9; 1 Jn. 1:3, 7.

Paul's letter to the Romans is like a great theological symphony. Justification is God's pronouncement of forgiveness which brings us back into a right relationship with God. Sanctification is the work of the Spirit in our minds and hearts, making us more and more like Jesus. This symphony comes to a resounding conclusion in chapter eight with the pronouncement, "There is therefore now no condemnation for those in Christ Jesus" (8:1). The Spirit is with us in times of suffering, gives us hope, and is at work in all things, bringing us good.

Nothing shall separate from his unbounded love,
Neither in depths below nor in the heights above;
And in the years to come, He will abide with me;
I am the Lord's, I know, for all eternity.
—Charles Naylor

O for a closer walk with God, a calm and heavenly frame,
A light to shine upon the road that leads me to the Lamb.
—William Cowper

Personal Prayer. I'm so glad to be in your presence, Lord. As I read the revealed Scriptures, my mind is enlightened and I have clearer insights into how I may bring good into the lives of those around me. Thank you for your Word and the privilege I have to study it and live by it. Thank you especially that I now am "in Christ" and thus in restored fellowship with you and a member of your church. Rather than pushing anyone out on the basis of my narrow preferences, make me an evangelist of good news to all I meet.

My Growth Need:
Unity so that the world can really know.
Jn. 13:34-35; Rom. 14:17-19; 1 Cor. 1:10; Gal. 3:28;
Eph. 4:1-6; Phil. 2:2-3; Col. 3:13-14.

Reading 48

PROPER LIFE IN THE CHURCH

The letter of Ephesians is an outstanding piece of early Christian writing. It reports two things very clearly. To those believers hiding behind ideological iron curtains, separating Christians from each other according to their own preferences, the message is "Unite or perish!" And to those facing the hostile world under Christ's banner, it's "Onward Christian soldiers!" Proper life in the church involves unity among the members and mission as their main agenda together. Both depend on acknowledging Jesus Christ as the cornerstone of truth and destiny.

1. The Big Picture Verses.
Ephesians 3:19, 2:19-20. The Context:
The Book of Ephesians.

May you know the love of Christ that surpasses knowledge so that you may be filled with all the fullness of God. You are no longer strangers and aliens, but fellow citizens with the saints and members of the household of God, built upon the foundation of the apostles and prophets, with Christ Jesus himself as the cornerstone.

2. A Bit of Background

The letter to the Ephesians ranks high in the devotional and theological literature of the Christian church. It's been called "the Queen of the Epistles." Paul was nearing the end of his ministry, was in prison in Rome, and wrote to share his most matured thoughts on the themes of Christ and his church for the benefit of the Ephesian congregation and others, now us. It's a circular letter intended to be passed around among the churches.

With two clear divisions, theological and practical, Ephesians shows how closely the writer intends to link faith and action, two sides of the same coin. The purpose of God from eternity has been to make possible fallen humanity becoming daughters and sons of God who are gathered into a great family of mutual love and service. The life, death, and resurrection of Jesus now has made all this possible.

The family of God, the church, is described (1:1-3:21) and then its proper life together detailed (4:1-6:24). Paul, an ambassador of Christ now in chains, ends the letter with a flourish. Reflecting his regularly seeing Roman soldiers in the prison, he wants to identify the available spiritual resources of a Christian "soldier" who must fight in this world against the powers of evil and darkness. All believers must put on the full armor of God (6:10-18).

If the letter to the Romans is where Paul does his most careful theological argumentation, here he soars spiritually, even sings of the heights of God's now-arrived grace. Great passages include 2:19-22; 3:14-19; and 4:1-16.

3. The Message in Brief

The ultimate in all reality is the one God and Father of us all who has destined us in love to be his children (1:5), and then together to be the church. The creation now has a great rift in its heart, a fatal flaw of human making, and God's plan for its healing is centered in Jesus Christ. He is the reconciling agent for all humanity and creation. Through the church, Christ's body, God's plan is now to be realized (3:9). In the church, the dividing wall disrupting the human community is broken down (first the one between Jew and Gentile). None are now aliens in a foreign land, but potentially fellow citizens in God's one household (2:19), forming one living temple, a common home with God through the Spirit of Christ (2:22).

The call is for Christ to dwell in the hearts of all believers through faith, enabling them to be rooted and grounded in love. All in Christ's body are to walk in a manner worthy of their calling, making every effort to maintain the unity of the Spirit in the bond of peace (4:1-3). We are to be the church of Christ, meaning at least this. Beyond mere forms and practices of the faith, true church members are to be seeking the power of godliness, uniting in prayer together, regularly hearing proclaimed the Word of God, helping each other mature in faith. As these happen, we believers emerge as a body of the Spirit that's a staging ground for the mission of the church in the whole world.

Paul was writing from Rome, the center of the *Pax Romana*, an amazing uniting of much of the then known world into a peace rarely seen on that scale. He saw this as a human symbol of God's divine intention of uniting all things in Christ, to a depth and breadth never before known. The glue holding all together would not to be armies and brutality but the love and forgiveness of Christ, the cornerstone of it all.

4. The Present Challenge

A good way of determining what the church should be doing on earth is to noting what's now happening in heaven. The rule is, "on earth, as it is in heaven." The heavenly kingdom is characterized by reconciliation, healing, communion, and family. God's present goal is hardly to build and protect a "religion" or formulate the final cultural rules of "righteousness." The focus is to be on Jesus, the church's cornerstone. We are to maintain proper and growing relationships with him, and through his Spirit with each other.

Emphasized in the church's life are to be forgiveness, reconciliation, and the unity of a restored humanity through a universal reign of love. Such loving unity within God's church is essential to its integrity. If not in the church, then where? If not now, how else can the church's mission to the world be seen as credible and desirable?

How are difficult decisions to be made by Christians? Judgments should come through the three root metaphors common to the whole message of the New Testament. The church is to (1) embody a manner of life that shows the redemptive purposes of God. It is to do this (2) in the manner of the cross of Jesus, joining the fellowship of his sufferings (Phil. 3:10), with church members bearing each other's burdens (Gal. 6:2). When living like that, the church will (3) reflect as it should the power of the resurrection of Jesus in the middle of an unredeemed world.[1]

5. Response from the Heart

My Growth Need: Unity so that the world can really know.
Jn. 13:34-35; Rom. 14:17-19; 1 Cor. 1:10; Gal. 3:28; Eph. 4:1-6; Phil. 2:2-3; Col. 3:13-14.

The beautiful prayer in chapter three of Ephesians is that believers may experience the love of Christ, be filled with the fullness of God, and join their hearts so they can be formed into a body in which God dwells. They are to be a shining witness to the world by uniting in Christ, even in the diversity of their spiritual gifts. They are to be mature in Christ by speaking the truth in love and being willing to confront without condemnation.

> Fill me with Thy Spirit, Lord, fully save my longing soul;
> Through the precious cleansing blood, purify and make me whole.
> Come, O Spirit, seal me Thine, Come, Thy fullness now bestow;
> Let Thy glory in me shine, let the fire within me glow.
> —Daniel S. Warner

Personal Prayer. O Lord, I thank you for the church, followers who have been faithful through the centuries and have brought the message to me. How wonderful, Father of love, that you were with Paul even in prison and assisted him to share the truth so beautifully in his ancient and still modern letter. I thank you for fellow believers all over the world, some facing great adversity and yet living lives of love and concern. I pray earnestly for them, my spiritual sisters and brothers. I ask that your Spirit keep them safe and true. I am so grateful to be counted among their number, all together as your church.

---

[1] See Richard B. Hays, *The Moral Vision of the New Testament.*

Reading 49

THE MINISTRY OF RECONCILIATION

God's purpose in this world goes beyond the saving of souls, healing of bodies, and feeding of the poor. While these are critical, to be sure, it may be that God's primary agenda is *reconciliation*, bringing all things together in Christ. Jesus prayed that we *may be one* as Jesus and his Father are one (Jn. 17:18-22). Our world is so torn apart. The call is for disciples of the Master to be agents of oneness, wholeness, reconciliation. When they are, the healing and feeding ministries will proceed most effectively.

1. The Big Picture Verses.
2 Corinthians 5:17-18. The Context: 2 Corinthians.

If anyone is in Christ, there is a new creation: everything old has passed away; look, new things have come into being! All this is from God, who reconciled us to himself through Christ and has given us the ministry of reconciliation.

2. A Bit of Background

The human struggles often are with each other as self-centered people. We have ghetto tendencies. We build relational boxes, live inside them, and view with suspicion and even hatred those outside. Even in the church, we build closed systems around particular interpretations of Scripture, preferred spiritual experiences and leaders, making unity in diversity almost impossible.

Reconciliation is the process of the love of God moving against the ghettos of exclusion and discrimination. How can it be known that we actually are disciples of Jesus? If we have reconciling tendencies, are displaying self-sacrificing love for each other (Jn. 13:35), and are insisting on building bridges that link people instead of walls that keep them away.

Some of the problems of the church at Corinth were noted in Reading 46. They also included mistrust of Paul's motives and his very person. His teaching authority was under attack. He poured himself into the task of saving this church and his own dignity as a representative of Jesus Christ. Paul vigorously defended himself (2 Cor. 10 and 13). Why? "I wrote to you out of much distress and anguish of heart and with many tears, not to cause you grief but to let you know the abundant love that I have for you" (2:4). Under these most awkward circumstances, genuine love required more than surface politeness. The result of "tough love" was some actual repentance and humility on the part of the congregation. What a joyous relief!

We believers are ambassadors for Christ. God is making an appeal through us that all people be reconciled to God and to each other (5:17-20). As an immediate instance of needed reconciliation in the larger Christian fellowship, Paul turns attention to the urgent physical need of fellow Christians in Jerusalem and a proposed offering for them. This would further a healing of the breach between believers of Gentile and Jewish backgrounds. It was to be a gracious act of reconciliation and community building.

3. The Message in Brief

Paul wrote these wonderful lines: "So if anyone is in Christ, there is a new creation: everything old has passed away; look, new things have come into being. All this is from God who reconciled us to himself through Christ and has given us the ministry of reconciliation" (5:17-18). There had been one particular offender in the Corinthian congregation. Paul asks the congregation to forgive and restore this person (2:5–11). That appeal had and still has bigger implications than reconciling a single person. They lie at the very heart of church mission.

Religious extremism has spread discord and death worldwide. Unfortunately, the story is not that different in the faith communities arising from the Old Testament revelation. Jewish Zionism and Moslem extremism and Christian crusading have terrorized whole peoples in the name of defending the true faith from unbelievers. Christians in the Western world have tended to declare virtual "war" on secularism, atheism, and nationalism. Even within Christian ranks, the high level of anger and disrespect is alarming. It often seems to flow from political ideologies more than the reconciling love of God.

The New Testament message is that Christ has given the church the ministry of reconciliation. We are to be witnesses to and living models of a coming new world, the kingdom of God, created only by the reconciling grace of God. "The church can become a compass for a disoriented world *if* it embraces the qualities that exemplify good evangelism--hospitality, relationship, integrity, a reconciling message of the good news of the gospel. This sort of community embodies and *is* the good news."[1]

4. The Present Challenge

God is the author of reconciliation and we human beings are to carry out the reconciling process that God has initiated. Genuine reconciliation begins first between God and human beings through the atonement of God's Son, Jesus Christ. The reconciled then are empowered to become agents of reconciliation. It's a work, a ministry of unconditional love. It demands respect for the inherent dignity of every human being, different or not.

Persons who are new creations in Christ, truly reconciled to God, will engage in the reconciliation ministry because that's now *who they are*. Samuel Hines was a true Christian reconciler because he was indwelt by Christ himself and was keenly aware of the disastrous results of dividers in our contemporary world. Hines was born in Jamaica where first the Spaniards and then the British had come and conquered by superior arms. Then they brought slaves to work the sugar, coconut, and banana plantations. "Neither of the invaders came to reconcile anyone to anything."

---

[1] Priscilla Pope-Levison, *Models of Evangelism*.

Nonetheless, Hines reports, "I do not have the energy or inclination to remain bitter about this history or to hate any of the nationals involved. God has put in my heart an unconditional love for all people--particularly those who hurt me. When we accept the atoning work of Jesus, the love of God fills our hearts. When this happens, reconciliation becomes a feature of our own lifestyle because we see people *from God's point of view.*"[2]

5. Response from the Heart

My Growth Need: Reconcile the way Jesus graciously did.
Matt. 18:16; Rom. 5:8-11, 12:18; 2 Cor. 5:19-20; Gal. 5:22-26; Heb. 12:14.

God's goal is the ministry of Christ through the church. It's bringing persons into a right relationship with God and then each other. We must look deeply within ourselves. Are our hearts in tune with the unifying work of the Spirit of God? Do I long to know God better each day? Do I live so that others may come to know God through me and then reconcile with each other through Christ's Spirit?

> Because you belong to Christ, you are akin to me;
> One in the bond unbreakable, made for eternity.
> Spirit with spirit joined, who can the ties undo?
> Finding the Christ in my heart, with the Christ in you.
>
> Because we belong to Christ, we must exalt His name;
> Letting the world see Christ in us, His love for all proclaim.
> Lift up the cross of Christ, His resurrection show,
> Until we all shall see Him, and His fullness know.
>
> —Duane Blakley

Personal Prayer. O Lord, I love the church. It has nurtured me in the Spirit. It has taught me the truths of Jesus Christ and called me to love his good news and all others because of it. Send me out, Lord, to be a self-sacrificing bridge builder. As you have come as a healer

---

[2] Samuel G. Hines, with Curtiss Paul DeYoung, *Beyond Rhetoric.*

of bodies and relationships, please send me as one of your agents of reconciliation. As I lift up the cross of your Son in my own life, may I also show his resurrection in how I deal with others. It's nothing short of his fullness that I want to know and display.

My Growth Need:
Rejoice! God is enfolded in Christ.
Ps. 32:1, 86:4-5; Mt. 6:14-15, 18:21-22;
Lk. 6:37-38; Eph. 4:32; Col. 3:13-14.

Reading 50

HE'S EVERYTHING TO US!

How would you define the church? At a minimum, it's not to focus on those of us who happen to comprise its human membership now. It's the community *of Jesus* that is living *in and for his Spirit*. In recent readings we have realized that the church too often has significant internal problems. The solution? We together must focus on the "mystery" of Jesus Christ in whom are hidden all the treasures of wisdom and knowledge and forgiveness and redemption and reconciliation.

1. The Big Picture Verses.
Colossians 2:3, 1:14. The Context: The Book Colossians.

May you have all the riches of assured understanding and have the knowledge of God's mystery, that is, Christ, in whom are hidden all the treasures of wisdom and knowledge. God has rescued us from the power of darkness and transferred us into the kingdom of his beloved Son, in whom we have redemption, the forgiveness of sins.

2. A Bit of Background

Not to know one's personal heritage, be ignorant of the past, is to be orphaned in the present. In his letter to the Colossians, Paul addresses the identity question for them as Christians. He insists that the good news of Jesus Christ is the necessary touchstone for realizing who and whose they were and we now are to be. He makes clear certain foundational assumptions. The essence of the true gospel of Christ, the basic theological identity of Christian believers, is centered in a right view of God as known in Jesus and a commitment to holiness of life that leads to peace, hope, deep gratitude, and sacrificial service. Believers are urged to be rooted deeply and built up in this true gospel so that they might abound in thanksgiving (2:7).

Paul greets this congregation as a "holy" faith community. Believers in Jesus are to have a quality of relationship with God that yields conduct corresponding to that relationship—being holy as God is holy. The heart of such God-like conduct is love. In a Christian believer, "love sits upon the throne erected in the inmost soul and reigns without a rival."[1] Paul was aware that around and maybe even in the Colossian congregation were dangerous false teachers threatening to confuse and distract the church's identity and functioning (2:8-10). He was anxious to encourage mature discipleship that knows how to be *in* the world without being *of* it. They must know clearly *whose* they are and *for whom* they are.

3. The Message in Brief

Jesus Christ is the all-sufficiency of life for us who believe. In Jesus have been hidden all the treasures of wisdom and knowledge (2:3) because all the fullness of God dwells in him (1:19). Therefore, he alone is necessary and sufficient for our salvation (1:14). Christian identity must rest on awareness of and thanksgiving for this magnificent truth. Jesus Christ is the visible expression of the invisible God, the Alpha and Omega (Rev. 22:13), the full alphabet of past, present, and future reality (Col. 1:15-18). Nothing greater can be conceived and nothing less is adequate for Christian belief and life.

This grand conviction of the supremacy of Jesus Christ has practical meanings for congregations of God's people. We are to be living demonstrations of the divine grace that reconciles all things to God's will. Christ is the principle of cohesion that is to inform a faithful community, enabling it to rise above typical gender, class, and race distinctions and discriminations. In Christ we humans are all to be one. The life of God's people is to reflect a Christ-likeness,

---

[1] John Wesley, in the sermon "On Zeal."

becoming an extension of the life of Jesus through the power, wisdom, and gifting of the Spirit of Christ.

Adequately conceiving of God must include the crucial Christian doctrine of the *Trinity*. By knowing the One who has come to be with us, Jesus, we can glimpse the One who was long before us, the Father, and the One who now is present to sustain us, the Spirit. They all are one and the same—God! The one God *stands* (Father), *saves* (Son), and *stays* (Spirit).[2] God is more verb than noun, formlessness (Father), becoming form (Son), and always enlivened by the life and energy flowing between these two, and now to and through us (Spirit).[3]

4. The Present Challenge

The purposes of the church are not for their own sake or any wonder-working show that enjoys a large audience and massive income. The power of the Spirit is to function as the church's very heart, enabling it to live for engagement in the mission of the Spirit. All spiritual gifts are given by God for the well-being of the church and the accomplishment of its mission. The identity of the church is just this, being an instrument of the Spirit, the body of Christ--who is Lord of all! True Christian life is not primarily about gaining specialized religious knowledge and affirming right creedal statements. It's more about accepting Jesus Christ as Lord of all and living accordingly by his grace and power.

If the church abides in God, God will dependably abide in the church (Jn. 15:4). If the church does not, however, neither will God. Divine power is not exercised automatically apart from appropriate human response and partnership. Divine sovereignty chooses to *empower* rather than *overpower*. John Wesley was fond of saying that God works "strongly and sweetly," meaning that God's will for human salvation can be resisted. We have been given *response–ability* by God's grace, which renders us *responsible* for receiving and actively employing the salvation and mission of God. Knowing the truth and doing nothing about it is an option, and a path to spiritual disaster.

---

[2] Barry Callen, *God As Loving Grace*.
[3] Richard Rohr, *Immortal Diamond*.

5. Response from the Heart

My Growth Need: Rejoice! God is enfolded in Christ.
Ps. 32:1, 86:4-5; Mt. 6:14-15, 18:21-22; Lk. 6:37-38;
Eph. 4:32; Col. 3:13-14.

The most powerful therapeutic idea in the history of the world is the forgiveness of God. To be forgiven is to be set free to live. The gospel puts forgiveness at the center and provides resources for doing it. There can be no enduring marriages, families, friendships, or communities without the practice of forgiveness. Jesus came show us forgiveness and show us how to forgive.

In order for us to forgive, we must have experienced the reality of God's forgiveness. The primary purpose of the coming of Jesus was to reveal and activate in our midst the nature of God. The heart of God is loving forgiveness. Forgiveness is freeing and enlivening for both the giver and receiver. "As God's chosen ones, holy and beloved, clothe yourselves with compassion, kindness, humility, meekness, and patience. Bear with one another and, if anyone has a complaint against another, forgive each other, just as the Lord has forgiven you" (Col. 3:12).

Personal Prayer. May these inspired lines be the constant prayer of my own heart:

> "Forgive our sins as we forgive" you taught us, Lord, to pray,
>   but you alone can grant us grace to live the words we say.
> How can your pardon reach and bless the unforgiving heart
>   that broods on wrongs and will not let old bitterness depart?
> Lord, cleanse the depths within our souls, and bid resentment cease;
>   then, bound to all in bonds of love, our lives will spread your peace.
>
> —Rosamond Herklots

Reading 51

ADVICE TO YOUNG LEADERS

If only church life were simple and all questions answered definitely and even in advance! Since that's not the case, Christian believers must be fully committed to their common Lord and actively pursuing unity with each other regardless of their differences. Much depends on good leadership. Church leaders in particular must be skilled at knowing the faith and handing with the dynamics of human relationships. Church life will not always be a smooth community experience. Difficulties must be handled wisely to avoid interfering with the all-important mission.

1. The Big Picture Verses.
1 Timothy 1:5, 6:12, 20; 2 Timothy 1:2. The Context: 1 & 2 Timothy and Titus.

We have a glimpse here into needed wisdom for today's church. It arose from circumstances in the early church causing Paul to counsel young leaders. The aim of his instruction was for these leaders to be healing and upbuilding agents of love that comes from a pure heart, good conscience, and sincere faith. They were to fight the good fight of faith and take hold of the eternal life to which we all are called. They (we) are to guard the precious deposit of the gospel of Christ entrusted to us. Paul prays that grace, mercy, and peace would flow to them (us) from God the Father and Christ Jesus our Lord.

2. A Bit of Background

These three short New Testament books often are called the "pastoral epistles." They are written to young church leaders for the purpose of strengthening the resident ministry of the church, standardizing its teaching, and checking dangerous deviations from the apostolic faith as originally handed down by Paul. The local churches were having to find their way with no precedents, and certainly they were facing very challenging environments. They were trying to clarify their identities while false belief options were pushing in and they were getting organized for stainability and mission.

There was a particular "heresy" troubling these young churches. Apparently it was a mixture of rash speculation, secret rituals, extreme aesthetic practices, and the old Jewish legalism. Whatever the particulars, the result was trying to restrict Christianity for the select few who could be highly disciplined and completely obedient to set rules. Paul calls this a subtle shift away from focus on Jesus, thus a dangerous deviation from the true gospel.

Church leaders must be selected carefully and trained well. Ministers are watched carefully by the public (1 Tim. 3:1-7) and must be especially careful with money and responsible as family and congregational leaders. In a world where we cannot all be expert theologians or profound mystics, the need is for a plain, straightforward Christianity that's clear about apostolic foundations and conduct expectations. Leaders must keep things focused on *relationship with the Master* and not on human personalities and standards. These letters to young leaders in the early church were meant to encourage guidance in doing just that.

3. The Message in Brief

We find here the essentials of an early Christian "creed," maybe originally framed as a hymn sung with great joy (1 Tim. 3:14-16). The heart of the faith is belief in the man Jesus who came as God among us and triumphed over suffering and death by his resurrection through the power of the Spirit. He now is exalted to his rightful place, being proclaimed as Lord of all. Required of believers is discipline and endurance. If with Jesus we have died, then with him to life we will rise. If we firmly endure, a throne with him will be our prize.

The Christian faith, true "spirituality," is more than a set moral program, a list of mandatory religious rules. It must not be reduced to a complex creed to affirm, or an expected level of ethical achievement to be reached. It's life lived "in Christ." It's rising with Jesus and by him coming to new life. A wise church leader once met and befriended a wealthy man on shipboard. He became ready to accept Christ, except that he didn't want to give up his cigarettes. "Wouldn't I have to do that?" he inquired. She responded wisely, "I suggest that first you become personally acquainted with Jesus, and then ask him your question." Relationship comes before rules.

4. The Present Challenge

While times and places have changed radically for the church since the first century, it seems like there is little really new under the sun. Some difficult issues clearly persist in church life. Included are how best to be united in the midst of diversity, the role of women in church leadership, the fact of human trafficking, and the challenge of how best to prepare quality ministry leaders. They've all been addressed in a variety of ways by Christians, but without full resolution.

We learn that the Bible is an "inspired" and essential record of what initially was taught in the church, but it's not intended to provide the last word on numerous culturally conditioned issues of attitude and conduct that appear in new times and places. This presents a real challenge for church leaders. The church must go on with a loving harmony that only the Spirit of Christ can provide. While unity and diversity aren't necessarily opposites, they do create tension that must be handled with care by leaders.

Pastors usually lead as they were inspired by others. Eugene Peterson was the son of a butcher long before being author of *The Message* paraphrase of the Bible. He learned important lessons from his father's way of functioning. "Don Peterson welcomed all his customers as they were, valuing them, whether they unfolded crisp bills for the finest rib eyes or fished in their pockets for coins and walked out with packages of hot dogs. He treated each person with dignity, whether an elder from the Methodist church or one of the women from the brothel a couple of blocks away. Eugene later viewed his father's work as priestly work and considered it one of his dad's great gifts to him."[1] Good modeling is crucial for the church's future.

5. Response from the Heart

My Growth Need: Lead by patience, example, and love.
Deut. 4:9; Ps. 119:11-16; Prov. 22:6; Mt. 18:15-20; Eph. 5:18-21; Col. 3:16-17.

A pastor's choice of preaching themes is crucial for the balanced health of a congregation. Prominent should be staying true to Jesus through hardship and testing. Be prepared to pass on to others what has been given. Stay focused, especially in the Scriptures which are God-breathed and useful for training in righteousness. If the church is to continue its ministry with effectiveness, the development of young leaders is essential.

> O master Teacher, teach us now that we in turn may teach.
> Reveal Thy truth and teach us how the hearts of all to reach.
>
> Enlighten now each seeking mind with Thy great mind of love,
> That in our seeking we may find the wisdom from above.
>
> Instruct our souls that we may learn the lessons of the heart,
> That taught by Thee, we may, in turn, Thy saving truth impart.
> —Carlton C. Buck

Personal Prayer. O Lord, a lifetime of study is not enough to grasp the full meaning of the gospel of Christ. I slowly come to know that only as I live the gospel and share faithfully over time. Thank you for your continuing to instruct my mind and heal my relationships so that I may become more adequate in communicating the great truths I have learned. I may not be a pastor but still I am a church leader with responsibility for the well-being of others. Guide me, Lord, that I might guide others wisely.

---

[1] Winn Collier, *A Burning in My Bones*, a biography of Eugene Peterson.

Reading 52

THE GOD WHO NEVER DIES

What's the ultimate answer to the question about everything and all time? Amazingly, there actually is one. It's the ever-living "Person," the eternal One whose name is "I AM" (Ex. 3:14). God always was and ever will continue to be. The God who has no beginning also will have no ending. The Bible begins with his creating and ends with his recreating. Origin? Destiny? Meaning in the meantime? It's all God. To God be the glory!

1. The Big Picture Verses.
Deuteronomy 6:4-5; Revelation 22:13. The Context: All

of Scripture. Here, O Israel: the Lord is our God, the Lord alone. You shall love the Lord your God with all your heart and with all your soul and with all your might. I am the Alpha and the Omega, the First and the Last, the Beginning and the End.

2. A Bit of Background

Everything dies, people, animals, institutions, planets, all that we know. Well, almost all. God *was* before the whole creation existed and *will be* after it all has run its course and is gone. If Genesis is the Bible's prologue, "in the beginning," the Book of Revelation is its epilogue, "Come, Lord Jesus!" There will be an ending to what once was begun by the creating God. Before, during, and after all phases of creation's existence, is the loving and reigning Lamb of God. He says, "I am the Alpha and the Omega, the First and the Last, the Beginning and the End" (Rev. 22:13).

While never knowing God *fully*, we humans are enabled through the unfolding plot of the biblical story to know God *truly*. The intended purpose of this knowing is practical, enabling present lives of integrity, fulfillment, and relevancy. The Bible's primary focus is not on some philosophical view of God's being, but on how life is to be lived and reality construed in light of God's character as depicted in the stories of Israel and Jesus.

The great question, of course, is learning the intentions of this ever-present and eternal One. Israel was informed of the answer as it was preparing to claim its promised land (Deut. 7:6-8). God is *love* and thus stoops down to raise us up. God stooped to Israel not because it was special but because of God's great love even for the undeserving. God is faithful "to a thousand generations." God has come, especially in Jesus, and promises future presence—"See, I am coming soon!" (Rev. 22:7). God is and shares "eternal life."

God's amazing love is without time limit. Eventually, faith, hope, and love alone will remain, and the greatest of these is love (1 Cor. 13:13). Our response is to be like John's when exiled on the island of Patmos because of loyalty to Christ. He managed to describe heaven as awash in song. It's victory notes already could be heard faintly, even in his place of human crisis. "Then I heard every creature in heaven and on earth and under the earth and in the sea, and all that is in them, singing, 'To the One seated on the throne and to the Lamb, blessing and honor and glory and might forever and ever!' And the four living creatures said 'Amen!' And the elders fell down and worshiped" (Rev. 5:13-14).

3. The Message in Brief

We live in a planned universe, not in a chaos of meaningless or endless time. Within this plan is the eventual vindication of goodness and the punishment of evil. Before all of it ever was, and beyond when it will be no more, is one overarching reality. *God is!* God's name is *I Am Who I Am* (Ex. 3:14). That is, God is the great mystery beyond all lesser realities. God is not defined in or bound by time but is the constant presence who creates time and gives it meaning. That meaning requires that those who know God are to be faithful to his special way of life. Jesus may be paraphrased as saying this to his disciples of all times:

> I realize that seeing me on the cross was devastating to your faith. How could the true Messiah be so humiliated by this world? It would take my resurrection for you to realize that what you saw on the cross was not the triumph of this world's power. It was an unexpected presentation of the amazing power of the love of my Father for all lost humankind. That awful death of mine was completely voluntary and totally for you! When all else is gone, that sacrificial love will stand for all eternity. Receive my Father's gift and be that holy love in action in your time!

The biblical God can be reached by desperate humans who cry out in faith to the God who already is reaching for them. God is willing and able to enact radical new circumstances that we could never bring about for ourselves. It's everywhere in the biblical revelation. *Creatio ex nihilo* (creation from nothing), justification by faith (salvation by God's sheer grace), and resurrection of the dead (even death will die!). These are about the amazing God who chooses to be in mutual relationship with us. "I've read the back of the book," an old Southern gospel song says, "and we win!"

4. The Present Challenge

The technological world of today is reaching dramatic new distances and unknowns with its giant telescopes and spacecrafts. What's out there, where did it originate, and what's in the future? The more we little humans see the more we are coming to realize how much is yet to be seen and how much we don't yet understand. The Bible sees this as merely touching the edge of God's garment. The ultimate is not a *what* but the one and ultimate *WHO*. We so love our freedoms and struggle to realize that the greatest of all freedom is restored relationship with God as known in Christ and voluntary obedience to the will of God that's built into the fabric of the creation itself.

Despite all that has been said in the 52 Readings of this book, the fact remains that our words and concepts about God are fragile and incomplete at best. So wise are words of St. Bonaventure (1217-

1274): "God is everywhere, with a circumference that is nowhere. God is within all things, but not enclosed, outside all things but not excluded, above all things but not aloof, below all things but not debased." God is all in all (1 Cor. 15:28). God is not far from any of us since it is "in him that we live and move and have our being" (Acts 17:27-28).

God accepts and receives us in our weakness. Praise be to our wonder-full God! May we realize as much as possible that for which Paul prayed so long ago:

> And may you be able to feel and understand how long, how wide, how deep, and how high God's love really is, and experience this love for yourselves, though it is so great that you will never see the end of it or fully know or understand it" (Eph. 3:18-20, *LNT*).

5. Response from the Heart

My Growth Need: Bow Down to the ultimate of all reality!
Gen. 1:1-2; Psalms 90:1-2; Isa. 40:28-31; I Tim. 1:17, 6:15-16; Rev. 22:12-13.

According to Psalm 22, God is to be praised for his dominion over all people and circumstances and times. God is to be celebrated even if some divine plans are yet unknown, even unimaginable. We must praise, celebrate, and serve regardless of the unknowns and risks. Praise changes things. It brings humility and needed answers.

African-American spirituals like "Great Day" and "My Lord, What a Morning!" reflect a people who knew well great suffering and yet survived by declaring great faith in God right in the teeth of it all. After all, "the dominion belongs to the Lord and he rules over the nations" (vs. 28) and over all of our personal circumstances. Prayed A. W. Tozer:

> O God, the Triune God, I want to want Thee;
> I long to be filled with longing,
> I thirst to be made more thirsty still;
> Show me Thy glory, I pray Thee,

So that I may know Thee indeed![1]

Paul announced to the Ephesian church (3:21, *The Message*):

> Glory to God in the church!
> Glory to God in the Messiah, in Jesus!
> Glory to God down all the generations!
> Glory through all millennia! Oh, yes!

Personal Prayer: My prayer should be that I want to want God more and more, becoming overwhelmed by who God is and that he should know and care about me. Glory to God in the church, in the world, and in my own life! When I think of God in any of my dark nights, may I sing with the Africa-Americans, "My Lord, What a Morning!" As Paul expressed to the Ephesians, may I "be able to feel and understand how long, how wide, how deep, and how high God's love really is!"

---

[1] A. W. Tozer, *The Pursuit of God*.

www.ingramcontent.com/pod-product-compliance
Lightning Source LLC
Chambersburg PA
CBHW050338230426
43663CB00010B/1902